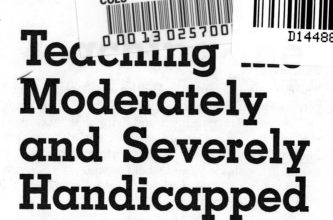

Teaching the Moderately and Severely Handicapped

Volume I
Second Edition

A Functional Curriculum for Self-Care, Motor Skills, and Household Management

Michael Bender

Peter J. Valletutti

5341 Industrial Oaks Blvd.
Austin, Texas 78735

Authors' Note

The curriculum is published in three volumes. Volume I contains objectives and activities in the areas of self-care, gross motor, fine motor and prevocational skills, and household management and living skills. Volume II contains objectives and activities in communication, interpersonal skills, sex education, drug education, and leisure skills. Following consultation with educators, the authors concluded that a three-volume format would organize the extensive amount of information contained within the curriculum into a manageable form suitable for use in instructional situations.

While the complete curriculum is meant specifically for use by the teacher, the material in Volume I is of special interest to other professionals such as physical therapists, psychologists, and nurses. The material in Volume II is of particular interest to professionals such as speech/language and hearing, recreational, and music therapists. Volume III is a valuable resource for those teaching functional academics to the mildly and moderately handicapped and those who are teaching the areas of prereadiness and readiness skills to nonhandicapped students as well. Each volume is organized to meet many different learning needs in a variety of educational and habilitative settings. With such diversity of use in mind, the authors have designed each volume as a self-sustaining unit, and teachers may use each one independently of the others, according to the specific interests, needs, and abilities of their students.

Volume II **Functional Curriculum for Communication and Socialization**

Contents **Introduction and Curriculum Overview**
Nonverbal Communication Skills   **Sex Education**
Verbal Communication Skills   **Drug Education**
Interpersonal Skills   **Leisure Skills**

Volume III **Functional Academics for the Mildly and Moderately Handicapped**

Contents **Introduction**   **Functional Arithmetic**
Curriculum   **Numerals**
Functional Academics   **Money**
Functional Reading   **Measurement**
Functional Writing   **Time**
                                        Consumer Skills

Teaching the Moderately and Severely Handicapped

Volume I
Second Edition

Library of Congress Cataloging in Publication Data

Bender, Michael, 1943–
    Teaching the moderately and severely handicapped.

    Contents: v. 1. A functional curriculum for self-care, motor skills, and household management.
    1. Handicapped children—Education.   2. Handicapped children—Education—Curricula.   3. Handicapped—Life skills guides.   I. Valletutti, Peter J.   II. Title.
LC4015.B37   1985   371.9   84–22861
ISBN 0–936104–52–X (v. 1)

5341 Industrial Oaks Blvd.
Austin, Texas 78735

10 9 8 7 6 5 4 3 2 1   84 85 86 87

Dedication

to my wife Madelyn for her understanding, love, and support.

M.B.

to my good friends Bernard Pine and Howard Honig, and to my best friend, my wife Billie.

P.J.V.

Contents

Preface

This new edition of the curriculum provides functional educational goals designed to assist teachers, other professionals, and parents in facilitating the performance of moderately and severely handicapped students in the full variety of life situations and environmental contexts.

This book is *not* a methods book nor does it contain presentations and/or charts of task analyses. It presumes a basic understanding of teaching methods and a fundamental level of expertise in analyzing educational tasks so that they may be used as a framework for evaluation and as a means of focusing on discrete behaviors requiring remedial or instructional attention. A task analysis approach to instructing moderately and severely handicapped learners is insufficient for teaching within a functional framework because it is too atomized to be of significant value in preparing students for life's reality contexts. Real situations involve diverse and interrelated cognitive judgments as well as varied environmental settings. Reality contexts can only be effectively simulated in a classroom setting if the entire behavior is demonstrated with all its applicable dimensions (psychomotor, affective, and cognitive) expressed as a total, integrated act. A task analysis approach is also inadequate, from a functional perspective, whenever small steps are tangibly reinforced because such frequency of reinforcement does not occur naturally in the environment.

Although specific objectives have generally been placed in their developmental sequence, known sequences have only been considered if they make functional sense. Developmental milestones have been deemphasized if the specific behavior does not contribute to the functional success of moderately and severely handicapped students (e.g., drawing a geometric shape or matching wooden blocks of different colors).

The curriculum is not intended as a model one for profoundly handicapped individuals; in fact, many high level goals are purposely included to encourage program implementers not to have a restricted and limiting view because there are many mildly handicapped students who are functioning at a lower than expected level and would benefit appreciably from the activities in this curriculum. Further, it is to be remembered that there are many moderately and severely handicapped students who are not primarily cognitively restricted but rather are physically, emotionally, and/or language impaired.

This new edition of the curriculum has been developed as a guide to preservice and inservice teachers and other professionals who work with moderately and severely handicapped students.

Parents, surrogate parents, and other family members as well as house parents in group homes/apartments or other alternate living arrangements will find this curriculum valuable as they interact with and instruct the handicapped individuals with whom they work and/or live.

This curriculum is designed, in addition, to serve as a text for students taking courses in curriculum development and teaching methods in special education at undergraduate and graduate levels.

The Suggested Readings appended to each curriculum section not only contain recent publications but some of the older, classic materials as well. These classic materials have been included because they have maintained their immediacy and, therefore, should not be automatically dismissed out of a passion for newness.

The Materials Lists attached to each curriculum section are deliberately brief because the materials of a functional curriculum are ordinary materials invariably found in the home, school, and community and because teacher-made materials are usually more appropriate, better focused, and more motivating to students.

The area of safety education has been eliminated from this new edition of the curriculum because safety factors must be diligently addressed in meeting *each* of the other identified objectives and in implementing *all* suggested motivational activities. Safety considerations are of such great importance that they must be integrated into the total curriculum and not treated as a separate curricular entity.

Finally, this curriculum does not address all the dimensions of a functional curriculum because that is neither practical nor possible. It does not provide all the possible instructional activities that are interesting or applicable to individual students; it simply provides a structure out of which a creative professional can extrapolate additional objectives and activities and provide answers to the challenging questions that arise from the actual implementation of the curriculum.

Acknowledgments

The material for this revised curriculum has been developed over a period of years. It has been developed by the authors from their deep conviction that a functional curriculum is critical to the development of handicapped learners. Functional materials and approaches are valued not only for their sake as the end goals of educational programming for moderately and severely handicapped persons but also because they result in greater learner interest and involvement. Developing functional learning experiences is not an easy task, primarily because we have all been conditioned to think in traditional educational ways by virtue of the mistakes of our own schooling. Therefore, it was necessary to seek the help of others. We wish to thank those individuals who helped us complete this work. We are deeply grateful to:

Gail McGregor, Shelley Hammerman, Edith Garrett, Anne Smith, and Candice Suggars, who teach and/or work with moderately and severely handicapped individuals.

Susan Harryman, Director of Physical Therapy, and Lana Warren, Director of Occupational Therapy, at the John F. Kennedy Institute.

We especially wish to thank Irene Gray for her understanding, commitment, and tireless efforts in typing and retyping the manuscript. The quality of her work and advice is greatly appreciated.

1 Introduction and Curriculum Overview

When establishing curricula for students who are nonhandicapped or mildly handicapped, the range of skills that must be included is much narrower than that for a population of students with moderate and severe handicaps. It is axiomatic that the greater the handicap the greater the educational need, and, thus, the more comprehensive the curriculum must be. The skills needed by moderately and severely handicapped students continue to expand as society becomes more complex. The curriculum must encompass all of the functional domains, including: self-care, gross motor, fine motor, and prevocational skills; household management and living skills; and communication, inter-personal, sex education, drug education, and leisure skills.

For the past 7 years, the first edition of this curriculum has been used extensively by educators and other human service professionals working with the moderately and severely handicapped. Feedback provided by "hands-on" users of the curriculum, including parents, and by college and university professors, coupled with input from the authors' own teaching experiences, has resulted in modifications and refinements that have been incorporated into this new edition.

A Functional Orientation

A functional orientation to curricula for handicapped students can be readily accommodated while operating in a subject-oriented structure and setting. For example, a traditional way of teaching color concepts is to introduce young children to various colored shapes, beads, and blocks. A functional approach, on the other hand, involves the learner with objects he or she will come into

1

contact with while functioning in real-life situations and activities. For example:

1. In the dressing area, show the learner a blue shirt, and ask him to find a pair of socks of the same color on a mock store counter. Tell him that the socks he wants may not always be on display, and he may have to ask the store clerk for them. For example, he may say, "Do you have a pair of blue woolen socks, size twelve?"
2. Give the learner a swatch of cloth from her "new" dress, and ask her to match it to the shoes on display in a glass case. Tell her to ask the clerk for help in locating a pair of red shoes to match her new red dress.
3. In the food area, show the learner a green banana, a yellow banana, and a brown, overripe one. Ask him which one is ready to be eaten. Ask him which one is not ripe yet and which one is overripe.
4. In the community, show the learner a traffic light. Tell him that he is going to visit his Aunt Rose. While walking or cycling to his aunt's house, he will come to four corners where there are traffic signals. Show him the color green and tell him he can walk when the light is green if it is safe. Remind him not to cross when it is red. Role play and practice.
5. Show the learners a map of a stadium where sections are color coded. Tell them to find their seats using color clues.
6. In a simulated work experience, give the learner a wiring task in which wires of the same color have to be properly connected or the system will not work. Ask him to perform the wiring task.
7. In a consumer setting, send the learner to the "store" to buy red apples, green grapes, blueberries, and/or oranges.
8. In a school setting, tell the learner to get a workbook (e.g., the orange book on the top shelf).
9. Discuss the fish in the aquarium. Tell the learner to describe any unusual identifying characteristics. Then, ask him to describe the fish in terms of their colors.
10. As part of a leisure experience, take the learner on a nature walk, and ask him to note nature's colors: the green of the grass, the blue of the sky, and the red of the sunset.
11. Play games that involve moving markers along colored paths. Encourage the learner to take turns along the colored path as designated by spinners or game card directions. Tell him to select his game marker by the color of his choice.

Teaching colors from a functional perspective makes them come alive because you have infused them with reality. A functional approach is much more motivating than the more traditional unidimensional approaches.

The holistic nature of a functional curriculum requires that it be taught within the context of its functional reality. A skill must be taught in its total context. For example, it is unwise to teach the motor skill of turning on water faucets unless water is drawn for a real purpose (e.g., filling an ice cube tray or a pet's water bowl or washing one's hands) and then used for that purpose—the ice cube tray must be carried to the freezer with any spillage cleaned up; the pet's water bowl must be put in its customary spot; the washed hands must be ready for a nutritious snack or meal. A functional approach to curriculum development and implementation reflects the demands of living independently in society.

Developing a Functional Curriculum

The development of a functional curriculum is not an esoteric task. A functional curriculum is based on the total life events of people as they meet the challenges and demands that are an integral part of functioning in their society. Therefore, looking at life from a "reality" perspective is all that is needed to begin to design a curriculum that is functional because it is natural.

Curriculum Steps

The first step is *to conceptualize those general behaviors that are critical to successful independent functioning*. These general behaviors become the focus and framework of a functional curriculum. They are written as general objectives (i.e., those long-range objectives that when acquired will enable individuals to lead a more productive, satisfying, and enriching life). General objectives, because they are long range, may be written in nonbehavioral terms, since their total acquisition is an ideal toward which the individual is striving. However, the identification of general objectives is not an idle process, because it provides the basic framework of the curriculum from which all other structures evolve.

Once the general objectives of a functional curriculum are identified, the second task is *to articulate those specific objectives that will contribute to the realization of each of the identified general objectives*. Thus, all of the specific objectives subsumed under each general objective address those behaviors that will enable the learner to realize more closely the ideal that is implicit in the words of the general objective. Specific objectives are stated in behavioral terms because they describe skills that are to be demonstrated by the individual learner, whenever possible, in natural settings and in real-life contexts.

Once the specific objectives are identified, the next step is *to explore possible functional activities that will lead to their acquisition*. The authors have identified three functional settings: the *school*, the *home*, and the *community*. Suggested activities for the home and the community are meant to be communicated by teachers as they form partnerships with parents and utilize the natural settings of the home and the community to structure and reinforce learning. Suggested activities for the school are meant to stimulate teacher creativity while utilizing the natural environment of the classroom, the school building, and its immediate surroundings.

It is expected that as readers carry out the curriculum they will continue to find new bits of the universe of skills, will reject some suggested activities, and will create others. These modifications are encouraged because professional educators must not be automatons who blindly and unthinkingly follow any guide. Rather, they must be creative, dynamic leaders who, through judicious educational evaluation and a creative spirit, design learning experiences that will enrich the lives of the handicapped students they teach, no matter where that learning takes place. A learning area is not the physical setting itself but the nature of the human interaction. Readers no doubt will find gaps in the curriculum. A recurrent nightmare is that something vital has been left out. If gaps are found, *then fill them*.

As an aid to brainstorming for possible instructional activities, *functional emphases are identified* because they are the keys to creating instructional experiences that are reality based and are not divorced from the world in which we expect individuals to function. Failure to observe the functional elements of a learning experience renders the instructional act as disfunctional as the more traditional disconnected approaches common to subject-oriented curricula.

Developing Instructional Plans

Once the sequence and scope of general (or unit) objectives and their supporting specific objectives are charted, the structure for educational evaluation and programming is present. These objectives serve as the framework for systematically observing and assessing the student's performance in terms of both processes and products. Evaluation occurs as the learner functions on a daily basis in natural settings and responds to structured and simulated activities presented by parents, instructors, instructional aides, and other human service professionals. These observations aid in determining those general and specific objectives appropriate for the individual. Once these decisions are made, planning can commence as follows:

1. The design of a specific instructional plan begins with the articulation of a general objective that represents a major curriculum segment, followed by identification of a relevant specific objective.
2. Following the selection of a specific objective, a pertinent instructional objective is then constructed. The instructional objective, like the specific objective, is student oriented and has the dual purpose of: (a) structuring the instructional sequence and (b) suggesting the assessment strategy and assigned performance criterion levels. Toward these ends, an instructional objective has three elements:

    a. The definition of the stimulus situation or conditions (e.g., "When given . . ." or "After being shown . . .").

    b. The specification of the desired response (e.g., "The learner will . . .").

    c. The establishment of a mastery level (e.g., "The learner will do so in 4 out of 5 trials," or "He will do so correctly within 5 minutes.").

3. Next, materials and equipment are listed. The instructional segment is placed early in the plan for ease in reading as one skims the written plan prior to its implementation.

4. Individualized reinforcement and reinforcement schedules are then identified in recognition of: (a) the different reward preferences and needs of individuals, and (b) their varying response rates.

5. The motivating activity is then stated. For many, this is a challenging task, because it may be difficult to specify age-appropriate motivating activities that will capture the attention, imagination, and interest of those individuals for whom the instruction is designed.

6. Instructional procedures are then enumerated. They are instructor oriented and are sequenced in logical steps from initial motivation to assessment. Attention must be paid throughout to instructional steps that illuminate the teaching-learning process. Evidence that some teaching is taking place must be included. Demonstrations, assistance, and problem-solving challenges must be an integral part of explaining the instructional procedure.

7. The assessment strategy to be used is then specified. This strategy reflects the desired response and mastery criterion or criteria stated in the instructional objective. It is instructor oriented and includes record-keeping requirements.

8. At this point, a proposed follow-up activity or objective is written to ensure that the sequence of instruction is observed. A follow-up objective is specified when the instructor believes that the specific objective will be mastered and that the learner will then be ready to proceed to a new functional context, the next specific objective, or, at times, to a new general objective. If the learner, despite the best laid plans, fails to meet criteria, then a new plan must be written on an ad hoc basis to meet the specific problem demonstrated by the learner. A remedial instructional experience is likely to concentrate only on a cognitive dimension, a psychomotor aspect, or a health and safety factor.

    For example, an individual learner may have failed to meet mastery criteria in making a bed because he was unable to select new linen in the right size. In this case, remediation is then pursued through an instructional design and experience that concentrates solely on developing this skill. As a further example, the learner may not meet performance criterion because he was unable to put on new pillowcases. In this case, remediation is then pursued through an instructional experience that concentrates on developing the skill of putting on pillowcases. As a final example, the learner may not select clean linen to make up the bed;

therefore, attention must be paid to developing the awareness that clean linen is needed to make a bed.

9. Recommended instructional resources are identified next. These suggested readings and resources are meant to support the instructional design and to provide relevant information to readers and implementers of the instructional plan. It should be noted that they are not materials used during the implementation of the plan. They are simply the materials used in the design process.

10. Finally, a concluding section is appended for the purpose of recording observations and their programming implications for later reference and for use in completing checklists, writing progress reports, and designing individualized educational programs (IEPs). For educational and treatment purposes, the instructor should schedule a time for recording observations that provide special insights into the individual's learning characteristics and interests. Certainly, this is the place where relevant observations are recorded that specify program modifications, especially when the learner fails to meet criteria.

A final note relevant to the final presentation of the instructional plan should be heeded. Introductory information at the beginning of the plan should include basic organizational details, such as:

The topic area
The proposed date of instruction
The plan designer and primary instructor
The names of the individual or group members for whom the plan is designed
The time allotted or recommended
Special notes or precautions, including general health and safety factors and
    individual needs and concerns

A sample instructional plan is presented in Chapter Appendix A to further clarify the elements identified above.

Developing the Functional Curriculum

Education of moderately and severely handicapped persons is viewed as a lifelong endeavor that continually strives to add more and more skills to the student's repertoire and eternally seeks to reinforce previously acquired behaviors. All the objectives in the curriculum have been included because they are expected to facilitate the individual student's accommodation to society on the one hand and society's acceptance of the handicapped individual on the other. This socially functional orientation demands a lifetime effort. Therefore, artificial and arbitrary upper age limits are primitive and must be removed if this population of citizens is to be served educationally.

Some of the skills and their accompanying activities may appear to be scaled at too *high* a level for moderately and severely handicapped students. They are included *deliberately*, to reinforce the concept of lifelong education, to establish higher horizons for this population, and to suggest appropriate educational goals for mildly handicapped students and perhaps even for non-handicapped students.

The functional curriculum has been designed for handicapped students without designating traditional diagnostic labels. This approach was taken because it is clearly recognized that categorical labels such as "mentally retarded" and "autistic" are nonproductive for educational programming purposes. A specific label does not suggest a specific educational program; what is of concern is the student's unique profile of abilities and disabilities. Knowledge that a student is retarded avails little, but an appraisal of what the student can and cannot do provides key evaluative/diagnostic information.

Parent Involvement

Parents can be most helpful in reinforcing learning that has taken place in the school, acting as carry-over agents, and offering suggestions about motivating materials and activities. Therefore, the curriculum is also meant for parents and other adults who have primary responsibility for and/or will want to facilitate learning in children and adults with moderate and severe handicaps. Parents must play a critical role in the education of their handicapped children, especially when the natural setting for learning is in the home environment and when they can more effectively and consistently use the community as an instructional setting.

Teaching Strategies and Programming Considerations

Success in educating moderately and severely handicapped students requires extensive knowledge, a broad range of professional skills, and a positive attitude. Primary among the skills needed to teach moderately and severely handicapped persons is the understanding and use of a variety of effective and proven teaching strategies. As with their nonhandicapped peers, teaching moderately and severely handicapped students requires individualization. What is a successful approach on one day might be the antecedent for a behavioral problem on another. It is therefore important to have in one's instructional repertoire a variety of teaching strategies.

Listed below are instructional, programming, and organizational strategies that have been used successfully by classroom teachers of moderately and severely handicapped learners. These strategies are also appropriate for teachers of nonhandicapped students who have looked to special education for innovative ways to manage behavior, organize classrooms, and personalize instruction.

Normalization Considerations

Age Appropriateness   Always select instructional materials and activities that would be considered suitable for nonhandicapped individuals of the same age.

Appearance   Program, at all times, to help the student behave and look as appropriate as possible. If the student looks and behaves in deviant ways, he will be stigmatized by others.

Avoidance of Stereotypic Judgments   Do not assume that a handicapped person is unable to perform certain skills and participate in specific activities and events just because he is handicapped.

Cultural Background   Choose materials and activities that reflect the student's cultural and ethnic background and expose him to new cultures that reflect the cultural diversity of his society.

Nonhandicapped Peers   Involve the student, whenever possible, in activities with nonhandicapped peers. The handicapped student can usually participate in some way.

Peer Interest   Encourage the student's interest in the welfare of his friends and peers (e.g., make him aware of a friend's/peer's illness and the need to send a get-well card). Match students with different skills so that they can assist each other.

Privacy   Remember to respect the student's privacy. For example, respect his privacy when teaching self-care skills such as toileting and bathing. However, do not sacrifice safety for privacy.

Teacher Behavior

Communication   Use your voice as a means of communicating your feelings and wants to the student, especially with the nonverbal student who does not comprehend oral language. Be aware that monotonous voice patterns turn a student off. It is also important to supplement vocal communication with gestures whenever possible to optimize the student's understanding of your message and to facilitate his comprehension of total communication.

Control   Remain calm and poised no matter what happens. A student often will react negatively to a teacher who is losing or has lost control.

Cooperation Seek the cooperation of other teachers, professionals, and support staff. Bus drivers, school custodians, and community helpers can assist immeasurably in normalizing the lives of your students.

Enthusiasm Show enthusiasm when a student progresses or attempts to comply with your requests. Remember that what may seem to you like very little progress may be a giant step for the student.

Expression of Affection Express sincere affection for the student. React to the human qualities in the student no matter how handicapped he is. Your warmth, interest, and love will elicit positive responses. Do not express affection by touching, hugging, and kissing the student too much; this will provide a poor model of behavior if carried into his adult years. Also, do not infantilize the student by mothering him too much.

Flexibility Demonstrate flexibility in carrying out lesson plans. If an unexpected negative behavior occurs that requires immediate action on your part, change your schedule. For example, suppose a student begins to eat someone else's food during lunch. Stop the student immediately, and work on the idea of "my food" versus "not my food," even if you had previously scheduled an outdoor event or another activity. Always keep your priorities in mind. *Seize the moment* to teach, because you might not get a good opportunity for a long time. Do not wait to create an artificial situation; react when the real situation occurs.

Humor A sense of humor that is not hostile or sarcastic always helps.

Modeling At all times serve as a model of behavior in the way you look, act, talk, walk, eat, etc. Verbalize models of behavior. For example, "Other people like to be near a person who smells pleasant."

Materials

Assistive Devices Become familiar with assistive devices. If you can operate these devices yourself, you will be more likely to use them properly in instructional situations. The use of walkers and hearing aids is an important skill for the teacher to master.

Diversity Discover and use exciting materials and activities from other disciplines. Music, art, dance, and physical education activities can serve to stimulate different students. Do not be restricted by a narrow view of educational programming and goals.

Familiarity Use familiar games and songs in activities. Do not waste time searching for educational games or special songs when there are familiar ones available. Keep in mind ethnic, cultural, and geographic preferences.

Progress Charts Construct charts that graphically demonstrate student progress. For example, draw a picture of a stopwatch or clock face to show the time it took the student to run a specified distance. Encourage the student to try harder. Chart his progress and urge him to chart his own progress, when feasible.

Relevancy   Use current materials, toys, games, television shows, and records to motivate the student. Dancing to a current favorite top tune usually will be more stimulating than dancing to the *Nutcracker* Suite. However, remember that some old favorites have lasting appeal.

Reminder Charts   Construct charts that will help the student keep track of required behaviors (e.g., a Shopping List Chart that the student uses to match food on hand with the pictures on the chart). When he has less food at home than is pictured on the chart, he will know that he needs to go food shopping.

Variety   Vary activities and materials whenever possible; take advantage of the motivating effects of surprise, suspense, and novelty. For example, a personal computer can bring magic to a class session.

Instructional Considerations

Activity Alternation   Alternate quiet activities with activities involving gross motor actions. This alternating of activities acts as a motivating factor and as an aid to classroom management.

Changing Activities   Activities should be changed frequently enough so that students do not have time to become disinterested. There also should be opportunities for the student to select alternate activities, including a non-participatory one.

Consistency   Students need to continually know what is expected of them and what the consequences of their actions will be. Consistency is one of the most important assets in a well-managed classroom.

Developmental Learning   Plan your learning experiences so that they are developmental. Always keep in mind the hierarchical arrangement of skills. Consult other members of the team before you teach a skill that does not follow the usual developmental sequence.

Disturbing Behaviors   Program, at all times, to reduce inappropriate and disturbing behaviors. If these behaviors persist, they will interfere with attempts to successfully normalize the lives of handicapped persons.

Goal Planning   Be realistic in planning goals. Do not develop objectives at so high a level that you and the student become frustrated. Also, do not develop objectives and activities that are too low in level. Review your objectives, and, if their levels are too high or too low, modify them.

Imitation   Tell the student to imitate your actions after he has observed you. For example, tell the student to watch you as you wash your hands. Next, tell the student to do what you just did. Praise the student for approximating or imitating the task. Use peer models whenever practical. Verbalize the peer's behavior and reward that behavior.

Individualized Instruction   Individualize instruction, because there is such wide diversity in handicapped populations that personalizing instruction is essential. Remember that individual programs can be implemented and be successful within a group setting.

Instructional Grouping   Although one-to-one instruction may be necessary, overuse of this procedure is often impractical in most classrooms and minimizes the natural opportunities to learn from others.

Instructional Programming   Set up your instructional program in small steps so that the student is likely to be successful. Use successful experiences to encourage the student to attempt more advanced steps. If possible, end each activity with student success.

Lifelong Skill Sequences   When selecting instructional targets, it is important to keep in mind where a child may be functioning in the future. Instructional time should be directed to those skill areas that will ultimately be most functional. Minimize the amount of time spent on relatively unimportant skills.

Model Demonstration   Demonstrate the finished product whenever possible. For example, when the student is expected to assemble a wooden puzzle, show him the complete puzzle before you ask him to assemble the pieces. In an arts and crafts project, show him the completed project. For example, when making Halloween masks, show him a sample mask so that he has a model available to refer to as he is working. The model also may act as motivation.

Music   Incorporate music into activities whenever possible. As an example, you can play a tune on an autoharp and sing the instructions appropriate to an activity, such as, "Johnny, line up, line up, line up."

Nutrition   Serve nutritious snacks instead of junk foods and other non-nutritional foods that may be unhealthy for the students. Foods and beverages such as candy, cookies, cake, pretzels, potato chips, and soda have little nutritive value. Do not offer these foods to students as rewards, for snacks, at mealtimes, or at parties. Nutritious snacks such as fresh fruit, raisins, nuts, sunflower and pumpkin seeds, milk, and pure fruit juices are liked by students and are healthy. Also, avoid food reinforcers whenever possible.

Pantomimed Instruction   Use pantomime to demonstrate a skill. For example, in pantomime show the student how to thread a needle and sew on a button. This approach helps to isolate the required movements; it also is an enjoyable activity.

Past Experience   Inquire about the experiences the student has had whenever possible. Talk to his parents, guardians, or past teachers. References to these experiences often will provide the needed motivation for lessons.

Peer Tutoring   Organize your lessons in such a way as to take advantage of the benefits of peer tutoring and buddy systems. The student may learn a skill more readily when it is demonstrated by a peer.

Physical Prompting   Physically guide the student through an activity whenever he is unable to do the activity himself. For example, if the student is unable to cut with scissors, use a pair of training scissors and guide him through the activity. In writing activities hold the student's hand and the pencil, and move his hand in the desired pattern. Whenever you physically guide a student through an action or series of actions, encourage him to remember how his body feels when he moves it in a specific way.

Practice   Practice a task often. Even after you are convinced that the student has mastered a particular skill, practice and reinforce it periodically. Schedule practice sessions. Vary the activities as much as possible to maintain student interest and to promote generalization.

Resource People   Seek the help of resource people who can enrich the educational program. Store managers, bus drivers, police officers, and road repair people not only can provide interesting demonstrations and lectures, but also may allow you the use of their facilities so that the student can have first-hand experiences. For example, a bus driver can provide you with the use of an empty bus to practice getting on and off.

Reverse Programming   Program in reverse when working on some motor skills that consist of a series of separate motor events. For example, the *backward chaining* approach is helpful in teaching the tying of shoelaces. Starting in the middle of a sequence may also be appropriate for some students.

Role Play   Use role playing, puppet play, and creative dramatics to simulate real experiences and to practice skills.

Routines in Learning   When dealing with an activity that has several steps, establish a routine for the student to follow. "First you do this, then this, then this . . .," etc. Practice the steps in sequence.

Seasonal Activities   Program activities appropriate to the seasons. Plan for those activities, such as shoveling snow and planting seeds, to coincide with the seasons. Outdoor recreation and camping activities should be planned according to the weather.

Skill Demonstration   Demonstrate the skill you are attempting to facilitate. Explain what you are doing as you are doing it. For example, say, "Look at me as I button my shirt. I take the button between my thumb and index finger of one hand; look. Then I take the buttonhole with the same fingers of my other hand; look. And then, I push the button through; look. Now let's do it together."

Skill Instruction   Teach a skill at the time of its functional use (i.e., when it occurs naturally). For example, show the student how to wash his hands after he has gone to the toilet. Also, schedule practice sessions at times of functional application. When the student has developed skills in the use of eating utensils, plan parties, invite guests for dinner, and practice during snack and cafeteria times. Schedule practice sessions often.

Task Analysis   Use a task analysis approach whenever possible. For example, teaching the brushing of teeth may have to be broken down into holding a tube of toothpaste, unscrewing the cap, and placing the toothpaste on the brush. While teaching the individual steps, do not lose sight of the total task.

Teaching Environment   Always consider the environment in which teaching activities should be presented (i.e., the home, the school, and/or the community).

Understanding Objectives   Let the student know the specific objective on which you are working and why it is necessary. Tell him, "You must know how to regulate the water in the sink so that you can wash your hands and face without burning yourself. Together we'll work on it. First you . . ."

Useful Skills   Do not waste time teaching a skill that can be circumvented by modern styles or modern technology. For example, if a student has inordinate difficulty in telling time using a regular watch or clock, teach him how to tell time with a digital watch or clock. If a student has excessive difficulty in tying shoes, encourage him to wear loafers.

Visual Monitoring   Use mirrors for visual monitoring so that the student can see how he is doing a task while he is doing it. Mirrors are especially valuable in observing the movements required to make speech sounds. (Remember to use unbreakable mirrors.)

Classroom Management

Activity Substitution   Substitute a constructive activity whenever a student is engaged in a maladaptive behavior such as a destructive or self-stimulatory activity. For example, if the student is waving his fingers and hands in a perseverative manner, provide him with something to do with his hands, such as modeling clay or playing with a toy with movable parts. Demonstrate how to use these objects appropriately.

Appropriate Assistance   A teacher should provide only enough assistance to allow the student to participate in or complete a task he is not able to do independently.

Correction If a student is behaving or performing inappropriately or incorrectly, correct him in a positive manner. Say, "This is the way to play the game" and simultaneously demonstrate the desired behavior.

Directions Be explicit in your directions and commands. Be sure the student knows exactly what behaviors are expected. Classroom organization, behavioral management, and success of student performance are, to a large degree, dependent on the instructor's explicitness.

Ignoring Behavior Ignore inappropriate behavior whenever possible. For example, the student who continually talks out, if ignored, will not be reinforced for this behavior. As with other strategies, ignoring should not be overused, or it will lose its effectiveness.

Reprimands Use reprimands whenever necessary. Reprimands are not punishment and can be effectively used in the structuring of behaviors. For example, say, "No," if you want to discourage a student from taking someone else's food or materials.

Responsibility Assign the student a classroom responsibility no matter how severe his handicap and no matter how small the task. Program responsibility from the beginning. Use class assignments as rewards.

Timeout Remove a student who is disruptive from the class or learning area and place him in social isolation for a short period of time. Make sure that you explain to him the reason for his removal. It is important that the student not be returned to the exact milieu he left when the timeout period is completed. It is advisable to place him near other students, right next to you, or in a new activity when he returns.

Reinforcement

Appropriate Reinforcement Be reinforcing at appropriate times, but do not overreinforce or it will lose its effectiveness. For example, you may praise the student for being quiet during quiet time by saying, "I'm glad you're being quiet." However, if this is repeated too many times, the student may feel this is an automatic response and will not accept it as reinforcement. Always use age-appropriate reinforcers.

Carry-Over Agents Train and encourage teacher aides, parents, foster parents, foster grandparents, and house parents, to be effective carry-over and practice agents. If the significant persons who interact with the student are consistent in reinforcing desired behaviors, the program will be more successful in a shorter period of time and will facilitate generalization of skills to the natural environment. Make sure you are consistent too.

Immediate Feedback Provide the student with immediate feedback of results (i.e., reward him as soon as possible after he has attempted, approximated, or achieved a task). Also, if a student is performing a task inappropriately or incorrectly, stop him from continuing the task, and indicate your disapproval in any way that he will understand. Demonstrate the acceptable behavior.

Inappropriate Reinforcement Never reinforce any behavior that, if it persists, will cause the student problems later in life. For example, when teaching handshaking, encourage the student to shake hands only when a new acquaintance offers his or her hand first. Do not reinforce the student if he continually initiates handshaking. This behavior, if it persists and is abused, might prove to be annoying and/or might accentuate the student's handicap. Do not overly encourage a young student to clap his hands in glee when a peer does well. This behavior may be carried over into his adult years, and he may clap whenever he is pleased or happy. Although clapping is viewed by many as acceptable behavior for the young, it may be inappropriate in older students. Always try to reinforce the student during naturally occurring situations.

Interests Find out what the student's interests are. Knowledge of a favored toy, a favorite person, a special game, and a preferred food can mean the difference between success and failure in an activity. Keep a list of these preferences for each student and continually update it.

Peer Reinforcement Show the student's peers how to behave in reinforcing ways. Encourage them to reward the student's desirable behaviors.

Reinforcement Preferences Discover the student's reinforcement preferences. What might be reinforcing to you or to other students you have taught might not be reinforcing to a specific student. You may have to search for a reinforcer.

Token Economies A token economy may be an effective management strategy on an individual, classroom, or school-wide basis. Assigning units of value or tokens for particular behaviors enables a teacher to reward behaviors as they occur or at a later time when they are "cashed" in.

Environmental Considerations

Community Resources Become familiar with community resources, and use them as learning environments. Make the entire community your classroom. For example, the neighborhood supermarket is the best place to facilitate learning in the purchase of foods. The office building and the department store offer opportunities in learning how to use elevators, revolving doors, and automatic doors.

Ecology Behave in an ecologically minded way (e.g., when teaching a student how to cut up newspapers to make paper designs, use old papers). Become a model for conservation and pollution control whenever possible.

Geographic Area   Take into consideration the geographic area in which the student lives and its impact on the program. Lessons designed to facilitate locomotion skills in the use of a subway only make sense when subway travel is part of the student's environment.

Learning Area   Make your learning area as attractive and pleasant as possible. However, beware of the dangers of overstimulation. Make your room interesting with plants, animals, books, toys, and games that are motivating.

Safety Hazards   Be aware of potential safety hazards in all activities. For example, do not use sharp tools with the student who is destructive, and do not use miniature objects with the student who puts nonedible objects into his mouth.

Work Displays   Display the student's work on bulletin boards, in display cases, and at school exhibits. The joy and pride of displayed work are reinforcing.

Evaluation

Assessment   Instruction should always be preceded by assessment. This will provide the teacher with a general profile of a student's skills as well as identifying areas for future instruction.

Continuousness   Evaluation should be a continuous process. It is important to develop criteria to assess how effective a particular technique or activity is in achieving a desired goal.

Self-monitoring   Some students react positively when they are actively involved in keeping track of their own performance. Whenever possible, and when appropriate, this type of monitoring should be encouraged.

Evaluating Individual Performance and Progress

Teachers who fully appreciate the essential role of educational evaluation in designing instructional programs are aware that learners continually provide diagnostic information as they interact or fail to interact with people and objects in their environment. Strategies for observing and recording performance and progress are necessary to a systematic evaluation process; in addition, a framework must be provided that will structure and formalize observations.

The scope and sequence of curriculum objectives provide that needed framework, because learners should be evaluated in terms of the tasks you require of them. Therefore, a suggested companion to any curriculum is a complementary checklist that mirrors the objectives stated there.

A sample completed checklist is provided in Chapter Appendix B to clarify its composition and use. A response legend accompanies the checklist to illuminate the nature of possible responses and, when applicable, the types of assistance employed to obtain the desired responses.

Chapter Appendix A: Sample Instructional Plan

Topic Area:	Household Management and Living Skills
Date:	March 20, 1985
Designed by:	Mr. Ferris
Time Recommended:	35 Minutes
Students Involved:	L. Banks, M. Krishnan, R. Kim, R. DeStefano, W. Carter, E. Partridge, M. Kasabian, E. Lane, G. Parks, M. Marten, and J. Goldberg

Special Notes or Precautions

1. General health and safety factors
   a. remind the students to wash their hands after changing the soiled linen
   b. caution them to select clean linen from the linen closet or bureau drawer
2. Individual needs and concerns
   a. because G. Parks is often reluctant to participate in an unfamiliar activity, do not pressure performance
   b. W. Carter is frightened of going near closets; therefore, for him, use a bureau drawer to store the clean linen

General Objective III[1]

The student will be functionally independent in caring for his living quarters, appliances, and furnishings in a manner that allows him to perform optimally.

See Chapter 5, "Household Management and Living Skills," for suggested instructional activities and functional emphases for this specific objective and others under this general objective.

Specific Objective G[1]

The student makes his own bed.

Instructional Objective

When shown two beds, one with soiled linen and the other with clean linen, the students will unmake the soiled bed, wash their hands, and then make the bed up with clean linen. They will do so using the correct-size linen, selecting linen that is color/design coordinated whenever feasible. They will change and make the bed in 5 minutes without any assistance.

Materials and Equipment

1. Two beds
2. Soiled linen
3. Sheets of different sizes, styles, and colors/designs
4. Linen closet or bureau
5. A laundry bag, basket, or hamper

Individualized Reinforcement and Reinforcement Schedules

R. DeStefano needs frequent verbal reinforcement. M. Marten should be praised upon completion of the task and also whenever he has difficulty, and should be helped until successful. E. Lane is working with a token reinforcement system. L. Banks enjoys assisting the instructor in completing tasks.

Motivating Activity

Ask students to tell you which bed looks cleaner, that is, which one they would prefer to sleep in. Reinforce them if they select the clean bed; explain the reason for selecting the clean bed if they fail to identify it.

Instructional Procedures

1. Tell the students to help you fold and put away the clean bed linen that has been washed and dried the day before. Tell them to find the place

---

[1] See Chapter 5, "Household Management and Living Skills," for suggested instructional activities and functional emphases for this specific objective and others under this general objective.

where the clean linen should be kept. Help them if necessary.

2. Ask them then to unmake the soiled bed. Demonstrate how to avoid touching the soiled parts as much as possible. Ask them if they should wash their hands. Then ask them to explain why. Provide help with the hand-washing and drying sequence if needed.

3. Encourage them to find appropriate replacement linen. Help them, if necessary, in locating and then selecting the appropriate linen. Ask them why they selected the linen in the colors, amounts, and sizes chosen.

4. Ask them to make the bed, giving them whatever help is needed. Demonstrate bed-making procedures whenever necessary.

5. Remind them to place the dirty linen in the laundry bag, basket, or hamper when necessary.

Assessment Strategy

Observe each individual as he carries out the process. Check to see whether he:

1. Identified the soiled bed
2. Removed soiled bed linen appropriately
3. Washed and dried his hands properly
4. Located clean bed linen
5. Selected the required and appropriate bed linen
6. Made the bed properly
7. Completed the total task in 5 minutes

Note any help or demonstrations required during the instructional experiences in the "Observations and Their Programming Implications" section below. Record each student's performance on his "Household Management and Living Skills Checklist."

Follow-Up Activity or Objective

If the students achieve the instructional objective, proceed to an instructional experience in which the students practice changing the bed linen in preparation for overnight guests.

Recommended Instructional Resources

Halchin, L. O. (1976). *Home economics for learners with special needs.* Washington, DC: Home Economics Education Association.

Parnell, F. B. (1981). *Homemaking skills for everyday living.* South Holland, IL: Goodheart-Willcox.

Observations and Their Programming Implications

Chapter Appendix B: Sample Completed Checklist

Student's Name: Michael Peters, Jr.

General Objective III (Self-Care: Dressing)

The student will be functionally independent in dressing and undressing himself in a manner that allows him to perform optimally in diverse situations.

Special Physical Restrictions/Conditions (if any):

minor involuntary movements

of his right hand

Evaluator(s):

Ms. Rosenbaum, teacher

Ms. Peters, mother

Mr. DeVito, occupational therapist

Specific objective	Response[a]	Number of observations/ by whom[a]	Dates	Observations and their programming implications
A. The student puts on and removes clothing with no fasteners	PP	4/P	10/23/84 10/24/84 10/25/84 10/26/84	Michael demonstrates the motor skills to put on his underpants. However, 50% of the time he puts them on back-to-front. Work on cognitive skill of identifying front of underpants.
B. The student puts on and removes clothing with zippers	PP	4/T and P	12/08/84 12/10/84 12/11/84 12/13/84	Michael zips his pants zipper. However, he fails to zip it completely up 25% of the time. Work with oversize zippers and give verbal prompts.

Specific objective	Response[a]	Number of observations/ by whom[a]	Dates	Observations and their programming implications
C. The student puts on and removes clothing with snaps	CAR (V)	3/T	11/03/85 11/10/85 11/17/85	Michael is able to snap his painting smock in preparing for art activities. However, he sometimes leaves several snaps open. Remind him to complete his dressing. Gradually fade out verbal prompt.
D. The student puts on and removes clothing with buttons	CAR (P)	2/OTM (O.T.) and confirmed by T	02/02/85 02/02/85	Michael unbuttons his shirt successfully but has difficulty buttoning his shirt completely 100% of the time. Needs physical prompting.
E. The student puts on and removes clothing with hooks and eyes	N/A			
F. The student removes clothing with Velcro fasteners	IF	3/T and P	09/06/84 09/10/84 09/12/84	
G. The student adjusts clothing when necessary	DFS	4/P and T	10/02/84 10/07/84 10/20/84 10/22/84	Michael consistently adjusts his clothing after toileting activities and when his clothes are changed.
H. The student chooses clothing appropriate for the weather	N/ATT			
I. The student chooses clothing appropriate to the time of day, situation, and occasion	PP	1/P	03/07/85	Michael is just beginning to differentiate play clothes from school clothes.

[a]Legend: N/A—not applicable; NR—no response; N/ATT—not attempted; PP—partial performance; CAR—completed/assistance required; P—physical guidance; G—gestural prompts; V—verbal cues; IF—independent functioning; DFS—demonstrated in functional situation; T—teacher; P/SP—parent/surrogate parent; OTM—other team member (specify).

2 ∥ Self-Care Skills

Programming for moderately and severely handicapped individuals in the area of self-care skills is essential. Skills such as toilet training (Anderson, 1982; Azrin & Foxx, 1974; Bettison, 1978), cleaning and grooming (Dreith & Kreps, 1975; Swain, Allard, & Holborn, 1982), dressing and undressing (Adelson & Sandow, 1978; Edgar, Maser & Haring, 1977), and drinking and eating (Barnerdt & Bricker, 1978; Edwards & Bergman, 1982) are skills of daily living that need to be mastered if the student is to become an acceptable and functioning member of society. The following reasons have been offered as a rationale for priority programming in self-help skills:

1. The student who physically is capable of being toilet trained, but for some reason has not been trained, will be excluded from most social and community interactions.
2. The student who is not functionally independent in drinking and eating will require supervision that is likely to be continuously burdensome to caregivers. Furthermore, required care may not be available as the student becomes older. Moreover, he will be greatly limited in his opportunities for positive social interaction and for productive work experiences.
3. The student who is not functionally independent in dressing and undressing skills will require significant amounts of attention from caregivers, including teachers. Attention to the mechanics of self-care, if it continues for many years, will take time from teaching those higher level skills involved in communicating and interacting with others. The development of social interaction skills will be restricted if inordinate attention has to be paid to personal care experiences.
4. The student who lacks essential cleaning and grooming skills invariably will be denied many interpersonal and social experiences.

Proficiency in self-care skills helps handicapped students develop responsibility for their personal needs and enhances self-esteem while it increases the likelihood that others will view them as acceptable friends, coworkers, peers, acquaintances, and mates. An individual who is dependent or semidependent for his personal care cannot possibly lead a life that is remotely normal. The appearance of normalcy, if not normalcy itself, is critical to successful functioning in society's mainstream (Nutter & Reid, 1978).

The objectives and activities suggested in this unit of the curriculum were developed after a review of the professional literature and after consultation with physical and occupational therapists, nutritionists, psychologists, pediatricians, and nurses. As the teacher uses this unit of the curriculum, he or she may soon see that students gain in self-confidence as they begin to master basic self-care skills. Mastery of the environment is perhaps the greatest joy of the developing person. The self-concept of the student will also be enhanced if he is enthusiastically praised for growth in specific areas. Functional independence will contribute to personal usefulness in the home, neighborhood, and society and to greater fiscal independence.

Although self-care skills must be given early attention, they cannot be given undue or prolonged emphasis at the expense of other curricular areas. Concentration on these fundamental skills can result in monotonous school days for students and teachers alike. A variety of instructional experiences is important, especially when teachers have to program in the area of self-care. Burnout, an omnipresent spectre in high-stress teaching assignments, is a less likely result of instructional programming that is multidimensional and varied.

Suggested readings are provided at the end of this chapter that represent a review of current as well as past self-care information, techniques, and programs. The reader may also wish to review the Special Materials List at the end of this chapter for additional information on specific resources in this area.

General Objectives of the Unit

I.   The student will be functionally independent in toileting, provided there are no physical reasons why he is not capable of being trained.

II. The student will be functionally independent in drinking and eating in a manner that allows him to perform optimally in diverse situations.

III. The student will be functionally independent in dressing and undressing himself in a manner that allows him to perform optimally in diverse situations.

IV. The student will be functionally independent in cleaning and grooming himself in a manner that allows him to perform optimally in diverse situations.

General Objective I

The student will be functionally independent in toileting, provided there are no physical reasons why he is not capable of being trained.

General Information

It is important that the teacher who is working in the area of toilet training first consider whether the student is ready to be toilet trained (after he or she has been medically evaluated to be in such a program). Readiness is usually indicated when the student:

1. Is ambulatory and can walk to the toilet.
2. Has enough vision to see where the toilet is and to see gestures made by the teacher.
3. Has enough motor control to undress himself below the waist.
4. Has sufficient receptive language skills to understand simple commands.

Specific Objectives

The student:

A. when he requires supervision or assistance, indicates in an acceptable manner that he needs to go to the bathroom.
B. when independent in toileting, closes the bathroom and/or stall door for privacy.
C. removes, lowers, unfastens, and/or opens appropriate clothing before toileting.
D. when appropriate, either raises a toilet seat for voiding or uses a urinal.
E. sits on the toilet seat for eliminating or for voiding.
F. wipes himself after voiding or eliminating.
G. flushes the toilet after wiping himself or flushes the urinal after voiding.
H. washes and dries his hands after toileting.
 I. dresses and/or arranges clothing after toileting.
 J. locates and uses a bathroom or public restroom independently.

Specific Objective A

The student, when she requires supervision or assistance, indicates in an acceptable manner that she needs to go to the bathroom.

Functional Settings and Suggested Instructional Activities

School

1. If one does not exist, set a specific time or times during the school day (e.g., before recess or during free time) when the student is free to go to the bathroom. Check to see if the student uses an appropriate gesture to let you know that he has to go to the bathroom.
2. Make a time chart for the student. Chart each time the student indicates he needs to go to the bathroom (Figure 1).
3. Make maintenance checks for those students who are being trained to stay dry and reinforce them if they are dry. Say "No" if their pants are wet or indicate displeasure in some other way. Do this check at fixed intervals and later at intermittent intervals. Make a maintenance check chart for each student (Figure 2).

Home and Community

1. Ask the parents if they notice time patterns when their child is wet. Tell them to ask the child to go to the bathroom 10 to 15 minutes before these times occur.
2. When possible, go for a walk through the student's immediate community or go to a community event (e.g., a ball game, the movies, or a puppet show). Encourage the student to gesture appropriately or tell you when he has to go to the bathroom. Assist him in finding a public restroom.

Functional Emphases In designing your own instructional activities and plans, emphasize the following elements:

1. Use of a gesture that is socially acceptable.
2. Use of a gesture that is as widely recognized as possible.
3. Use of an appropriate gesture in an unobtrusive way (i.e., the student does not wave his hand frantically or interrupt others unnecessarily).
4. Use of a verbally appropriate statement that is neither unacceptable nor infantile.
5. Termination of requesting assistance when he is able to function independently.

Specific Objective B

The student, when independent in toileting, closes the bathroom and/or stall door for privacy.

Time Chart — Student's Name

	7-8	8-9	9-10	10-11	11-12	12-1	1-2	2-3	3-4	4-5	5-6	6-7	7-8	8-9
Monday		8:15	9:20		11:15		1:30							
Tuesday		8:10	9:00		11:11									
Wednesday		8:15	9:30		11:15		1:15							
Thursday														
Friday														
Saturday														
Sunday														

Figure 1. Time chart for toileting.

Maintenance Check Chart—Student's Name

	7-8	8-9	9-10	10-11	11-12	12-1	1-2	2-3	3-4	4-5	5-6	6-7	7-8	8-9
Monday	7:30 dry	8:30 dry	9:30 wet	10:30 dry	11:30 dry	12:30 dry	1:30 dry							
Tuesday	wet	dry	dry	dry	dry	dry								
Wednesday	dry	dry	dry											
Thursday														
Friday														
Saturday														
Sunday														

Figure 2. Maintenance chart for toileting.

Functional Settings and Suggested Instructional Activities

School

1. Set specific times during the school day (e.g., before or after lunch and during recess) when students are free to go to the bathroom. Chart if they remember to close the door after entering the bathroom. If they forget, remind them.
2. At toileting time, indicate through gesture and/or words that toileting takes place only in the bathroom, and students in other rooms should not be able to see us or we see them. Indicate that closed doors stop others from seeing into the bathroom. (*Note:* Locks should be placed on bathroom doors only after the student has developed the cognitive and fine motor skills involved in unlocking a door. Doors at all times should be capable of being opened from the outside in case of an emergency.)

Home and Community

1. Ask the parents to observe whether or not their child closes the bathroom door when he goes to the toilet. If the student fails to close the door, encourage the parents to remind him while closing the door.
2. Before taking the students on an outing, field trip, or community visit, check to see what bathroom facilities are available, e.g., public restrooms (movie) or individual bathrooms (private residence). Observe to see if the student closes the bathroom or stall door during toileting. If he forgets, encourage him to close the door.

Functional Emphases In designing your own instructional activities and plans, emphasize the following elements:

1. Use of acceptable safety procedures when closing a bathroom door (e.g., not locking the door unless the child is capable of unlocking and locking a door in a public restroom).
2. Avoidance of a toilet that is occupied, not functioning, or being cleaned or repaired.

Specific Objective C

The student removes, lowers, unfastens, and/or opens appropriate clothing before toileting.

Functional Settings and Suggested Instructional Activities

School

1. During bathroom time(s) observe how the student removes, lowers, unfastens, and opens his clothing. If the student is having difficulty, assist him while explaining orally and/or through gestures what you are doing.

2. Practice dressing and undressing with oversize clothing worn over the student's regular clothes.

Home and Community

1. Ask the parents to monitor whether their child is having difficulty lowering, removing, fastening, or opening his clothing before she goes to the bathroom. If difficulties exist, provide suggestions (e.g., loose clothing, fewer buttons, and the use of Velcro fasteners) about ways the parents can help to improve the situation.
2. Plan a visit to a store or event in the community. Before the trip, provide time for the student to practice (in a bathroom) removing, lowering, unfastening, and/or opening specific clothing that would interfere with or restrict him from going to the bathroom. If this part of the activity is successful, proceed to the community event, allowing time for at least one community restroom stop.

Functional Emphases In designing your own instructional activities and plans, emphasize the following elements:

1. Use of appropriate clothing that can be easily removed, lowered, unfastened, and/or opened.
2. Avoidance of clothing that has too many buttons, snaps, zippers, or fasteners.
3. Use of clothing that is not too tight.
4. Use of clothing that is age appropriate (e.g., no elastic waist bands for older students).
5. Placement of the student's clothing so that it is not soiled by touching the bathroom floor.

Specific Objective D

The student, when appropriate, either raises a toilet seat for voiding or uses a urinal.

Functional Settings and Suggested Instructional Activities

School

1. During toilet time, take the student to the bathroom. Point out the toilet seat and explain that it should be down when someone is going to sit on the toilet and raised when someone is going to urinate while in the standing position.
2. During bathroom times, remind the student to lift the toilet seat before voiding. (It is important that this reminder be made privately to avoid any embarrassment for the student.) If the student continues to forget to lift the toilet seat, place a set of rules in either written, picture, or rebus form by

the toilet (i.e., lift the seat, flush, and lower the seat). Ask him to read or identify these rules before he goes to the bathroom.

Home and Community

1. Enlist the help of the parents in monitoring whether their male child lifts the toilet seat before voiding when at home. Tell the parents to demonstrate to their child how to lift the toilet seat before voiding. Remind them to emphasize lowering the toilet seat after voiding.
2. When on a community outing or activity, set a specific time to go to the bathroom. Select a place that has restrooms with urinals as well as toilets (e.g., theaters, department stores, recreation parks, or shopping centers). Encourage the male student to use the urinal correctly. It may be necessary for a male teacher to demonstrate how to stand in front of a urinal, how to flush, and in certain instances how to decide which size urinal is appropriate.

Functional Emphases   In designing your own instructional activities and plans, emphasize the following elements:

1. Use of good health habits after voiding (i.e., washing and drying hands).
2. Use of good health and sanitary procedures before voiding (e.g., avoiding urinals or toilets that are unclean or have excessive odors).
3. Awareness of situations when other people are waiting to use the same toilet or urinal (e.g., at ball games, theaters, and department stores).
4. Avoidance of deodorizers or screens placed in urinals.
5. Use of appropriate behavior when using a toilet or urinal (e.g., not putting in excessive paper, unnecessary flushing, and discarding foreign objects).

Specific Objective E

The student sits on the toilet seat for eliminating or for voiding. (Note: Female teachers should implement activities with female students and male teachers with male students when possible.)

Functional Settings and Suggested Instructional Activities

School

1. During bathroom time, observe how the student sits on the toilet seat. Provide him some stability if he is having difficulty. Gradually decrease assistance until the student appears at ease when sitting on the toilet seat. (*Note:* Adaptive equipment should be used when necessary.)
2. During bathroom time and only when necessary, monitor to see that the student is sitting correctly on the toilet seat. Because the privacy of the student is very important, only observe if there is a need to monitor this behavior.

3. If the student appears to be having difficulty sitting on the toilet seat, hold him so that he feels secure. When he is steady, remove your hands. Never leave the student alone until he has mastered the total toileting procedure. Support the student whenever he appears afraid or uncertain of his balance.

Home and Community

1. Enlist the help of the parents to monitor how their child is sitting on the toilet seat. Provide suggestions and/or help if they are experiencing difficulties.
2. When the student has to go to the bathroom, provide him with experience sitting on a variety of toilet seats that are typically found in community restrooms (i.e., split seat, round, and oval).

Functional Emphases In designing your own instructional activities and plans, emphasize the following elements:

1. Use of safety procedures during toileting, especially for students with balance problems.
2. Observance of good health habits (e.g., sitting on a clean toilet seat).
3. Avoidance of public restrooms that are dirty or in unsafe areas.
4. Arrangement for having a responsible person with the student if problems are anticipated.
5. Use of adaptive equipment when needed.

Specific Objective F

The student wipes himself after voiding or eliminating. (*Note:* If the student is a boy, tell him to practice wiping himself with toilet paper. Boys may wipe from front to back or back to front. If the student is a girl, tell her to practice wiping herself with toilet paper, using a front-to-back movement).

Functional Settings and Suggested Instructional Activities

School

1. Observe to see whether the student is wiping himself using the proper movement and is doing so thoroughly.
2. Develop a checklist for bathroom objectives. Include on this list an objective on wiping oneself after using the toilet. Post this chart on or near the bathroom door. If more privacy is preferred, give each student his own checklist. At specific times, observe to see if he is using the checklist.

Home and Community

1. Set up a time each month, or, if necessary, more often to call the student's parents. Ask them to monitor whether their child is remembering to wipe

himself after using the toilet. Send a note home as a reminder for those parents who cannot be reached by phone.

2. Before visiting a community restroom, remind the student of acceptable bathroom behaviors. Monitor how well he uses the bathroom, wipes himself, and flushes the toilet.

Functional Emphases In designing your own instructional activities and plans, emphasize the following elements:

1. Use of appropriate wiping procedure (i.e., wiping front to back for females).
2. Inclusion of all apropriate health habits (e.g., washing hands, covering the toilet seat with paper when necessary, and, when necessary, flushing the toilet before use).
3. Selection of public restrooms that are clean and in safe areas.
4. Selection of public toilets that have toilet paper, appropriate-size seats, and, when necessary, adaptive equipment.

Specific Objective G

The student flushes the toilet after wiping himself or flushes the urinal after voiding.

Functional Settings and Suggested Instructional Activities

School

1. Randomly check to see that the toilet has been flushed after the student has used it. When necessary, or if the child is only partially flushing the toilet (i.e., does not put enough pressure on the handle or flusher), demonstrate the correct way to flush the toilet.
2. Once the student has acquired the motor skill to flush the toilet, remind him (verbally or nonverbally) to flush. If he completes the act, reward him immediately. (*Note:* Activities involving flushing should be limited to those that are purely functional so that flushing for fun is not encouraged or reinforced.)

Home and Community

1. Call the parents and ask them to unobtrusively monitor whether their child flushes the toilet after he uses it. Suggest that they not interfere with the child's privacy when the child is independent.
2. Visit a variety of public restrooms so that the student has experiences with the various kinds of flushing mechanisms.

Functional Emphases In designing your own instructional activities and plans, emphasize the following elements:

1. Selection of bathrooms or public restrooms that have toilets that are clean and in working condition.
2. Use of appropriate health and social behaviors after going to the bathroom (e.g., disposing of used toilet paper in the toilet and flushing the toilet).
3. Application of appropriate hygiene and grooming skills after toileting (e.g., wiping himself properly and straightening his clothes).

Specific Objective H

The student washes and dries his hands after toileting.

Functional Settings and Suggested Instructional Activities

School

1. Ask the parents to help you provide each student with his own grooming aids, including his own bar of soap. These can be kept in a special place in the student's desk, locker, or learning area. Initially remind the student to check his area for any grooming aids he may need before toileting. Congratulate the student when he appropriately washes and dries his hands after using the toilet.
2. Wait for the student to finish using the toilet. Ask the student, "Did you wash and dry your hands?" If he has, reward him. If he has not, take him back to the bathroom and assist him in washing and drying his hands.
3. Tape a $3 \times 5''$ index card with the student's name on it next to the bathroom. Each time the student appropriately washes and dries his hands after using the toilet, tell him to record it by using a check mark, stars, etc.

Home and Community

1. Send home a checklist on bathroom behaviors to the student's parents. As part of this checklist, list several behaviors that require the parents to observe whether their child is washing and drying his hands after toileting. If this behavior is not occurring, provide suggestions to the parents such as leaving a bar of soap or a liquid soap dispenser near the toilet. The soap and/or dispenser can be in the child's favorite color.
2. After a community activity and/or when there is a need to go to a community restroom, observe to see if the student washes and dries his hands after using the toilet. It may be necessary to demonstrate how to use some of the soap dispensers typically found in public restrooms. When the student appropriately and correctly washes and dries his hands, record it. Later review the trip and praise the student for his appropriate social behaviors. Be sure to state exactly the behaviors for which you are praising him.

Functional Emphases In designing your own instructional activities and plans, emphasize the following elements:

1. Selection of bathrooms that have properly functioning sinks or wash basins.
2. Use of public restroom equipment for washing and drying hands (e.g., soap and towel dispensers).
3. Identification of hot and cold faucets by letters, colors, or rebuses.
4. Use of a variety of bathroom faucets, including those with single-lever action for hot and cold and spring-loaded faucets that automatically turn off when released as well as typical faucets.
5. Regulation of water temperature by first turning on the cold faucet and gradually turning on the hot faucet until the desired temperature is reached.
6. Avoidance of used bars of soap placed in public restrooms and of continuous cloth towel rolls.
7. Use of public restroom equipment for drying hands (e.g., paper towel dispenser and hand blower).
8. Disposal of paper towels after drying in appropriate receptacles or containers.

Specific Objective I

The student dresses and/or arranges clothing after toileting.

Functional Settings and Suggested Instructional Activities

School

1. After the student has voided or eliminated and wiped himself, indicate through gesture and/or words that he must dress himself before he leaves the bathroom and goes back to his class.
2. Place an unbreakable mirror in the inside of the bathroom door. Instruct the student to check his appearance before he leaves the bathroom, making sure his clothing is arranged properly (i.e., tucked in, zipped, buttoned, snapped, or closed).

Community

1. On trips to public restrooms and at home encourage the student to use the mirrors placed there to arrange his clothes properly. Remind him especially of the need to check that his fly is closed.
2. As part of a community outing, set aside time to go to a public restroom. Observe how the student's clothing looks after he uses the bathroom. If his appearance is inappropriate, take him aside *privately* and tell him to correct or improve his appearance. When possible, ask him to look at himself in a mirror to verify what you are saying.

Functional Emphases In designing your own instructional activities and plans, emphasize the following elements:

1. Use of appropriately fitting clothing.
2. Avoidance of decorative snaps or fasteners that are difficult to open and close.
3. Use of appropriate dressing skills.
4. Selection of bathrooms that are well lit, clean, and in safe areas.
5. Use of mirrors to check appearance.
6. Closing of the fly.

Specific Objective J

The student locates and uses a bathroom or public restroom independently.

Functional Settings and Suggested Instructional Activities

School

1. Check to see how independent the student is in finding the school bathroom. Provide opportunities to use bathroom(s) that are in or near his room as well as in different parts of the school. Check to see that the student uses the appropriate bathroom. Provide help when needed.
2. If the student might be transferred to another school in the district (e.g., he is moving from the middle school to the senior high), visit that school with the student and ask him to locate the restrooms there.

Home and Community

1. Ask the student's parents if their child knows where the bathroom(s) are located in his home. If the student has difficulty in finding the bathroom, provide suggestions to the parent on how to achieve this objective (e.g., placing a rebus or symbol outside the bathroom and developing a toilet schedule that includes going to each bathroom in the house if there is more than one).
2. Review the various signs and symbols found on public restrooms. Make a chart of these signs and locate them in the community.
3. When taking interstate bus, plane, or train trips, use the toilet facilities on these conveyances. Remind the student that other people may be waiting to use the same facilities.

Functional Emphases In designing your own instructional activities and plans, emphasize the following elements:

1. Avoidance of public restrooms in unsafe areas.
2. Avoidance of public restrooms that need repair and/or cleaning.
3. Use of appropriate social behaviors during bathroom use (e.g., closing bathroom door, use of bathroom deodorizers, and flushing after voiding and eliminating).

4. Identification of sex-appropriate bathrooms by symbols, rebuses, or words appearing on bathroom doors.

General Objective II

The student will be functionally independent in drinking and eating in a manner that allows him to perform optimally in diverse situations.

General Information

Initially, control of the muscles involved in the eating/drinking processes (sucking, swallowing, and chewing) must be evaluated. The utensils used in feeding should be assessed relevant to type of material, strength, size, and appropriateness (plastic utensils are not recommended). Initial feeding stages such as grasp of utensil, plate-to-mouth movement patterns, and scooping of food all occur normally between the ages of 12 to 18 months, but vary considerably in students with moderate and severe handicaps. Consultation with an occupational therapist is necessary before the above objectives are incorporated into instructional experiences.

Teachers utilizing this section should continually chart the progress of the student. His appearance as he eats is an important aspect of the feeding program.

Specific Objectives

The student:

A. drinks from a cup.
B. drinks through a straw.
C. drinks from a glass.
D. drinks from a container (can).
E. drinks from a water fountain.
F. eats with a spoon in an appropriate manner.
G. eats with a fork in an appropriate manner.
H. uses a knife appropriately during eating activities.
I. uses a napkin appropriately.
J. eats in a socially acceptable manner.

Specific Objective A

The student drinks from a cup.

Functional Settings and Suggested Instructional Activities

School

1. During lunch time, observe how the student uses his cup. Provide assistance if he appears to be unstable in handling the cup or if there is excessive spilling. Practice with the variety of cups the student may come in contact with while in the community.
2. Assign a peer who can successfully drink from a cup to sit next to the student when in the cafeteria or lunch room. Ask the peer to provide assistance to the student when appropriate.

Home and Community

1. Assist the parents in selecting a variety of drinking cups that are appropriate for their child. Ask the parents to monitor how well their child uses a specific cup. Use the same type of cup or cups in class that the student uses at home.
2. When possible, take the student to a sporting or recreational event where he is to be a spectator. At specific intervals, ask him if he is thirsty and if he is, encourage him to use his drinking cup. Assist when necessary.

Functional Emphases   In designing your own instructional activities and plans, emphasize the following elements:

1. Selection of a variety of cups ranging from spill proof to those typically found in restaurants.
2. Selection of the right size of cup.
3. Use of safety procedures when drinking hot beverages.
4. Practicing of good grooming habits after drinking from a cup (i.e., wiping the mouth).
5. Use of special cups when there are motor involvements.

Specific Objective B

The student drinks through a straw.

Functional Settings and Suggested Instructional Activities

School

1. At snack or lunch time and when appropriate, encourage the students to drink their beverages through a straw.

2. Conduct a beverage tasting party where all the beverages are suitable for drinking with a straw (e.g., water, milk, soda, and lemonade).

Home and Community

1. Ask the parents to observe how well their child uses a straw. If the child is having trouble, ask them to describe what problems the child is having. Offer suggestions according to the specific problem cited (e.g., cut size of the straw, increase diameter of the straw, and/or change material of the straw).
2. Take the students to a fast food restaurant and ask them to use straws to drink their beverage. Ask one student to model appropriate drinking with a straw (i.e., no slurping, dribbling, or pinching of straw).

Functional Emphases In designing your own instructional activities and plans, emphasize the following elements:

1. Use of a variety of straws.
2. Use of acceptable health habits while drinking with a straw (e.g., not sharing the straw with others).

Specific Objective C

The student drinks from a glass.

Functional Settings and Suggested Instructional Activities

School

1. During lunch, practice with the student who is just learning to drink from a glass. You may wish to fill the student's glass to a certain point, help him lift the glass, and/or show him ways of tipping the glass so a minimum amount of liquid comes to his mouth.
2. Conduct a safety lesson on drinking glasses. Bring in a variety of glasses and ask the student to identify which ones are the most fragile (easily broken and/or difficult to hold).

Home and Community

1. When appropriate, ask the parents to use drinking glasses during their child's meals. Suggest that they may initially use a plastic or unbreakable glass. Ask them to monitor how well their child uses the glass and provide suggestions when necessary.
2. Ask the parents to take their child out to eat for his birthday or for a special occasion. Ask them to observe how well the child uses a glass. Ask the student to discuss this event in school the next day. Ask him what kind of glass he drank from in addition to asking questions about the meal.

Functional Emphases In designing your own instructional activities and plans, emphasize the following elements:

1. Use of good health habits when drinking from a glass (e.g., not sharing someone else's glass).
2. Use of good safety habits when drinking from a glass (e.g., selecting the right size and weight of glass and not using a glass that is chipped).
3. Awareness of situations and areas where glasses should not be taken (e.g., near a swimming pool or at public events such as ball games).

Specific Objective D

The student drinks from a container (can).

Functional Settings and Suggested Instructional Activities

School

1. Serve drinks in containers during special times at school (e.g., parties and school events). Observe how well the student drinks from the container and provide assistance when necessary.
2. Plan a beverage tasting party where the students have to taste beverages that come in containers (i.e., soda, juice, and tea). Monitor how well they drink from the containers. Praise the student if she does well.

Home and Community

1. Encourage the parents to purchase a containerized drink from a vending machine while out shopping with their child. Ask them to observe how the child drinks from the container. (Caution! The parents may have to help the child to safely open the container and to safely get rid of metal strips.)
2. Encourage the parents to take their child to social and/or sporting events in the community. Tell them to purchase drinks that come in containers (usually from vending machines) at these events. Ask them to monitor how their child drinks from a container.

Functional Emphases In designing your own instructional activities and plans, emphasize the following elements:

1. Selection of containers that are safe, appear to have no sharp edges, and are easily opened.
2. Observance of good health habits while using containers (e.g., not sharing a can and making sure the top of a container is clean).
3. Awareness of procedures to follow after finishing drinking from a container (e.g., discarding container in appropriate place).

Specific Objective E

The student drinks from a water fountain. (Note: For younger and/or physically handicapped children, the water fountain may need to be adapted for their use, e.g., provided with stools or railings.)

Functional Settings and Suggested Instructional Activities

School

1. Plan breaks during the day that allow the student to go for a drink from the school's water fountain. Monitor how well the student drinks from the fountain, how courteous he is in allowing others to drink, and how careful he is in not getting the water all over him or the floor.
2. When visiting other schools for activities or events, observe the location of the water fountains. Point these places out to the student. When he is thirsty, direct him to one of these places.

Home and Community

1. Encourage the student's parents to visit or shop at places that have water fountains. Suggest that they direct the child to the fountain when he is thirsty and assist him when necessary in obtaining a drink.
2. Locate water fountains in the community that have a variety of mechanisms that turn on the water (e.g., push buttons, pedals, and turn mechanisms). Provide the student with opportunities to try a variety of these mechanisms.

Functional Emphases In designing your own instructional activities and plans, emphasize the following elements:

1. Selection of water fountains that are in safe areas and are properly working.
2. Selection of water fountains that are clean and appear to be well maintained.
3. Use of water fountains that have a variety of switches, buttons, and other mechanisms that turn on the water.

Specific Objective F

The student eats with a spoon in an appropriate manner.

Functional Settings and Suggested Instructional Activities

School

1. Show the student a variety of spoons, including those with looped handles for children who have difficulty grasping a utensil. Ask him to hold and try

each spoon as if he were eating a specific meal or dessert. During lunch, ask him to use the correct spoon that corresponds to the type of food he is eating.

2. Prepare a luncheon in the classroom. Serve foods that can be eaten with a spoon (e.g., Spaghetti-o's, applesauce, and pudding). Praise the student for his appropriate use of spoons.

Home and Community

1. Ask the parents to provide their child with a variety of spoons during different meals. Tell the parents to demonstrate to the child how to use each spoon with a variety of foods. It will be necessary to consult with an occupational therapist if the child has specific feeding problems.

2. Suggest that the parents prepare certain meals or desserts that require eating with a spoon (i.e., soups, stew, and chili). Tell them to observe how their child uses a spoon in eating these foods and to provide assistance only when needed.

3. While dining in the community, order foods that are eaten with spoons. Praise the student if he eats appropriately and with good manners.

Functional Emphases In designing your own instructional activities and plans, emphasize the following elements:

1. Selection of the most appropriate size and shape of spoon.

2. Selection of spoons that are made of suitable material (i.e., metal and heavy plastic); avoid wooden spoons because they tend to splinter.

3. Modifications of spoon when necessary, such as wrapping tape around the handle, bending the spoon (see Figure3). (See also Special Materials List at end of chapter for source of modified cutlery.)

4. Utilization of a correct holding position for maximum comfort and stability.

Specific Objective G

The student eats with a fork in an appropriate manner. (*Note:* The use of a fork should not be taught unless the teacher has made the judgment that the student will be able to use it safely. Students who are destructive to others and themselves should be carefully monitored during these activities.)

Functional Settings and Suggested Instructional Activities

School

1. Encourage the use of a fork during lunch.

2. Look through magazines for pictures of foods that can be eaten with a fork. Paste these pictures on index cards. Next, ask the student to select foods that are difficult or impossible to eat with a fork. Ask him to paste

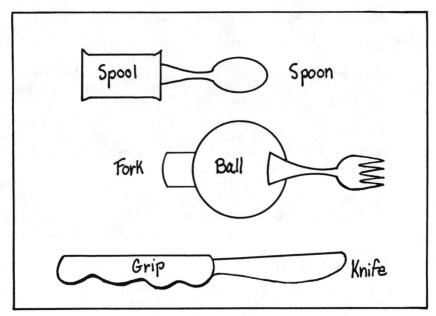

Figure 3. Modifications of eating utensils.

these pictures on index cards. Also, mix up the cards and ask him to pick out the cards that show pictures of foods that are eaten with a fork.

Home and Community

1. Encourage the parents to serve food their child likes and that is easy to handle with a fork (e.g., french fries, string beans, and carrots). Tell them to gradually include other foods that are more difficult to handle with a fork, such as spaghetti, noodles, and pie.
2. Dine out with the student. Select foods that are best eaten with a fork. Praise the student for eating correctly and appropriately with a fork.

Functional Emphases   In designing your own instructional activities and plans, emphasize the following elements:

1. Selection of most appropriate fork for the student.
2. Adherence to safety procedures when using a fork.
3. Modification of forks when necessary (see Figure 3). (See also Special Materials List at end of chapter for a sample source of modified cutlery.)

Specific Objective H

The student uses a knife appropriately during eating activities. (Note: Do not engage in the following activities if the student is self-injurious or injurious to others.)

Functional Settings and Suggested Instructional Activities

School

1. Show the student a variety of knives (e.g., bread, table, butter, steak, and carving knives) and demonstrate their use. Always use a cutting board to avoid marking or cutting tables or work areas.
2. Demonstrate using a sharp knife (with caution) to cut a slice of Italian or French bread. Tell the student to imitate your actions. Help him to cut a slice of margarine or butter off a stick and then ask him to spread it on the bread. Tell him to eat the buttered bread.
3. Prepare a class breakfast. Demonstrate removing margarine or butter from its container and spreading it on toast (use soft butter or margarine for ease in spreading). Tell the student to imitate your actions and practice this. Have the student cut his toast in half and eat it with his breakfast.

Home and Community

1. Encourage the parents to allow their child to make his lunch on certain occasions. Suggest that they encourage him to make peanut butter and jelly or similar-type sandwiches that require the use of a knife for spreading purposes. Ask the parents to carefully monitor how he uses the knife and praise him if he does it correctly.
2. Take the student to a pizza parlor as part of a reward for good work or as part of an outing. Order a pizza and, when it arrives, ask the student to cut or recut the pizza and give each student a slice.

Functional Emphases   In designing your own instructional activities and plans, emphasize the following elements:

1. Observance of safety rules in handling and using any type of knife.
2. Selection of the correct type of knife for a corresponding food.
3. Adaptation or modification of knife handle when necessary (see Figure 3). (See also Special Materials List at end of chapter for a sample source of modified cutlery.)

Specific Objective I

The student uses a napkin appropriately.

Functional Settings and Suggested Instructional Activities

School

1. Show the student a variety of napkins (paper, cloth, and the type found in holders in fast food places) and demonstrate their use.
2. Demonstrate wiping your mouth with a napkin. During snack time and lunch, tell the student to imitate your actions and practice wiping his

mouth after every few bites of food and sips of milk or juice, and at the completion of the meal or snack.

3. Sing the song, "Children, Look in the Mirror" (see Special Materials List at end of chapter for source). Encourage the student to look in the mirror after eating a snack or lunch and use a napkin to wipe his mouth in response to the song.

Home and Community

1. Suggest that the parents serve food that requires the use of one or more napkins during the meal (e.g., chicken, ribs, and melon). Ask them to monitor how well and how often their child uses his napkin.
2. Take the student to a fast food restaurant. Ask him to find the containers that hold the napkins. Order a meal and see if he retrieves a napkin from the holder before he eats. If he appropriately retrieves a napkin and uses it, praise him. If he doesn't, remind him.

Functional Emphases In designing your own instructional activities and plans, emphasize the following elements:

1. Selection of an appropriate napkin.
2. Observation of good social skills while using a napkin (i.e., using a clean napkin and discarding a dirty one in an appropriate receptacle).
3. Identification of when one may need more than one napkin (for foods such as chicken, melon, and other foods eaten with the hands).
4. Use of a variety of napkin holders typically found in restaurants and cafeterias.

Specific Objective J

The student eats in a socially acceptable manner.

Functional Settings and Suggested Instructional Activities

School

1. During lunch or snack time, encourage the student to follow your examples by eating small mouthfuls of food, taking small sips of liquid, chewing with the mouth closed, and using a napkin.
2. At lunch, show the student how to pass requested food or condiments to another person. Practice.
3. Show the student how to request food to be passed. When he does this correctly, praise him.
4. Prepare and serve a family dinner. Invite parents to attend a potluck supper. Praise the student for using appropriate social skills at this dinner.

Home and Community

1. Ask the parents to demonstrate socially acceptable eating habits by eating with their child and pointing out acceptable ways of eating.
2. Take the student to a family-style restaurant. Encourage him to practice serving and requesting food. Praise him for doing it appropriately.
3. Make a reservation at a restaurant that requires special attire (i.e., suits, ties, and jackets). Monitor how well the student eats in terms of being socially acceptable. Discuss the dining experience the next time you are in class.

Functional Emphases In designing your own instructional activities and plans, emphasize the following elements:

1. Use of appropriate social skills during eating (i.e., wiping the mouth, taking small bites, and chewing with the mouth closed).
2. Selection of restaurants or dining facilities that serve food in a variety of ways and styles.
3. Application of the principle that the only food he should eat is food on his own plate and discouragement of eating food from someone else's plate even if he just wants to taste it.
4. Observation of appropriate eating skills (i.e., using appropriate utensils, not using fingers, and eating slowly).

General Objective III

The student will be functionally independent in dressing and undressing himself in a manner that allows him to perform optimally in diverse situations.

Specific Objectives

The student:

A. puts on and removes clothing with no fasteners.
B. puts on and removes clothing with zippers.
C. puts on and removes clothing with snaps.
D. puts on and removes clothing with buttons.
E. puts on and removes clothing with hooks and eyes.
F. puts on and removes clothing with Velcro fasteners.

G. adjusts clothing when necessary.

H. chooses clothing appropriate for the weather.

I. chooses clothing appropriate to the time of day, situation, and occasion.

Specific Objective A

The student puts on and removes clothing with no fasteners.

Functional Settings and Suggested Instructional Activities

School

1. When it is time to go out, put on a poncho or other sleeveless article without armholes and then assist the student in putting his head through the opening of a poncho or other sleeveless item. Use a mirror throughout so that the student may carefully observe your dressing and then monitor himself throughout his imitation of the activity. Encourage him to check on the way he looks when the item is completely on. Practice putting on and removing garments. Reward him for a job well done.

2. Put on a sleeveless article with armholes, such as an undershirt or slip (if an item is inappropriate to your gender or if putting on an article of clothing would embarrass you, you may use another student and/or life-size doll or mannequin). Assist the student in identifying front/back and top/bottom of his piece of clothing. Help him to put his hands and arms through the armholes and the garment over his head and onto his body. Use a mirror and tell the student to practice putting on and removing garments. Reward him for a job well done.

3. Put on an article of clothing with sleeves such as a sweater or a blouse with no fasteners of any kind. Use an oversize garment to begin with. Assist the student in identifying front/back and top/bottom. Help him to put his hands and arms through the length of the sleeve and then pull the item over his head and onto his body. Help him to straighten his sleeves. Use a mirror and tell the student to practice putting on and removing garments. Reward him and repeat the procedure with his own garment.

4. Put on a pair of oversize socks or stockings. Assist the student in identifying heel, toe, and sock opening. Help the student to put his toes into the opening and then to pull the socks over his foot with the heel of the sock over the heel of his foot. Help him to straighten the body and top of the sock. Reward him and repeat the procedure with his own socks.

5. Engage in dressing and undressing activities during actual dressing and undressing periods.

Home and Community

1. Ask the parents to assist their child in putting on and removing articles of clothing that have no fasteners. Male children should work with socks,

underpants, undershirt, sweaters, and shoes (encourage the student to wear loafers). Female children should work with socks/stockings, panties, slips, ponchos, slipover dresses and blouses, sweaters, and shoes (only slip-on type).

2. Take the student to an indoor event, such as a movie or museum. While there, ask the student if he is hot and would like to remove his sweater. Assist him when necessary.

Functional Emphases   In designing your own instructional activities and plans, emphasize the following elements:

1. Selection of clothing that is in style and age appropriate.
2. Selection of clothing that is well made and not flimsy or easily torn.

Specific Objective B

The student puts on and removes clothing with zippers.

Functional Settings and Suggested Instructional Activities

School

1. Help the student practice using zippers on nonclothing items such as handbags, carrying cases, makeup kits, and portfolios. Take the student on outings that require the use of these accessories.
2. Bring in or borrow several coats with different-size zippers. Ask the student to pick a coat he likes and see how quickly he can zip it up. If he is having difficulty, assist him and eliminate the time criterion.
3. Engage in zipping and unzipping activities during actual dressing and undressing periods.

Home and Community

1. Ask the parents to assist their child in putting on clothing with zippers that do not require starting when it is time for the child to go out. Male children should work with pants and female children with dresses, slacks or pants, and skirts. Ask the parents to use oversize clothing first and then tell the student to practice with his actual clothing. Suggest to the parents that they help dress their child in front of a mirror so he can monitor his zipping, or help a female child with reaching behind her back to zip up a dress or blouse.
2. Ask the parents to prepare their child for putting on a zippered coat by first having the child zip an oversized coat. Ask them to practice with their child in front of a mirror. When the child is successful, the parents should gradually phase out the oversize coat and use his regular zippered coat. When success is achieved again, the parents should reward him for his efforts by taking him to a special event or place.

3. Ask the student to wear a zippered coat and take him to a restaurant, as part of a reward for achieving some goal. Observe how he unzips and zips his coat. Provide assistance when necessary and praise him if he does it successfully.

Functional Emphases In designing your own instructional activities and plans, emphasize the following elements:

1. Selection of a variety of zippers on coats, clothing, and accessories.
2. Avoidance of very small zippers that get caught or are poorly made.
3. Avoidance of decorative zippers that are different to start or are in hard-to-reach places.
4. Awareness of safety procedures when zipping (e.g., getting skin caught in pants zippers).
5. Use of adaptive or modified zippers when necessary.

Specific Objective C

The student puts on and removes clothing with snaps.

Functional Settings and Suggested Instructional Activities

School

1. Make cardboard and felt snapping pictures (e.g., an apple tree with snap-on apples, a clown with snap-on facial features). Encourage the student to work with this during his free time activities.
2. Assist the student in snapping and unsnapping snaps, first on oversize clothing and then on his actual clothing. Practice the activity in front of a mirror. Reward the student.

Home and Community

1. Ask the parents to use toys that teach snapping, such as a Dapper Dan and/or a Dressie Bessie doll. It is important that this activity is age appropriate; it is not recommended for children who normally would be too old for such toys.
2. Plan a trip into the community. Select clothing that has snaps for the trip. Ask the student to remove and put on this clothing at appropriate times. Assist him when necessary.

Functional Emphases In designing your own instructional activities and plans, emphasize the following elements:

1. Selection of a variety of snaps on different types of clothing.
2. Use of large snaps when small snaps present difficulty.

Specific Objective D

The student puts on and removes clothing with buttons.

Functional Settings and Suggested Instructional Activities

School

1. Ask the parents to send in a coat with buttons. When dressing to go outside, put the student's finger on a button and then immediately put that finger in the buttonhole to develop the understanding that a button goes into a hole. Next, put your finger on the button and grasp the button and push it through the buttonhole. Take the student's finger and put it on the button and assist him in buttoning.
2. Practice getting dressed for a party. Stand the student in front of a full-length mirror. Assist him in lining up his shirt, jacket, coat, or sweater so that the appropriate button is adjacent to its corresponding buttonhole. Reward him for lining up his clothing correctly.
3. Play "dressing up" in costumes or oversize clothes with buttons for Halloween parties or class play activities.

Home and Community

1. Ask the parents to practice with their child how to put on and remove clothing during dressing time. Suggest that they use large buttons to begin with and gradually work down to shirt-size or blouse-size buttons. Use oversize clothing if necessary.
2. Ask the parents to engage in buttoning activities during actual dressing periods and engage in unbuttoning activities at toileting times, before showers and baths, before changing clothes for recreational and other activities, and before bedtime. Tell the parents to help their child select clothes for school, and to encourage him to select some with buttons. After he has lined up his clothing so that an article is ready for buttoning, the parents should assist him in the buttoning activity. Suggest that they establish a buttoning pattern (e.g., bottom to top) and reward the child for the successful completion of the task.
3. During recess and inclement weather, check to see if the student has a coat appropriate for the weather. If it has buttons, suggest that he button the coat all the way up (if it is cold) or partially (if it is not cold). Then take a walk in the community.

Functional Emphases   In designing your own instructional activities and plans, emphasize the following elements:

1. Awareness of decorative buttons that are hard to use and serve little functional purpose.

2. Use of large or modified buttons for students who have difficulty with small buttons.
3. Selection of clothing with quality buttons.

Specific Objective E

The student puts on and removes clothing with hooks and eyes.

Functional Settings and Suggested Instructional Activities

School

1. Plan a dress-up party where everyone has to dress up in different types of clothing. Include in the clothing selection some items that require the fastening of hooks and eyes. Praise the student if she correctly uses hooks and eyes while dressing.
2. Plan a Halloween party. Gather a collection of inexpensive Halloween outfits that require fastening by hooks and eyes. Ask the student to select an outfit and monitor how well she uses its fasteners. Provide assistance when necessary.

Home and Community

1. Suggest to the parents that they select clothing for their child that has hooks and eyes. Tell the parents to monitor how well the student puts on clothing with these type of fasteners when it is time to go out. Tell the parents to praise their child if he does a good job.
2. Ask the parents to plan a clothes-shopping trip with their child. Suggest that they shop for clothes that include hook-and-eye fasteners. Ask them to observe how well the child dresses when trying on clothing using these fasteners.

Functional Emphases In designing your own instructional activities and plans, emphasize the following elements:

1. Use of modified hooks and eyes (larger) when appropriate.
2. Avoidance of clothes that have hooks and eyes solely for decorative purposes.

Specific Objective F

The student puts on and removes clothing with Velcro fasteners.

Functional Settings and Suggested Instructional Activities

School

1. Plan an exhibit that shows all the types of fasteners used for clothing. Ask the student to include clothes with Velcro fasteners. Ask the student to demonstrate how to use all the fasteners, paying special attention to how he uses the Velcro fasteners.
2. Ask the student to bring in any clothes he has that have Velcro fasteners. If he does not have any, provide him with some, if possible. Ask the student to demonstrate how he uses the fastener as part of getting dressed. Because the privacy and wishes of the student should be kept in mind, this activity should be closely monitored for possible causes of embarrassment.

Home and Community

1. When the parents are required to make a costume for a class play or a Halloween or other party, ask them to use Velcro fasteners. Ask them to demonstrate how to use these fasteners to their child.
2. Take the student window shopping and see if you can find any clothes that have Velcro fasteners. Point out these fasteners.

Functional Emphases   In designing your own instructional activities and plans, emphasize the following elements:

1. Use of Velcro when other fasteners are inappropriate for the skill level of the student.
2. Use of Velcro when fastener modifications are necessary.

Specific Objective G

The student adjusts clothing when necessary.

Functional Settings and Suggested Instructional Activities

School

1. Wait until the student's clothes need adjusting, as when buttons are unbuttoned, zippers are unzipped, a pant cuff is down, underwear is showing, or the shirt or blouse is out. Take the student to a full-length mirror and indicate in some way what is wrong. Assist the student in adjusting his clothing. Comment on the fact that he looks better, and reward him.
2. Wear your own clothes in a way that needs adjusting. Look in a full-length mirror. Comment that your clothes need adjusting. Adjust your clothes and praise yourself for looking better.

Home and Community

1. Provide the parents with a dressing skills chart for their child (see Figure 4). Ask them to encourage the child to use this chart and to look in the mirror to make sure his clothes are adjusted correctly.
2. Plan a trip into the community. Before you are ready to go, ask the student to check his appearance in the mirror. If he looks good, praise him. If he needs to have his clothing adjusted, assist him.

Functional Emphases   In designing your own instructional activities and plans, emphasize the following elements:

1. Selection of clothes that require minimum care and adjust quickly.
2. Use of appropriate social skills while adjusting clothes (i.e., adjustment is done in privacy and at appropriate times).
3. Application of skills after toileting.
4. Application of skills after trying on clothing in a clothing store.

Specific Objective H

The student chooses clothing appropriate for the weather.

Functional Settings and Suggested Instructional Activities

School

1. Take the student on trips outside the school building in the following types of weather conditions, wearing the articles of clothing listed below:

   a. Snow or cold weather: rubbers or boots, hat or head scarf, neck scarf, mittens or gloves, heavy or insulated coat or jacket, sweaters, and insulated or thermal underwear (optional).
   b. Rain: clear umbrella for better visibility, rubbers or boots, rain hat or scarf, and raincoat.
   c. Warm and hot weather: male—lightweight pants, shirts, jackets, coats, and suits; female—light coat, lightweight dresses, slacks, blouses, skirts, and lightweight pantsuits.
   d. Cool or fall weather: transitional polyester cottons or knits.

2. Discuss with the student what might happen if inappropriate clothing were worn. Demonstrate what would occur if someone wore clothes unsuitable to the weather (provided it does not present a health hazard). For example, the student could put on heavy clothes when the weather is hot. When the student begins to perspire, the teacher should assist him in changing his clothes while indicating that he had been dressed inappropriately for that day.

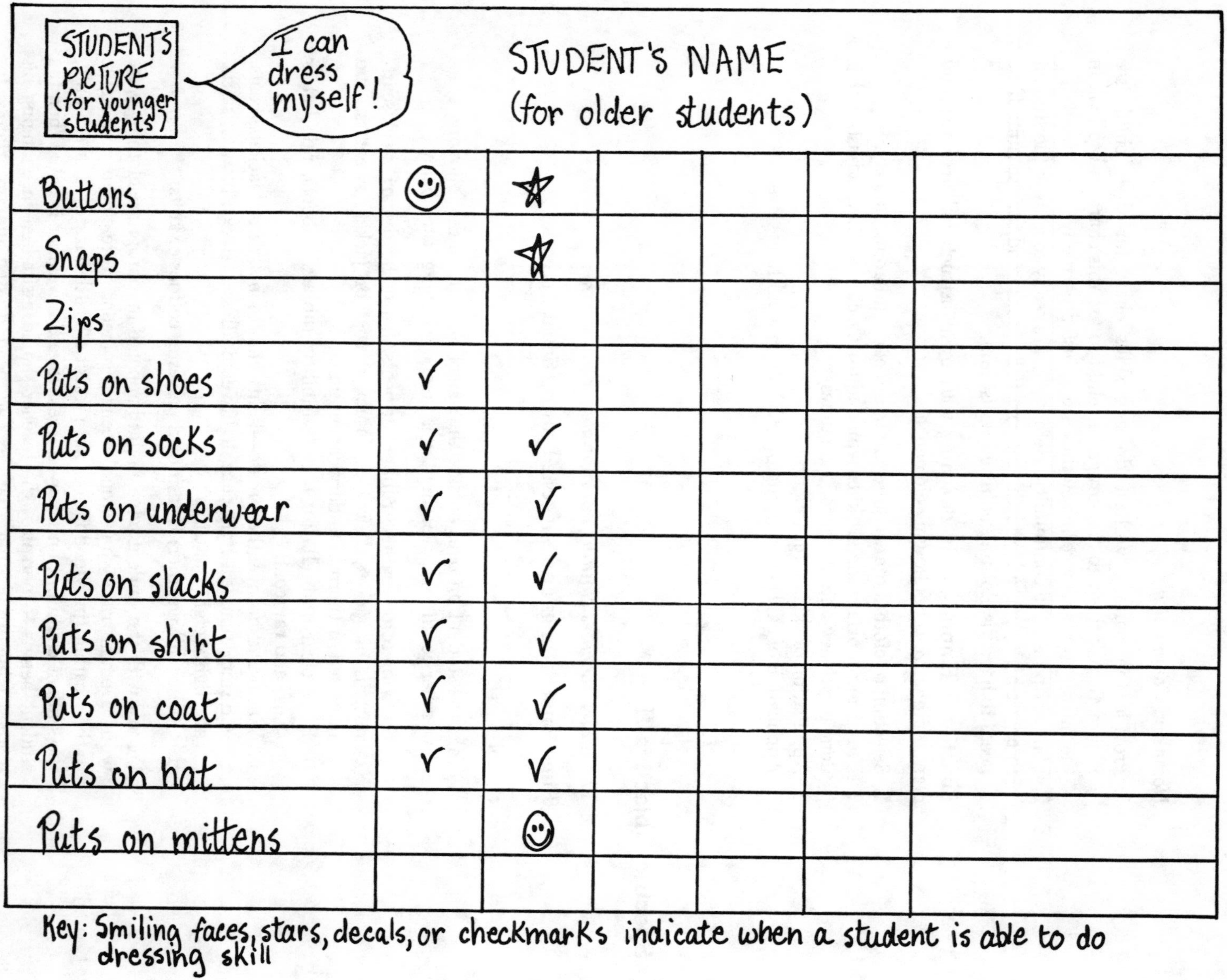

I can dress myself!

STUDENT'S NAME
(for older students)

STUDENT'S PICTURE
(for younger students)

Skill		
Buttons	☺	★
Snaps		★
Zips		
Puts on shoes	✓	
Puts on socks	✓	✓
Puts on underwear	✓	✓
Puts on slacks	✓	✓
Puts on shirt	✓	✓
Puts on coat	✓	✓
Puts on hat	✓	✓
Puts on mittens		☺

Key: Smiling faces, stars, decals, or checkmarks indicate when a student is able to do dressing skill

Figure 4. Dressing skills chart.

Home and Community

1. Ask the parents to encourage their child before he gets dressed to check the weather in some way: looking out the window, listening to the television or radio, or calling the weather service. Ask them to assist him in finding the way he is most capable of using.
2. Plan to go shopping for a class supper on a day when the weather is calling for showers. Check to see if the student brings in his raincoat. If he does not, review why he should always be prepared for weather changes, especially when inclement weather is being forecast.

Functional Emphases In designing your own instructional activities and plans, emphasize the following elements:

1. Selection of clothing that is suitable to a variety of weather conditions.
2. Use of a variety of systems that forecast the weather (i.e., radio, TV, or calling up a friend).
3. Awareness of health consequences of wearing too many or too few clothes for a specific weather condition.
4. Selection of appropriate clothing for recreational events (e.g., skiing, swimming, and tennis).

Specific Objective I

The student chooses clothing appropriate to the time of day, situation, and occasion. [The four categories to be chosen from are: (1) everyday clothes, (2) work clothes, (3) recreation (regulation gym suits, swimsuits, or tennis shoes), and (4) special events (attendance at church, temple, weddings, bar mitzvahs, etc.).]

Functional Settings and Suggested Instructional Activities

School

1. Discuss a scheduled activity. Ask the student to indicate in some way what he should wear. Reward him for selecting appropriate clothes. When the student is dressed for the activity, take a picture of him and post it on a bulletin board or in a display case. Promise him another similar activity very soon and follow through.
2. Match situation pictures from magazines with pictures of appropriate clothing.
3. Take pictures with a self-developing camera of the student dressed for each of the four categories noted above. Make a chart of the student's pictures so that he can refer to it as a model at all times (see Figure 5).

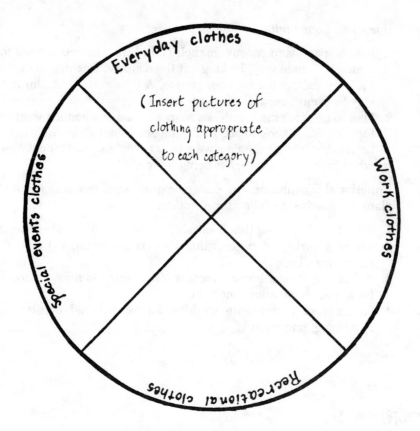

Figure 5. Appropriate clothing chart.

Home and Community

1. Ask the parents, when necessary, to assist their child in dressing appropriately for a specific activity by actively preparing him for that activity; for example, work clothes for gardening (work pants, work shirt, gardening gloves); recreational clothes for a picnic; and special events clothes for a school party.
2. Plan a function outside the school that requires semiformal attire (e.g., attending a concert and/or visiting a museum). Check to see if the student is aware of how he should dress. Discuss with him his options. If he comes in dressed appropriately, praise him. If he does not come dressed appropriately, review what he should wear.

Functional Emphases In designing your own instructional activities and plans, emphasize the following elements:

1. Selection of clothing that is well made, in style, and clean.
2. Relationship of sportswear to specific recreational events.
3. Use of appropriate social skills when dressed for specific occasions (e.g., weddings, funerals, bar mitzvahs, and confirmations).

General Objective IV

The student will be functionally independent in cleaning and grooming herself in a manner that allows her to perform optimally in diverse situations.

Specific Objectives

The student:

A. controls drooling when physically able.
B. controls the water flow or adjusts the water temperature for washing his hands and face.
C. washes and dries his hands and face.
D. washes his underarms and uses a deodorant.
E. brushes and flosses his teeth and rinses his mouth.
F. cleans and cares for his nails.
G. wipes and blows his nose.
H. takes a sponge bath.
 I. bathes in a tub.
J. takes a shower.
K. washes and dries his hair.
L. combs, sets, and/or styles her hair or has it done professionally.
M. shaves his face or body hair when appropriate.
N. uses facial blemish treatments when needed.
O. applies makeup when appropriate (female).
P. uses and cares for eyeglasses, hearing aids, and prosthetic devices when appropriate.
Q. cares for herself during menstruation.

Specific Objective A

The student controls drooling when physically able.

Functional Settings and Suggested Instructional Activities

School

1. At appropriate intervals, remind the student to swallow.
2. Place the student in front of a mirror when he is not drooling and point this out. Indicate your pleasure and reward him appropriately for not drooling.

Home and Community

1. Ask the parents to remind their child verbally and nonverbally to close his mouth to prevent drooling. They can touch the child's jaw as a reminder to keep his mouth closed.
2. Ask the parents to give their child a sip of his favorite beverage during meals. They should then encourage him to close his lips and then to swallow while not allowing the liquid to escape from his mouth.
3. Reward the student for not drooling when in public.

Functional Emphases In designing your own instructional activities and plans, emphasize the following elements:

1. Use of occupational therapists or other medical personnel as consultants in providing appropriate procedures concerning swallowing.
2. Use of nonverbal cues at appropriate intervals to remind the student to swallow.

Specific Objective B

The student controls the water flow or adjusts the water temperature for washing his hands and face.

Functional Settings and Suggested Instructional Activities

School

1. Before the student washes his hands, demonstrate how to turn the faucets on and off. Ask him to imitate your actions and praise him when he does it correctly.
2. Tell the student to touch hot and cold faucets when they are not being used. Color-code the faucets (red = hot, blue = cold) and indicate verbally and nonverbally which faucet is hot and which is cold.

Home and Community

1. Ask the parents to make certain that their child regulates water temperature by putting cold water on first. Tell them to demonstrate the temperature of both the water flow and the water in the basin of the sink.
2. Before and/or after eating in a restaurant, encourage the student to wash his hands. While in the restroom, observe how he adjusts the water temperature. Praise him if he does it appropriately.

Functional Emphases In designing your own instructional activities and plans, emphasize the following elements:

1. Consideration of fine motor skills necessary to complete and participate in activity.

2. Use of a variety of sinks (i.e., single faucet or double faucet and single spout or two spouts).
3. Observation of safety procedures involved in regulating water temperature (i.e., turning cold water on first and adding hot water and turning hot water off first and then cold water to avoid scalding).
4. Avoidance of faucets and sinks that are not working properly.

Specific Objective C

The student washes and dries his hands and face.

Functional Settings and Suggested Instructional Activities

School

1. When the student needs to wash her hands and face, show her a bar of soap. Demonstrate the use of the soap. For ease in handling, you may want to use hotel-size soap or break a regular-size bar in half. Assist her in using the soap to wash her hands and face.
2. After toileting, eating, and play activities, such as finger painting, pasting, and modeling with clay, indicate to the student that his hands should be washed and assist him in washing them.
3. Sing the song, "This is the Way I Wash My Hands":[2]

> This is the way I wash my hands,
> Wash my hands, wash my hands.
> This is the way I wash my hands,
> Whenever they get dirty.

As you and the student sing, pantomime the washing of hands.
4. Use a "Good Grooming Chart" on a daily basis to record all washing activities (see Figure 6).

Home and Community

1. Ask the parents to assist their child in washing and drying his hands during appropriate times (i.e., when hands are dirty, before going to bed, and before and/or after going to the bathroom).
2. Ask the parents to extend the washing of their child's hands after eating or strenuous play, and before or after bedtime to the washing of his face. After the child lathers his hands, the parents should encourage him to place the lather on his face and proceed to wash and rinse it. A facecloth may also be used when he washes his face.

---

[2]Sung to the tune of "This is the Way We Wash Our Clothes"; the words may be changed to suit varying activities.

Grooming Chart—Student's Name	S (or date)	M	T	W	Th	F	S	S	M	T	W	Th	F	S
Washes face	✓	✓	☺											
Dries face	✓	✓	☺											
Washes hands	✓	✓	☺											
Dries hands	✓	✓	✓											
Washes underarms	☺	☺	☺											
Uses deodorant	✓	☺	☺											
Brushes teeth	✓	✓	✓											
Cleans nails														
Showers														
Bathes	✓	✓	☺											
Washes hair	✓	✓	✓											
Dries hair	✓	✓	✓											

Key: ☺ means skill was performed
✓ means skill was attempted

Figure 6. Good grooming chart.

3. As part of a leisure-time experience, the parent may wish to pantomime and sing along with the Sesame Street record, "Everybody Wash" (see Special Materials List at end of chapter for source). It is important to emphasize that this activity should be age appropriate.

4. While in a restaurant, ask the student to wash his hands before his meal comes. Point out the type of soap dispensers in that particular restroom. Assist him in using the soap from the dispenser to wash his hands. While there, show the student the paper towel dispenser and ask him to use it after washing his hands. Assist him in removing a paper towel.

Functional Emphases In designing your own instructional activities and plans, emphasize the following elements:

1. Awareness of safety procedures in washing (e.g., avoiding soap in eyes and scalding water).
2. Use of good health habits (i.e., use of clean towels and clean soap).
3. Use of a variety of soaps and soap dispensers typically found in the home (e.g., small and large bar of soap, soft soap dispensers, and liquid soap).
4. Avoidance of restroom soaps and towels that are unclean or used.

5. Use of a variety of towel and soap dispensers typically found in community restrooms.

Specific Objective D

The student washes his underarms and uses a deodorant.

Functional Settings and Suggested Instructional Activities

School

1. When the student needs to wash under his arms (e.g., after strenuous play), assist him by demonstrating wetting and rinsing out a washcloth. Tell the student to imitate your actions and to wet and rinse a washcloth. Tell the student to practice wetting and rinsing the washcloth and using it to wash under his arms. Reward the student for using a well-rinsed washcloth.
2. As part of a grooming lesson and if the student is motorically able to use a spray deodorant, take the top off the spray can. Show the student the hole where the spray comes out. Place the student's finger on the nozzle and press down to spray. Tell the student to spray a small amount on his hand. Then assist the student in directing the spray to his underarms. Indicate in some way that only a small amount should be used.
3. Use a "Good Grooming Chart" to reward the student with check marks for washing and drying the underarms and using a roll-on deodorant (see Figure 6).

Home

1. Ask the parents to demonstrate to their child the use of a roll-on deodorant as part of being well groomed.
2. Ask the parents to encourage the student to use deodorant during morning washing.

Functional Emphases In designing your own instructional activities and plans, emphasize the following elements:

1. Awareness of good grooming procedures (i.e., washing at appropriate times and using deodorants).
2. Observance of good social skills (i.e., knowing when to use deodorant).
3. Selection of deodorants that may be nonallergic and/or suited to specific individuals or sexes.
4. Use of fine motor skills involved in washing and using deodorants.
5. Observation of good health habits (i.e., clean washcloths, soaps, and deodorants.).
6. Use of deodorants that do not pollute the environment.

Specific Objective E

The student brushes and flosses his teeth and rinses his mouth.

Functional Settings and Suggested Instructional Activities

School

1. Reward the student for brushing by saying, "Good," "Great," or some other word that indicates enthusiastic pleasure and by charting his daily brushing. Each time the student remembers to brush at the appropriate time, place a check mark beside his name on a "Good Grooming Chart" (see Figure 6).
2. Use (Colgate) red tablets to check teeth. Have the student chew a tablet and then stand in front of a mirror and check his teeth. If red appears assist the student in brushing to remove the stains. Use the "Giant Teeth and Brush" aid to demonstrate brushing (see Special Materials List at end of chapter for source).

Home and Community

1. Ask the parents to assist their child in his grooming by helping him brush his teeth. Suggest that they stand in front of a mirror and place their hands over his hand as he holds and uses the toothbrush.
2. Ask the parents to encourage their child to brush and floss his teeth semi-independently or independently and to brush daily.
3. Ask the parents to enlist the help of the dentist in demonstrating how their child should use dental floss as part of the child's scheduled visit to the dentist. Ask the parents to practice this procedure at home on a regular basis.

Functional Emphases   In designing your own instructional activities and plans, emphasize the following elements:

1. Awareness of the need to rinse out the sink and clean up after brushing, flossing, and rinsing.
2. Use of fine motor skills involved in uncapping the toothpaste tube, putting toothpaste on the toothbrush, and placing the cap back on the toothpaste tube.
3. Awareness of the need to use only a small amount of toothpaste on the toothbrush.
4. Observation of the sequence of steps involved in brushing the teeth.
5. Awareness of health habits, including using only one's own toothbrush and disposing of paper cups.
6. Use of age-appropriate activities, especially when using cartoon figures such as "Happy Tooth."

Specific Objective F

The student cleans and cares for his nails.

Functional Settings and Suggested Instructional Activities

School

1. After engaging in a work activity that is likely to lead to dirty nails (e.g., gardening), require the student to clean his nails. Praise the student when he attempts to clean his dirty nails independently.
2. Discuss the need for clean nails and hands during grooming activities. Reward the student for his clean nails by placing a check mark on his "Good Grooming Chart" (see Figure 6).
3. During leisure activities, play the Sesame Street song, "Everybody Wash" (see Special Materials List at end of chapter for source). Pantomime washing and pay special attention to the hands and nail area. Tell the student to practice using the nailbrush on his nails.
4. Show the film *Learning about Health—Questions about Health* (see Special Materials List at end of chapter for source). Encourage the student to discuss what it means to be clean and to have a good appearance.

Home

1. Ask the parents to call their child's attention to the cleanliness and good appearance of clean nails. When possible, ask them to use their nails as a model.
2. Ask the parents to demonstrate using a nailbrush to clean nails. Tell them to schedule clean nail checkups.

Functional Emphases In designing your own instructional activities and plans, emphasize the following elements:

1. Awareness of signs that indicate when nails need cleaning (e.g., after working in the garden, painting, or working with materials that leave dirt on the hands).
2. Observation of safety factors involved in cleaning nails (e.g., not using knives, paper clips, or other inappropriate materials).
3. Observation of safety factors involved in soaking hands (i.e., temperature of water).

Specific Objective G

The student wipes and blows his nose.

Functional Settings and Suggested Instructional Activities

School

1. During class, call the student's attention to his nose when it needs blowing or wiping. Do this verbally or nonverbally, or have the student view his appearance in the mirror before wiping or blowing his nose.
2. When the student is sniffling or appears to have a cold, show him a box of tissues. Demonstrate removing tissues from the box. Tell the student to imitate your actions and to remove a tissue from the box. Practice.
3. Place a check mark on a "Good Grooming Chart" (see Figure 6) when the student wipes or blows his nose independently.

Home and Community

1. Suggest that the parents demonstrate to their child in front of a mirror how they wipe and blow their noses. Ask them to tell the child to imitate their actions and to practice blowing and wiping his nose.
2. Suggest to the parents that they praise their child for wiping and blowing his nose at appropriate times.
3. Remind the student to carry tissues with him at all times, especially when he has a cold. Plan a trip into the community and check to see whether the student has taken tissues along.

Functional Emphases   In designing your own instructional activities and plans, emphasize the following elements:

1. Procedures for appropriately disposing of used tissues.
2. Observation of health habits (i.e., not using someone else's used handkerchief or tissue).
3. Use of a handkerchief only when tissues are not available.

Specific Objective H

The student takes a sponge bath.

Functional Settings and Suggested Instructional Activities

School

1. During grooming time, discuss sponge baths. Indicate that they are convenient to use when one is sick or in a hurry.
2. Provide an opportunity for the student to sponge bathe, when necessary, during class time (for example, following recess, physical education, work, or toilet accidents).
3. Show the film *Learning About Health—Questions about Health* (see Special Materials List at end of chapter for source). Discuss keeping clean and smelling clean.

Home

1. Ask the parents to explain to their child how to use a sponge and take a sponge bath. Tell them to practice with him wetting a sponge, squeezing it out, and washing his body starting with his face and working down.
2. Ask the parents to supervise their child as he independently gathers the materials for a sponge bath (i.e., sponge, washcloth, and towel) when he needs to bathe. Tell them to provide assistance when necessary in gathering the materials and taking the bath.

Functional Emphases In designing your own instructional activities and plans, emphasize the following elements:

1. Awareness of those times when it is necessary to take a sponge bath.
2. Selection of sponge bath materials.
3. Observance of good safety procedures (i.e., regulating water temperature).
4. Observance of good health habits (i.e., using clean bathing materials: washcloth, sponge, soap, and towel).

Specific Objective I

The student bathes in a tub.

Functional Settings and Suggested Instructional Activities

School

1. When appropriate, and *with* parental permission, show the Harris County Center film on *Bathing* (see Special Materials List at end of chapter for source).
2. Role play staying at a motel where there is only a bathtub and no shower is available. Use a sink to practice running and regulating the water temperature for a bath. Review the safety factors in taking a bath.

Home

1. Ask the parents to assist their child in taking a tub bath when she needs to bathe. Tell them to provide assistance only when necessary.
2. Ask the parents to use a doll (when age-appropriate) to demonstrate taking a bath. Tell them to point out the parts of the body that require special attention, such as the genital area and the anus.

Functional Emphases In designing your own instructional activities and plans, emphasize the following elements:

1. Adjustment of water temperature before getting into tub.
2. Observance of the safety procedures of getting in and out of a tub.
3. Placement of dirty clothes in a hamper.
4. Modifications of tub when necessary (e.g., hand rails).

5. Selection of bathing accessories (i.e., soaps, washcloth, and towels).
6. Appropriate washing of all areas of the body including genitals.

Specific Objective J

The student takes a shower. (*Note:* This activity is only for those students who will not require supervision for safety factors.)

Functional Settings and Suggested Instructional Activities

School

1. With parental permission, show the Harris County Center film on *Showering* as part of a grooming lesson (see Special Materials List at end of chapter for source).
2. Role play a scene in which the student spends a day at the beach or at a pool. Engage in a showering pantomime.

Home

1. Ask the parents to encourage their child to shower as well as taking sponge and tub baths. Suggest that they provide maximum supervision if they feel he cannot shower independently.
2. Suggest that the parents encourage their child to wash his body from head to toe while standing in the shower. They should also encourage safety habits such as checking the water temperature, moving slowly in the shower stall, picking up dropped soap carefully, and holding onto the towel rod with one hand.

Functional Emphases In designing your own instructional activities and plans, emphasize the following elements:

1. Observation of safety procedures involved in taking a shower (e.g., standing on a rubber mat).
2. Observation of the safety procedures involved in getting in and out of a shower (e.g., holding onto hand rails and standing on a bath mat).
3. Awareness of the need to gather items necessary before showering (i.e., soap, washcloth, towels, and shower cap).
4. Adjustment of water temperature before getting into shower.
5. Expenditure of a reasonable amount of time to shower (5 to 10 minutes).
6. Modification of showering area (e.g., use of hand rails).
7. Use of a variety of showers, including those that have a tub and shower curtain and those with a sliding door and a stall.
8. Modification of shower accessories (e.g., soap on a rope).

Specific Objective K

The student washes and dries his hair.

Functional Settings and Suggested Instructional Activities

School

1. In preparation for going out to a dinner, discuss with the student the need to wash his hair. If his hair happens not to be clean, point this out to him.
2. Show the Harris County Center film on *Shampooing Hair* (see Special Materials List at end of chapter for source). Discuss and explain it to the student. Show him pictures of dirty hair and ask the student what he would do to clean it.
3. Place a check mark on a "Good Grooming Chart" each time the student washes and dries his hair (see Figure 6).

Home

1. Ask the parents to assist their child in washing his hair when necessary. Provide them with basic steps and precautions to take (e.g., avoiding getting shampoo in his eyes and making sure that the water is not too hot or cold.
2. Ask the parents to make certain their child washes his hair on a regular basis and at special times when the hair needs washing (e.g., after swimming, after strenuous activities, and after working in dirty or dusty environments).

Functional Emphases In designing your own instructional activities and plans, emphasize the following elements:

1. Selection of shampoos that are nonallergic and safe for the eyes.
2. Practice of appropriate grooming skills (i.e., knowing when to wash hair).
3. Observance of safety procedures when in a tub or shower and when regulating water temperature.

Specific Objective L

The student combs, sets, and/or styles her hair or has it done professionally.

Functional Settings and Suggested Instructional Activities

School

1. During a leisure activity, sing "Children Look in the Mirror" (see Special Materials List at end of chapter for source) adding the line, "Do you see neat hair in place?" Tell the student to look in the mirror and answer "Yes"

or "No." If the answer is "No," assist the student in combing or brushing her hair.

2. Encourage the student to use grooming time to practice combing and brushing her hair. Assist the student in combing and brushing her hair until she is able to do it independently.

3. Once the student has begun to set her hair, schedule a class "hairstyle show." Ask the students to set and comb their hair independently and show their hairstyles to classmates and friends. Parents may be invited.

4. As part of an art activity, take "before" and "after" snapshots and make a display board of the pictures.

5. During grooming time, discuss beauty parlors and barber shops. Talk about appropriate behavior in public.

6. Read a high interest–low vocabulary story to the student about a trip to the barber or beauty shop. Discuss and demonstrate what goes on at these places.

Home

1. Ask the parents to look through magazines with the student and help her decide on an appropriate and flattering hairstyle.

2. Take a trip to a shopping mall. Ask the student to identify places where she might be able to get her hair cut and/or styled.

Functional Emphases In designing your own instructional activities and plans, emphasize the following elements:

1. Observance of safety procedures to follow in selecting chemicals for hair setting and in the use of scissors, razors, or other instruments.

2. Awareness of health factors involved in using clean materials and instruments (e.g., combs and brushes).

3. Selection of a variety of hairdressing places, including those that specialize in certain cuts or styles as well as schools for hairdressing that students could visit.

Specific Objective M

The student shaves his face or body hair when appropriate. (*Note:* Because of safety problems associated with shaving with a blade-type shaver, the activities presented and suggested use an electric or battery-operated shaver.)

Functional Settings and Suggested Instructional Activities

School

1. As part of daily activities involving grooming, schedule time for the student to demonstrate his ability to take care of his grooming aids. For example, take the student to a wastebasket. Demonstrate opening and cleaning the

electric shaver over the basket. Tell the student to imitate your actions and practice opening and closing the electric shaver over the basket. Practice cleaning the shaver with the small brush or other equipment supplied with it.

2. Demonstrate folding the electric cord into the storage space, putting the protective cap on the shaver head, putting the shaver in its case, and putting it away in a safe, secure, and suitable place. Tell the student to imitate your actions and practice the above steps.

Home

1. Ask the parents to practice with their child who needs to shave, turning on and off an electric or battery-operated shaver. Suggest that they may also wish to try the following procedures. For a male child, put a small amount of talcum powder on the student's cheek. Tell him to look in a mirror and shave off the talcum powder. Say, "Good," "Great," or any other word of approval. Gradually increase the area covered by the powder on his face until he proceeds to shave his entire face. For a female child, assist her in shaving off body hair (legs) in very gradual steps. Allow her to compare one leg that has been shaved with the other. Repeat activity for underarm hair.

2. Ask the parents to demonstrate how to prevent and/or treat razor burn.

Functional Emphases   In designing your own instructional activities and plans, emphasize the following elements:

1. Observation of safety procedures when using shaving appliances.
2. Use of a variety of safe shaving aids and shavers.
3. Awareness of the signs that suggest that he should shave.
4. Adaptation of shaving equipment.
5. Arrangement for supervision and monitoring when necessary.

Specific Objective N

The student uses facial blemish treatments when needed.

Functional Settings and Suggested Instructional Activities

School

1. As part of a grooming lesson, show the student pictures of people with clear skin and contrasting pictures of adolescents with acne. Indicate in some way that the people with acne can be helped to look better. Before-and-after pictures of the same individual or of a peer might be shown to demonstrate this.

2. During lunch, help the student differentiate between foods that contribute to facial blemishes (check with physician, if necessary) and those that do not.
3. Construct a chart or checklist of skin care activities (Figure 7); indicate with a check mark, a star, a decal, or other symbol those skin care activities the student observes.

Home

1. Ask the parents, as part of daily grooming, to supervise their child in washing his face with hot water and soap, ending with cold water. Ask them to encourage their child to wash his face in this manner at least three times daily. They should reward him for doing so and indicate that he is doing something that will help his face clear up or keep it blemish free.
2. Ask the parents to reward their child for substituting in his diet nongreasy and nonspicy foods for those that are acne producing. Provide them with a "Preferred Foods Chart" (Figure 8) to help them offer the child healthy foods.

Skin Care—Student's Name						
	M	T	W	T	F	Comments
Washes face	✓	✓	✓	✓	✓	
Treats blemishes				✓	✓	
Removes make-up					✓	
✳						
✳						
✳						
✳						

Key: Place stars/pictures/ happy faces next to each activity when student completes it.

✳ Add specific activities for each student's particular skin problem

Figure 7. Skin care chart.

```
┌─────────────────────────────────────────────────────────┐
│ PREFERRED FOODS CHART                                     │
├──────────────────────────────┬────────────────────────────┤
│            MILK              │          MEATS             │
│ milk                         │ hamburgers  salmon         │
│ cheese                       │ hot dogs    eggs           │
│ yogurt                       │ ham         liver          │
│ cottage cheese               │ bologna                    │
│ ice cream                    │ lamb chops                 │
│ pudding                      │ pork chops                 │
│ custard                      │ tunafish                   │
│        (4 cups per day       │ chicken    (2 servings     │
│         for teenagers)       │ turkey      per day)       │
├──────────────────────────────┼────────────────────────────┤
│      VEGETABLES/FRUITS       │    BREADS AND CEREALS      │
│ apples      asparagus        │ white bread                │
│ bananas     carrots          │ rye bread                  │
│ oranges     beets            │ whole wheat bread          │
│ grapefruit  celery           │ saltines                   │
│ pears       lettuce          │ oatmeal                    │
│ peaches     tomatoes         │ Cream of Wheat             │
│ apricots    cucumbers        │ Corn Flakes                │
│ fruit juices potatoes        │ Granola                    │
│             spinach          │                            │
│        (4 servings           │       (4 servings          │
│         per day)             │        per day)            │
└──────────────────────────────┴────────────────────────────┘
```

Figure 8. Preferred foods chart.

3. Suggest that the parents assist their child in establishing a routine for sufficient sleep.

Functional Emphases In designing your own instructional activities and plans, emphasize the following elements:

1. Use of fine motor skills in washing and using face cleansers and medications.
2. Selection of approved and safe skin blemish treatments.
3. Use of appropriate safety procedures when using hot water.
4. Avoidance of foods that contribute to facial blemishes.
5. Avoidance of purchasing unproved creams and lotions, especially those that are expensive.

Specific Objective O

The student applies makeup when appropriate (female).

Functional Settings and Suggested Instructional Activities

School

1. Plan social events that include females of adolescent years and older. Discuss the use of makeup as part of dressing for these events. In the discussion, point out that, just as there are different clothes, there are different types of makeup.
2. As part of grooming activities, show the student pictures of a made-up clown. Tell her that the use of a lot of makeup is funny, but just the right amount of makeup can make someone look prettier. Look through magazines with the student for pictures of the well made-up face of an everyday girl or woman. Ads for lipsticks, blusher, face powder, or cold cream are usually good pictures for this purpose.
3. Show the student pictures or slides of "before" and "after" applications of makeup. Tell the student to identify which is which. Discuss situations in which makeup might be worn. Draw up a list of words or pictures that portray situations appropriate for each student. Plan and carry out these identified events whenever possible. If not possible, role play the event. Assist the female student in dressing up for these occasions. Take both before and after pictures of the student. Display these on bulletin boards, in scrapbooks, display cases, or school newspapers, and on greeting cards.

Home

1. Ask the mother to demonstrate the use of standard makeup (lipstick and powder) on herself (when makeup is age-appropriate for the child). She should use a mirror for the application of makeup and encourage her child to use a mirror to imitate the motor activities involved in opening makeup containers and in applying makeup to her own face. She should stop immediately when she has reached the point beyond which the makeup would prove distracting to most people and indicate verbally and/or through gestures that she has put on enough makeup.
2. Ask the parent to demonstrate removing makeup. She should tell her child to imitate her actions and remove her makeup before she goes to sleep. She should reward her for completely cleansing her face before going to bed.

Functional Emphases In designing your own instructional activities and plans, emphasize the following elements:

1. Use of motor skills necessary for applying and removing makeup.
2. Purchase of nonallergenic and safe makeup.
3. Avoidance of using too much makeup.

4. Observation of health factors necessary after wearing makeup (e.g., removing makeup at night and washing the face).
5. Awareness of the age at which it is appropriate to wear makeup.

Specific Objective P

The student uses and cares for eyeglasses, hearing aids, and prosthetic devices when appropriate. (*Note:* The parent and teacher should work together on the activities listed below. When dealing with special aids and devices, it is important to consult and work cooperatively with appropriate medical and allied health personnel.)

Suggested Instructional Activities

Care

1. Show the student pictures of others, especially classmates or peers, who use the same device(s) used by the student. Point out persons around him, including the teacher, who use such devices. Indicate in some way that these people are using such devices because they need them and because these devices help.
2. Assist the student in putting on glasses and/or a hearing aid. Use a mirror if necessary and if it is not disturbing to the student. Comment on the help it is giving him.
3. If the student needs to wear eyeglasses, show him something of high interest that is difficult for him to see without his glasses. Put on his glasses, making it possible for him to see better. Comment on the improvement the glasses provided. Then remove his glasses so that he is unable to see well. Put his glasses back on. (*Note:* The same type of activity can be used with sound stimuli and the use of a hearing aid.)

Cleaning

1. Demonstrate cleaning of eyeglasses to the student. Assist him in using a tissue or Sight Saver.
2. Assist the student in identifying when his glasses are dirty. Show him pairs of clean and dirty glasses. Help him to distinguish between the clean and dirty pairs. Join him in cleaning the dirty glasses.
3. Help the student to identify when his glasses are dirty. Reward him for cleaning his dirty glasses.
4. Demonstrate removing glasses and putting glasses in a slip-in case. Assist the student to do so. Help him identify a safe and suitable storage place for his glasses.
5. Demonstrate removing a hearing aid and placing it in a safe and suitable place. Assist the student in successfully accomplishing the task and reward him.

6. Assist the student in keeping ear insert(s) clean. Help him keep cords untangled. Reward him for doing so.

Functional Emphases In designing your own instructional activities and plans, emphasize the following elements:

1. Consultation with appropriate professionals concerning the selection of eyeglasses, hearing aids, and prosthetic devices.
2. Appropriate selection of aids according to effectiveness, size, and comfort.
3. Consideration of where to store aids when not in use.
4. Awareness of procedures to follow to keep devices in proper working order.

Specific Objective Q

The student cares for herself during menstruation. (*Note:* The activities listed below can be modified for either the home, school, or community setting.)

Suggested Instructional Activities

1. For the female student who has not yet begun to menstruate, prepare her for its eventuality by showing the Harris County Center film on *Menstruation* (see Special Materials List at end of chapter for source). Show her pictures, read about it, demonstrate with a mannequin or science model, and discuss it. Tell the student that, when menstruation begins, it is something to feel good about because it means that she is growing up and becoming a woman. Assure the student that there is nothing to be afraid of, that it happens to all women.
2. Practice putting on a sanitary napkin. Use the kind of sanitary napkin that sticks to the panties because it is the easiest to handle and requires no belt. Show the student how to determine which is the sticky side by feeling both sides with her fingers, and assist her in sticking the sticky side to her panties. Show the student how to wrap up the used sanitary napkin and where to dispose of it.
3. Assist the student in identifying signs that menstruation is beginning. Help her put on the napkin.
4. Put the student on a napkin-changing schedule, perhaps every other time she goes to the bathroom to void. In the early stages, check to see if this is being done.
5. Help the student to wrap the used napkin and dispose of it in an appropriate receptacle. You may want to place a small wastebasket in the bathroom for disposal of sanitary napkins only.
6. Discuss the need for the student to be prepared by keeping a napkin with her at all times. Check first at regular, then irregular, intervals to see that she has one in her handbag.

7. Tell the student that she should not announce her period or discuss it with everyone. Help her to select someone whom she should discuss it with in case she needs help and for record-keeping purposes.

Functional Emphases In designing your own instructional activities and plans, emphasize the following elements:

1. Selection of the most appropriate type of sanitary napkins.
2. Observation of appropriate health habits when discarding used sanitary napkins.
3. Use of fine motor skills necessary for putting on and removing sanitary napkins.
4. Identification of appropriate ways and places to dispose of used sanitary napkins.
5. Awareness of signs that point to problems associated with menstruation.
6. Identification of steps to take when problems arise with menstruation.

Special Materials List

Kits

Giant Teeth and Brush. Kaplan School Supply Co., 600 Jonestown Road, Winston-Salem, NC 27103.

Self-Help Skills Instructional Kit. EBSCO Curriculum Materials, Box 1943, Birmingham, AL 35201.

Records

Everybody Wash (Sesame Street). Columbia Book and Record Library, 51 West 52nd Street, New York, NY 10019.

I Take My Little Hands and *Children, Look in the Mirror.* In *Musical Activities for Retarded Children* Abingdon Press, 201 Eighth Avenue South, Nashville, TN 37202.

Films

Bathing, Showering, Shampooing Hair, and *Menstruation.* Harris County Center for the Retarded, Inc., 3550 West Dallas Street, Houston, TX 77019.

Learning about Health: Questions about Health, Encyclopedia Brittanica, Educational Corp., 425 N. Michigan Ave. Chicago, Illinois 60611.

Assistive Devices

Build-up Handle Cutlery. Kaplan School Supply Co., 600 Jonestown Road, Winston-Salem, NC 27103.

Suggested Readings/References

Adelson, N., & Sandow, L. (1978). Teaching buttoning to severely-profoundly multi-handicapped children. *Education and Training of the Mentally Retarded, 13,* 178–183.

Alpern, G. D., & Boll, T. J. (Eds.). (1971). *Education and care of moderately and severely retarded children.* Seattle: Special Child Publication.

Anderson, D. M. (1982). Ten years later: Toilet training in the post-Azrin-and-Foxx era. *Journal of the Association for the Severely Handicapped, 7,* 71–79.

Azrin, N. H., & Foxx, R. M. (1971). A rapid method of toilet training the institution-alized retarded. *Journal of Applied Behavior Analysis, 4,* 88–89.

Azrin, N. H., & Foxx, R. M. (1974). *Toilet training the retarded.* Chicago: Research Press.

Ball, T., Seris K., & Payne, L. (1971). Long-term retention of self-help skill training in the profoundly retarded. *American Journal of Mental Deficiency, 76,* 378–382.

Barnerdt, B., & Bricker, D. (1978). A training program for selected self-feeding skills for the motorically impaired. *American Association for the Severely and Profoundly Handicapped Review, 3,* 222–229.

Bettison, S. (1978). Toilet training the retarded: Analysis of the stages of development and procedures for designing programs. *Australian Journal of Mental Retardation, 5,* 95–100.

Bromwich, R. (1981). *Working with parents and infants: An interactional approach.* Austin: PRO-ED.

Calkin, G. B., Grant, P. A., Bowman, M. M., & Gollop, D. F. (1978). *Toilet training: Help for the delayed learner.* New York: McGraw-Hill.

Campbell, P. H. H. (1977). Daily living skills. In N. G. Haring (Ed.), *Developing effective individualized education programs for severely handicapped children and youth.* Washington, DC: Bureau of Education for the Handicapped.

Colwell, C., Richards, E., McCarven, R., & Ellis, N. (1973). Evaluation of self-help habit training. *Mental Retardation, 11,* 14–18.

Crnic, K. A., & Pym, H. A. (1979). Training mentally retarded adults in independent living skills. *Mental Retardation, 17,* 13–16.

Dixon, J. W., & Saudargas, R. A. (1980). Toilet training, cueing, praise and self-cleaning in the treatment of classroom encopresis: A case study. *Journal of School Psychology, 18,* 135–140.

Dreith, R., & Kreps, A. (1975). *Community living skills guide—wardrobe II: selection and buying of clothing.* Denver: Metropolitan State College, The College for Living.

Edgar, E., Maser, J. T., & Haring, N. G. (1977). Button up! A systematic approach for teaching children to fasten. *Teaching Exceptional Children, 9,* 104–105.

Edwards, G., & Bergman, J. S. (1982). Evaluation of a feeding training program for caregivers of individuals who are severely physically handicapped. *Journal of the Association of the Severely Handicapped*, 7, 93–100.

Everyday eat the 2344 way. (1980). Rosemont, IL: National Dairy Council.

Ford, L. J. (1975). Teaching dressing skills to a severely retarded child. *American Journal of Occupational Therapy*, 29, 87–92.

Foxx, R. N., & Azrin, N. H. (1973). *Rapid training of the retarded.* Champaign, IL: Research Press.

Fredericks, H. B. D., Baldwin, V. L., Grove, D. N., & Moore, W. G. (1975). *Toilet training the handicapped child.* Marmouth, OR: Instruction Development Corporation.

Gallender, D. (1979). *Eating handicaps: Illustrated techniques for feeding disorders.* Springfield, IL: Charles C Thomas.

Gallender, D. (1980). *Teaching eating and toileting skills to the multihandicapped in the school setting.* Springfield, IL: Charles C Thomas.

Groves, I., & Carroccio, D. (1971). A self-feeding program for the severely and profoundly retarded. *Mental Retardation*, 9, 10–12.

Horner, R. D., Billonis, C. S., & Lent, J. R. (1975). *Project MORE: Toothbrushing.* Bellevue, WA: Edmark Associates.

Horner, R. D., & Keilitz, I. (1975). Training mentally retarded adolescents to brush their teeth. *Journal of Applied Behavior Analysis*, 8, 301–309.

Ingenthron, D., Ferneti, C. L., & Keilitz, I. (1975). *Project MORE: Nose blowing.* Bellevue, WA: Edmark Associates, 1975.

Keilitz, I., Horner, R. D., & Brown, K. H. (1975). *Project MORE: Complexion care.* Bellevue, WA: Edmark Associates.

Kramer, L., & Whitehurst, C. (1981). Effects of button features on self-dressing in young retarded children. *Education and Training of the Mentally Retarded*, 16, 277–283.

Lewis, P. J., Ferneti, C. L., & Keilitz, I. (1975). *Project MORE: Hairwashing.* Bellevue, WA: Edmark Associates.

Lewis, P. J., Ferneti, C. L., & Keilitz, I. (1975). *Project MORE: Use of deodorant.* Bellevue, WA: Edmark Associates.

Linford, M. D., Hipsher, L. W., & Silikowitz, R. G. (1972). *Self-help instruction, Systematic instruction for retarded children: The Illinois Program, Part III, Experimental Edition.* Danville, IL: Interstate Printers and Publishers.

Martin, G., Kehoe, B., Bird, E., Jensen, V., & Darbyshire, M. (1971). Operant conditioning in dressing behavior of severely retarded girls. *Mental Retardation*, 9, 24–31.

Martin, G., McDonald, S., & Omichinski, M. (1971). An operant analysis of response interactions during meals with severely retarded girls. *American Journal of Mental Deficiency*, 76, 68–75.

Matson, J. L., Marchetti, A., & Adkins, J. (1980). A controlled group comparison of procedures for training self-help skills to the mentally retarded. *American Journal of Mental Deficiency*, 84, 113–122.

Matson, J. L., Ollendick, T. H., & Adkins, J. (1980). A comprehensive dining program for mentally retarded adults. *Behavior Research and Therapy*, 18, 107–112.

Morris, S. E. (1973). *Program guidelines for children with feeding problems.* Unpublished document. Chicago: Illinois State Pediatric Institute.

Neely, R. A., & Smith, M. (1977). *Program for feeding training of developmentally delayed children.* Memphis: University of Tennessee, Child Development Center.

Nelson, G. L., Cone, J. D., & Hanson, C. R. (1975). Training correct utensil use in retarded children: Modeling vs. physical guidance. *American Journal of Mental Deficiency, 80,* 114–122.

Nutter, D., & Reid, D. H. (1978). Teaching retarded women a clothing selection skill using community norms. *Journal of Applied Behavior Analysis, 11,* 475–487.

O'Brien, F., Bugle, C., & Azmim, A. H. (1972). Training and maintaining a retarded child's proper eating. *Journal of Applied Behavior Analysis, 5,* 67–73.

Osarchuk, M. (1973). Operant methods of toilet behavior-training of the severely and profoundly retarded: A review. *Journal of Special Education, 7,* 423–437.

Perske, R., Clifton, A., McLean, B., & Stein, J. I. (Eds.). (1977). *Mealtimes for severely and profoundly handicapped persons.* Baltimore: University Park Press.

Piper, M. C., & Ramsey, M. K. (1980). Effects of early home environment on the mental development of Down syndrome infants. *American Journal of Mental Deficiency, 85,* 39–44.

Rotatori, A. F., & Fox, R. (1981). *Behavioral weight reduction program for mentally handicapped persons: A self-control approach.* Baltimore: University Park Press.

Sarber, R. E., Halasz, M. M., Messmer, M. C., Bickett, A. D., & Lotzker, J. R. (1983). Teaching menu planning and grocery shopping skills to a mentally retarded mother. Mental Retardation, 21, 101–106.

Smith, P. S. (1979). A comparison of different methods of toilet training the mentally handicapped. *Behavior Research and Therapy, 17,* 33–43.

Stainback, S., Healy, H., Stainback, W., & Healy, J. (1976). Teaching basic eating skills. *AAESPH Review, 1,* 26–35.

Stevens, C. J., Ferneti, C. L., & Lent, J. R. (1975). *Project MORE: Handwashing.* Bellevue, WA: Edmark Associates.

Stimbert, V. E., Minor, J. W., & McCoy, J. F. (1977). Intensive feeding training with retarded children. *Behavior Modification, 1,* 517–530.

Swain, J. J., Allard, G. B., & Holborn, S. W. (1982). The good toothbrushing game: A school-based dental hygiene program for increasing the toothbrushing effectiveness of children. *Journal of Applied Behavior Analysis, 15,* 171–176.

Thinesen, P. J., & Bryan, A. J. (1981). The use of sequential pictorial cues in the initiation and maintenance of grooming behaviors with mentally retarded adults. *Mental Retardation, 19,* 247–250.

Treffrey, D., Martin, G., Samals, J., & Watson, O. (1970). Operant conditioning grooming behavior of severely retarded girls. *Mental Retardation, 8,* 29–33.

Trott, M. C. (1977). Application of Foxx & Azrin toilet training for the retarded in a school program. *Education and Training of the Mentally Retarded, 12,* 336–338.

Tucker, D. J., & Berry, G. W. (1980). Teaching severely multihandicapped students to put on their own hearing aids. *Journal of Applied Behavior Analysis, 13,* 65–75.

Walls, R. T., Crist, K., Sienicki, D. A., & Grant, L. (1981). Prompting sequences in teaching independent living skills. *Mental Retardation, 19,* 243–246.

Weathers, C. (1983). Effects of nutritional supplementation on IQ and certain other variables associated with Down Syndrome. *American Journal of Mental Deficiency, 88,* 214–217.

Westling, D. L., & Murden, L. (1978). Self-help skills training. A review of operant studies. *Journal of Special Education, 12,* 253–283.

3 ‖ Gross Motor Skills

This chapter presents behavioral objectives and activities involving the student's gross motor skills, with emphasis on the use of the lower extremities. The student who is to function optimally, travel within his living and learning areas, and participate in diverse community and recreational activities will need to possess these skills, particularly those involving ambulation and movement in space and time (Presland, 1982; Wilson & Parks, 1976).

Educators are in agreement that moderately and severely handicapped individuals can make substantial gains in motor proficiency if they are provided with learning experiences that are functionally relevant and are diagnostically appropriate (Bobath & Bobath, 1975). Too often a gross motor program isolates skills that have been identified as developmentally significant, but that occur infrequently during everyday situations. Thus, although the handicapped student may become proficient in specific motor skills, a limited repertoire or a program that disregards cognitive and affective dimensions may restrict him from taking part in many work, social, and leisure-time activities and may limit his becoming a successful participant in community life. With this in mind, this curriculum presents a wide range of functional gross motor objectives concentrating on those that the student needs to perform in everyday situations (Galka, Fraser, & Hensinger, 1980).

In this chapter, preambulation skills are presented as the first general objective. Many students will require lengthy programming in this area, especially if they are developmentally young or are confined to a wheelchair. These skills serve as prerequisites to higher level skills and are often omitted from educational programs that promote gross motor development. It is important that teachers carefully consider whether their students need educational programming and/or therapeutic intervention in this area before they consider programming for more advanced skills. The use of a teacher-constructed, teacher-recorded behavioral diagnostic checklist as exemplified in Chapter 1 in addition to standardized assessment instruments can supply evaluative data as to whether or not a student requires additional programming in prerequisite gross motor skills before progressing to more advanced objectives (Hughes & Riley, 1981; Stone, 1977).

Many moderately and severely handicapped students have been denied educational, recreational, social, and work experiences because of their dependency on others for transportation or movement within their environment (Gruber, Reeser, & Reid, 1979). The use of assistive devices such as walkers, crutches, canes, and wheelchairs has enabled such persons to become more independent and has allowed them to participate more fully in society. The general objective regarding assistive devices serves as an introduction to this important area. The teacher should consult with occupational and physical therapists for additional information, especially in light of the rapid technological advances of recent years.

It should be noted that objectives and activities for nonambulatory students have been included in this chapter because a significant portion of the moderately and severely handicapped population is severely motorically impaired. This area has been neglected in gross motor programs that hold ambulation as the minimum performance level before programming for gross motor skills development. Many of the activities used with ambulatory students may be successfully applied to nonambulatory students.

The locomotion skills necessary within the home, school, and community have been determined after consultation with teachers, parents, and professionals working in alternate living units for the handicapped. The specific objectives presented involve travel within the community. Too often, moderately and severely handicapped individuals have been prevented from traveling because of their inability to navigate curbs, follow routing and detour signs, walk through automatic or revolving doors (Cipani, Augustine, & Blomgren, 1980), and negotiate stairways, elevators, or escalators (Cipani, Augustine, & Blomgren, 1982). Activities that help develop these skills are important learning areas for the moderately and severely handicapped.

The teaching of gross motor skills pertinent to recreational activities is also highlighted because of the great amount of nonworking hours or leisure time available to the handicapped. Even when sheltered workshops and activity centers are available, many handicapped students are unable to participate in sheltered work because of behavioral problems, lack of interest/motivation, or severe physical disability. Many are subjected to long periods of unoccupied time. Providing meaningful gross motor activities relevant to recreational activities will help these people to interact with others in leisure-time activities and reap the social and cognitive benefits therein (Stein, 1977; Wehman & Marchant, 1977).

The suggested readings and Special Materials List at the end of this chapter provide information on gross motor skills. The reader should decide which materials and information are applicable to a specific student or students being taught. Records and books are listed in the Special Materials

List by name only. They can be purchased at most local toy or record stores or through educational catalogs.

General Objectives of the Unit

I. The student will acquire those basic gross motor skills that will facilitate the later development of ambulation.

II. The student who requires assistive devices as an aid to ambulation will be able to use such assistive devices as canes, crutches, walkers, and wheelchairs to a degree that will allow him to function optimally.

III. The student will be able to move or walk, with or without assistive devices, to a degree that will allow him to function optimally in diverse settings.

IV. The student will acquire those gross motor skills that are an integral part of recreation activities.

General Objective I

The student will acquire those basic gross motor skills that will facilitate the later development of ambulation.

General Information

The term "ambulatory" is used to describe any student who walks, either independently or with the assistance of canes, crutches, or walkers. The term "nonambulatory" is used to describe any student who uses a wheelchair. The teacher should seek the consultation of appropriate medical and allied health personnel, especially physical and occupational therapists, for advice, approval, and programming suggestions for developing these skills.

Specific Objectives

The student:

A. lifts and turns his head.
B. steadies his head.
C. rolls over.
D. pulls himself to a sitting position.
E. sits without support.

    F. extends his legs.

    G. supports himself on one arm.

    H. crawls and creeps.

    I. pulls himself to a standing position.

    J. stands with or without support.

    K. cruises from object to object.

Specific Objective A

The student lifts and turns his head.

Functional Settings and Suggested Instructional Activities

School

1. Demonstrate head lifts and ask the student to practice head lifts. Put the student into a prone position and then tell him to lift his head and look at his toes. When possible, tell him to wiggle his toes. Ask the student to hold this position for a few seconds. At each attempt, gradually increase the length of time the position is held.

2. Encourage the student to practice head rolls. Ask him to roll his head to one side, focus on a target (favorite toy or object), and then roll his head the other way.

3. Show the student the Peabody Language Development Kit picture cards (use the level commensurate with the student's level of abilities and interests). Ask the student to lift or turn his head to look at or identify the pictures of familiar objects. (See Special Materials List at end of chapter for source.)

Home

1. Ask the parents to observe when their child lifts and turns his head. Tell them to assist him when necessary by placing a hand or arm under his neck and head. Tell them to support his head as he lifts and turns it.

2. Ask the parents to place a picture, mobile, television set, or other interesting object at the foot of their child's bed or crib. They should ensure that it cannot be seen by the child while he is lying flat on the bed. Ask them to tell him that there is a surprise at the foot of his bed, and encourage him to lift his head to see it. Tell them to change the object often to keep his interest.

3. Ask the parents to play "Hide and Seek" with their child. When he is lying flat on his bed, they should duck down below his level of vision and move around the bed and say, "Ready," when they want him to find them. They should tell him to lift or turn his head to find them.

Functional Emphases   In designing your own instructional activities and plans, emphasize the following elements:

1. Facilitation of lifting and turning the head to visual stimuli.
2. Facilitation of lifting and turning the head to sound stimuli.
3. Development of strength, control, and duration of response.

Specific Objective B

The student steadies his head.

Functional Settings and Suggested Instructional Activities

School

1. Ask the student to practice steadying his head. Tell the student to lift his head and steady it while looking at his toes. Tell the student to hold this position for a few seconds. Gradually increase the length of time he is expected to hold his head steady.
2. Use the Peabody Language Development Kit picture cards. Tell the student that he must lift and steady his head if he wants to see a surprise picture.
3. Tell a simple story using a flannel board. Place the flannel board in a position that requires the student to lift and steady his head to watch as you add flannel cutouts to the board.

Home

1. Ask the parents to assist the child to hold his head steady once he has lifted it by placing an arm or hand behind his neck and head. Tell them to support his head with headrests or pillows when needed.
2. Ask the parents to invite visitors or friends into their child's room. Suggest that they ask these visitors to stand so that the child has to lift and steady his head to see them.

Functional Emphases In designing your own instructional activities and plans, emphasize the following elements:

1. Facilitation of head control in response to visual and auditory stimuli.
2. Development of strength, control, and duration of response.
3. Development of head control as a means of surveying the environment.

Specific Objective C

The student rolls over.

Functional Settings and Suggested Instructional Activities

School

1. Place the student at the very edge of a mat. Tell him you are going to roll him over. Pick up the edge of the mat and roll the student over. Encourage him to roll the rest of the length of the mat on his own. Help him if he gets stuck before the end of the mat.
2. Ask the student to roll while music is being played in the background. Play music and encourage the student to roll first to one end of the mat and then back to the other end of the mat.
3. Place the student on his stomach on a mat. At the end of the mat, place a toy or object the student especially likes. Tell him he may have the toy to play with if he rolls to it.
4. Mark out a large circle on the floor with masking tape. Place the student on the floor at one point on the circle and tell him to roll around the circle.

Home

1. Ask the parents to assist their child in rolling over onto blankets that have been placed on the floor. Tell them to place one hand on the child's shoulder and one on his knees, say "Roll over," and help him to roll over. Suggest that they practice until he can roll independently. (This may also be done in a crib or a bed with sides; pad the crib bars or bed sides with bumpers, rolled-up towels, or blankets and follow the same procedures.) Tell the parents to remind the child that his arms and legs should be used to help him roll over, and have him practice rolling over on both sides.
2. Ask the parents to place their child in a crib or bed at the far side against the bars. They should then position a book, toy, or food that he especially enjoys at the other side and tell him he may have it if he rolls over to it. Suggest that they use musical toys as an added incentive.

Functional Emphases   In designing your own instructional activities and plans, emphasize the following elements:

1. Utilization of this behavior as a means of physical exercise.
2. Utilization of this behavior as a play activity.

Specific Objective D

The student pulls himself to a sitting position.

Functional Settings and Suggested Instructional Activities

School

1. Assign helpers to the student who is beginning to pull up to a sitting position. Instruct the helpers to help the student pull himself to a sitting position.

2. Use an inner tube to assist the student in pulling himself to a sitting position. Hold the inner tube and assist the student in locking his arms around the inner tube. Encourage him to use it as a support as he pulls himself to a sitting position.
3. Have an aide hold a shortened broom handle horizontally in front of the student. Assist the student in grasping the pole and pulling himself to a sitting position. Wrap tape around the handle for better grasping.

Home

1. Ask the parents to assist their child in pulling himself to a sitting position. Tell them to extend their fingers to him so that he may grasp them while he lies in a bed and help him pull himself to a sitting position.
2. Ask the parents to assist their child in a bed or crib to come to a sitting position by grasping the crib bar, bed rails, or headboard and pulling up. Tell them to place a mirror beside the crib or bed so he can see his progress.

Functional Emphases In designing your own instructional activities and plans, emphasize the following elements:

1. Utilization of this behavior to facilitate the viewing of the student's surroundings.
2. Utilization of this behavior to increase his ability to use his arms for play and for other functional activities.

Specific Objective E

The student sits without support.

Functional Settings and Suggested Instructional Activities

School

1. After the student is placed in a sitting position, push him gently to one side. Check to see if he puts his hands out to his side to brace himself. (This bracing to avoid falling is called a parachute reaction.) If he does not brace himself, assist him in doing so. Repeat activity, this time gently pushing him to the alternate side and then backward.
2. At music time, place the student in a sitting position on a mat. Sing songs that he enjoys and encourage him to sing along and clap to the music. Place the student who is at a beginning stage of sitting between two students who are able to sit independently.
3. Once the student is fairly confident of his sitting ability, begin to use furniture. Place the student or ask him to seat himself on a low bench with a back. Use the bench as a seat during snack time or at story time to keep the student interested in sitting.

4. Assign the student a specific chair in the classroom. Help the student put his name, color, or rebus on cardboard and attach it to his chair. Encourage the student to sit in his chair during all appropriate classroom activities. (*Note:* You may initially want to construct a 6-inch square box in which to put the chair so it will not flip over).

5. Seat the student on a backless stool or cafeteria seat. Point out that there is no back on this type of seat and that he must not lean back or he will fall. For a beginner, tape a piece of corrugated cardboard perpendicular to the seat, nearly at the back edge of the seat to remind the student not to sit back any further.

Home

1. Ask the parents to place their child in a sitting position on a mat or in his crib or bed. Suggest that they do a finger play or show him an interesting plaything such as blocks or small cars to keep him interested in remaining in the sitting position.

2. Ask the parents to assist their child in sitting without support. Tell them to place him on a mat or blanket in a corner and stand a second mat or cushion against the wall so he will not hurt himself if he falls. Tell them to assist him in sitting without support by gently helping him if he starts to lose his balance. Pillows may also be utilized to prop him up.

Functional Emphases   In designing your own instructional activities and plans, emphasize the following elements:

1. Utilization of this behavior to expand the child's control over his environment.

2. Utilization of this behavior to enable the child to manipulate toys and other objects without assistance from an adult.

Specific Objective F

The student extends his legs.

Functional Settings and Suggested Instructional Activities

School

1. Seat the student on a mat on the floor. Ask him to extend his legs as far as possible. Place a toy, game, or favorite object on the mat within reach of the student's legs when extended. If his toes touch the object, give it to him to play with.

2. Seat the student on the floor. Place a ball on the floor so that the student will be able to move the ball by extending his legs.

3. Place two students who are barefoot or wearing stockings on the floor on a mat, facing each other. Tell the students to extend their legs and tickle each other's feet.
4. Tape a balloon or punching bag to the floor. Seat the student on the floor and tell him to extend his legs to bounce or move the punching bag or balloon back and forth.

Home

1. Ask the parents to assist their child in extending his legs. If he sits in a chair, wheelchair, or other chair, tell them to lift his legs gently until they are extended in front of him. The parents should practice until their child can extend his legs as independently as possible, commensurate with his physical abilities (wheelchair children may be unable to do this independently).
2. Ask the parents to put a mark or picture on the footboard of their child's bed. Ask them to tell the child to extend his legs and touch the mark or picture. This is a good way to exercise cramped legs.

Functional Emphases   In designing your own instructional activities and plans, emphasize the following elements:

1. Utilization of this behavior as a means of increasing the child's ability to explore his environment.
2. Utilization of this behavior as a means of modifying the child's position.

Specific Objective G

The student supports himself on one arm.

Functional Settings and Suggested Instructional Activities

School

1. Give the student a box or container of wooden blocks or pegs. Tell him to support himself with one arm and dump the container of blocks with the other. Allow him to play with the blocks.
2. Help the student to play with blocks, small cars, or toy cowboys (any small plaything) on a mat, in his crib, or in bed. At cleanup time, ask the student to support himself on one arm and place the toys in a box or container. Use caution in selecting the size and type of object because students functioning
3. Ask the student to look through magazines or picture books while supporting himself on one arm as he lies on a mat, in a crib, or in bed. Use pop-up books as an added incentive.
4. Do exercises requiring the student to support himself on one arm. Tell the student to lie on his side and support himself with one arm. First, ask him

to raise his leg. Then ask him to raise it five times. Finally, ask him to lie on the other side and raise the other leg. Ask him to do this five times. If the student cannot lift his leg independently, ask a peer to help in raising his leg. This must be done on mats, in a crib, or in bed.

Home

1. Ask the parents to ask their child, while he is lying on a mat, in a crib, or in bed, to support himself on one arm. Tell them to demonstrate what they want him to do and encourage him to imitate their movements.
2. Ask the parents to place a toy, game, or favorite object within reach of their child as he lies in a prone position on a mat, in a crib, or in bed. Tell them to encourage him to support himself with one arm and reach for the toy or game with his free hand.

Functional Emphases In designing your own instructional activities and plans, emphasize the following elements:

1. Utilization of this behavior to increase the child's ability to manipulate objects in his environment.
2. Utilization of this behavior to facilitate body movement.

Specific Objective H

The student crawls and creeps.

Functional Settings and Suggested Instructional Activities

School

1. Tape cutout hand prints on the floor and connect them with yarn or masking tape. Ask the student to place his hands on the cutout hand prints and to crawl along the trail.
2. Construct an obstacle course of desks, chairs, and other large articles found in the classroom. Appoint a leader, and tell the students to crawl or creep through the obstacle course while following the leader.
3. Play a "crawling sweepstakes" on the floor. Make racing lines on the floor using masking tape or lines of colored yarn. Start a student in each lane. The first student to reach the end of his lane is the winner. Award prizes to each student who completes the race. Prizes may be stickers, stars, or a nutritious snack.
4. Play Musical Chairs using mats. Tape large colored circles of cardboard or construction paper on the floor or on large gym mats. Tell the students to crawl on the floor around the mats and onto a colored circle when the music stops. Remove a circle each time, until only one student and one circle are left.

Home and Community

1. Ask the parents to assist their child in crawling and creeping by demonstrating crawling to him. Tell them to help him to imitate them by moving his hands along or by giving him a gentle push. Suggest that they continually use verbal, facial, and gestural reinforcement.
2. Ask the parents to put a pillow under their child and place him on the floor (the pillow must allow his hands and feet to reach the floor). Tell the parents to gently move the pillow forward while encouraging the child to creep.
3. Take the student to a sandbox or a beach. Encourage him to creep or crawl in the sand. Make mountains and trenches of sand and ask him to crawl over and in and out of them.

Functional Emphases   In designing your own instructional activities and plans, emphasize the following elements:

1. Development of control over crawling and creeping movements.
2. Facilitation of speed and accuracy of creeping and crawling.

Specific Objective I

The student pulls himself to a standing position.

Functional Settings and Suggested Instructional Activities

School

1. Place the student so that he faces a classroom desk or table. Place his hands on the piece of furniture and assist him in pulling himself to a standing position.
2. Encourage the student, at appropriate times, to pull himself to a standing position. At snack time, lunch, or during a change of position between activities, encourage the student to pull himself to a standing position by holding onto someone's hand or a piece of stable furniture.
3. Conduct a "roll call." Seat the students on mats on the floor next to pieces of furniture. When you call each student's name, tell the student to pull himself to a standing position.

Home

1. Ask the parents to assist their child in pulling himself to a standing position. When he is sitting, they should offer their hands to him and help him pull himself to a standing position.
2. Ask the parents to seat their young child in a crib or playpen, facing the crib bars or playpen netting. Tell them to place the child's hands on the bars or netting and encourage him to gradually pull himself to a standing position.

Functional Emphases In designing your own instructional activities and plans, emphasize the following elements:

1. Use of a variety of equipment that aids and/or helps the standing process.
2. Identification of safe and appropriate places to practice standing.

Specific Objective J

The student stands with or without support.

Functional Settings and Suggested Instructional Activities

School

1. Play games that require the student to stand. For example, ask the student to pretend that he is a tree blowing in the wind and encourage him to bend his body in different directions. If the student needs support in standing, place him near a table or chair so he can grasp it for support.
2. Play Simon Says, with required standing movements. For example, say "Simon says, 'Stand up straight'. Simon says, 'March in place'."

Home

1. Ask the parents to tell their child to pull himself to a standing position. Tell them to assist him in standing with or without support.
2. Ask the parents to play music and encourage their child to stand and sway in time to the music. Tell them to modify the tempo and intensity of the music as he becomes more independent in the activity.

Functional Emphases In designing your own instructional activities and plans, emphasize the following elements:

1. Use of a variety of equipment that aids and/or helps the standing process.
2. Identification of safe and appropriate places to practice standing.

Specific Objective K

The student cruises from object to object.

Functional Settings and Suggested Instructional Activities

School

1. Construct cruising paths in the classroom. Arrange the furniture so that the student may cruise from one interest area to another (toy shelves to desk, table, and back, and from desk to bathroom).
2. Play a variation of Musical Chairs in which the student holds onto chairs and cruises until the music stops.

3. During class activities, ask the student to do things that require him to cruise (i.e., "John, will you please close the door?") Be sure there is a cruising path to the door. Gradually increase the distance between objects along the cruising path.
4. Once the student has started to cruise, gently insist that he do so rather than crawl. Encourage him to try to take a step or two, always within easy reach of you or the furniture in case he should feel unsteady or lose his balance.

Home

1. Ask the parents to assist their child as he cruises from object to object. Suggest that they initially use a long table for the child to hold onto and show him how to hold onto the table and cruise from one end to the other. Tell them to encourage imitation.
2. Ask the parents to arrange furniture in the room so that their child may cruise from one object to another and travel around the room. The furniture should be close enough so that he does not lose his balance when going from one piece of furniture to another. Furniture should also be stable enough not to tip over.

Functional Emphases In designing your own instructional activities and plans, emphasize the following elements:

1. Avoidance of furniture that has sharp or dangerous edges.
2. Selection of furniture that is stable.
3. Selection of cruising paths that are safe and free of hazards.
4. Selection and/or modification of games and activities that can help to promote cruising (e.g., Musical Chairs).

General Objective II

The student who requires assistive devices as an aid to ambulation will be able to use such assistive devices as canes, crutches, walkers, and wheelchairs to a degree that will allow him to function optimally.

General Information

The objectives and activities in this section are written from the viewpoint that the teacher may be the major provider of services in teaching the use of assistive devices to the student. It is important that activities taught in this section be shared with the parent so carryover, progress, and reinforcement can be enhanced. Appropriate consultation with medical and allied health personnel is necessary for prescription, measurement, and monitoring of activities and of all assistive devices.

Specific Objectives

The student:

A. uses walkers.
B. uses crutches.
C. uses canes.
D. opens, closes, and uses a wheelchair.

Specific Objective A

The student uses walkers.

General Information   There are several major types of walkers. The infant walker (Figure 9) is usually designed for children from 1½ to 4 years of age. It is adjustable in height from 18 to 24 inches. The child walker (Figure 10) is for children from 2 to 8 years of age who are not expected to be ambulatory in the future. Many of them have a padded body ring with an inside diameter of 10 inches. Many adjustable and select models are equipped with brakes. A walker that many adults and children use for functional ambulation is pictured in Figure 11. It usually has adjustable handrails.

Functional Settings and Suggested Instructional Activities

School

1. Place a rattle or toy on a chair in the corner of a room. Tell or gesture to the student who is in an infant walker to move across the room and retrieve the toy. Then ask him to bring it to you.
2. Tell or gesture to the student in an upright walker to follow a group of cardboard arrows that have been placed on the floor. Show him how to move the walker forward and then move his body in the same direction. Include curves or the turning of corners in the lesson. Encourage imitation.
3. Tape three weighted balloons to the student's walker. Place three empty cartons or baskets in different parts of the room. Tell the student to drop one balloon in each box as he reaches it. For the older student who has color matching abilities, tell him to drop the specific colored balloon in the box with the corresponding color on the outside.
4. Play a "retrieval" game. Tell the student to move forward in the walker to retrieve a toy or object from a chair. Tell him to move backward to another chair to retrieve another object. Be sure to tape on the walker a small bag in which he can collect the objects. Say the words (or gesture) "forward" or "backward" during the activity.
5. Set up a wastebasket in a corner. Give the student a small beachball or volleyball and help him to move toward the basket. When possible, tell the student to throw it in the basket. For older students, play a basketball-type game and reward the student when she scores a basket.

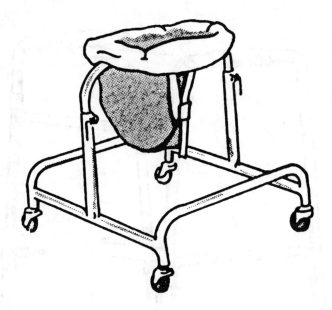

Figure 9. Infant walker.

Figure 10. Child walker.

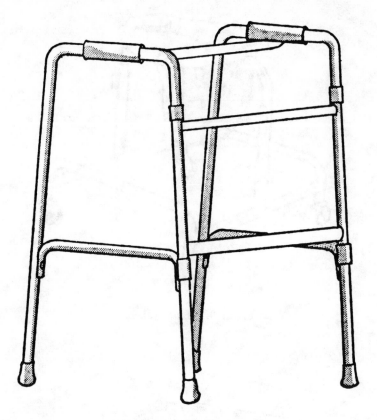

Figure 11. Adult walker.

Community   Community activities with walkers should emphasize functional ambulation. Walkers with a seat should not be used in the community.

1. Plan a trip in the community that requires the student to use his walker when moving from place to place. Assist him when necessary.
2. Shop at a store that has large aisles. Plan a time to do this shopping when there are minimal crowds. Tell the student to use his walker to go down the aisles. Assist him when necessary.

Functional Emphases In designing your own instructional activities and plans, emphasize the following elements:

1. Use of walkers for functional ambulation.
2. Use of walkers over different surfaces.
3. Use of walkers over different terrains.
4. Development of control of walkers when they are stationary objects.
5. Development of control of walkers when there are other people moving and walking around the student.

Specific Objective B

The student uses crutches.

General Information As with all assistive devices, crutches should be used only after the appropriate medical and allied health personnel have been consulted. During evaluations, the student's muscle, joint, and pain status can be ascertained and a determination made as to whether or not he can manage successfully with crutches. Crutches are used to increase balance and stability as well as to reduce or eliminate stress on weight-bearing joints. Basically, they compensate for a loss of muscle control. The major type of crutch, the axillary, has an underarm rest (Figure 12). Sometimes crutches are adapted for use within specific parts of the country or on different terrains. Figure 13 pictures the tip of a crutch specifically developed for walking on ice.

Functional Settings and Suggested Instructional Activities

School

1. Show the student the *four-point gait*. This gait offers maximum support because there are always three points of contact with the ground. The cycle for the student to follow is: (1) right crutch forward, (2) left foot forward, (3) left crutch forward, and (4) right foot forward. Assist the student in practicing this gait pattern. Tell the student to walk from one end of the room to the other employing this gait.
2. Show the student the *tripod gait*. Assist the student in practicing this gait pattern. [This gait is so named because of the triangle created by the crutch tips and the student's feet while in the standing position (Figure 14).]
3. For the student with a severe unilateral involvement of a lower extremity that needs to be protected from stress, practice a *three-point gait*. This is a weight-bearing type of gait. Tell the student to follow this cycle: (1) bring involved leg and both crutches forward at the same time and (2) bring unaffected leg forward.
4. When appropriate, tell the student to practice going from one end of the room to the other using a *two-point gait*. This requires the student to be

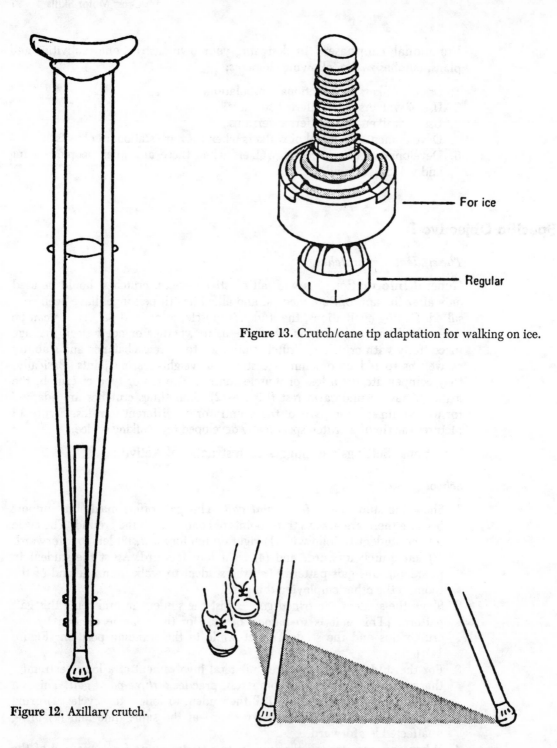

Figure 13. Crutch/cane tip adaptation for walking on ice.

— For ice

— Regular

Figure 12. Axillary crutch.

Figure 14. Tripod gait.

able to balance on one leg and involves a significant amount of skill. There is usually a progression from a four-point to a two-point gait. Show the student how to bring the right crutch and left foot forward at the same time and then bring the left crutch and right foot forward. Reward the student when he moves appropriately.

Community

1. Take the student to a community event such as a ball game or concert. Arrive early so he will be able to use his crutches without feeling the pressure of being in a crowd. Assist him when necessary.
2. Plan a trip in the community that requires the student to use his crutches over a variety of surfaces. Assist him when necessary.

Functional Emphases   In designing your own instructional activities and plans, emphasize the following elements:

1. Avoidance of areas where crutches are inappropriate or could prove dangerous.
2. Knowledge of maintenance of crutches (e.g., replacing tips).
3. Use of crutches on various surfaces.
4. Use of crutches on various terrains.
5. Use of crutches when moving around obstacles.

Specific Objective C

The student uses canes.

General Information   Canes provide less support than crutches. Some canes are weighted with lead to provide added stability, but most are not. Some have molded handles that have been developed to fit the contours of the hand. The tips of canes can vary from the traditional rubber ones to built-up ones made of tape and leather that provide a wider base of support. Various tips have been developed for walking on different surfaces (see Figure 13). There are five major types:

1. Wood cane—usually 36 inches with a curved handle (can be cut down to the appropriate length).
2. Telescopic aluminum cane—usually adjustable from 22 to 38 inches (adjustability allows for child's growth).
3. Tripod cane—three-legged, or crab, cane that allows for an "ankle"-type action to grasp the ground (thus providing additional support).
4. Quad cane—four-legged cane the provides maximum support with four points of contact with the ground.
5. *Loftstrand* and single point canes.

Functional Settings and Suggested Instructional Activities

School

1. Indicate to the student, by gesture and/or speech, that he should walk toward you using his cane. Indicate that he should bring the cane and affected leg forward simultaneously and then bring the unaffected limb forward. Practice with the student and correct him when this sequence is not followed. If necessary, move him through the activity.
2. Place taped X marks at different intervals in the room. Ask and/or gesture to the student who uses quad canes or crab canes to walk to these marks. Once he is there, reward him by praising him for a job well done.
3. Place empty paper cups next to the X marks on the floor. Plan a game in which the student walks to each X and picks up the empty cup. The student with the most cups at the end of a time limit wins the game and should be rewarded.
4. Ask the student with a telescopic or wooden cane to walk to the base of a set of stairs. Tell him to slowly climb the stairs by stepping up with the unaffected leg first. (It may be necessary to tap the student's leg to indicate the one he is to move.) Tell him by gesture and/or speech to then bring up the cane and the affected leg. Carefully supervise this activity. Reverse this procedure when coming down the stairs. Emphasize that the affected leg and cane should come down first.

Community

1. Take the student who is using a cane to a street where there is a high curb. Tell him to step up on the curb the same way he climbed stairs, that is, the unaffected leg first followed by the cane and then the affected leg.
2. Take the student to a department store. Practice walking over thresholds or steps leading into the store with him.
3. Assist the student in practicing walking into an elevator. Point out to him the crack in the floor where the door opens and closes. Demonstrate how to avoid the crack because it may cause him to lose his balance. Practice walking in and out of the elevator. (*Note:* It is important to gain permission from the appropriate personnel to use the store elevator. Many will allow you to practice before the store opens or during certain off hours.)

Functional Emphases In designing your own instructional activities and plans, emphasize the following elements:

1. Avoidance of areas where canes are inappropriate or could prove dangerous.
2. Knowledge of maintenance of canes (e.g., replacing tips).
3. Use of canes on various surfaces.
4. Use of canes on various terrains.
5. Use of canes when moving around obstacles.

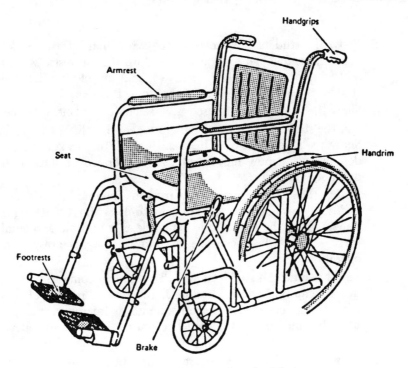

Figure 15. *Basic parts of a wheelchair.*

Specific Objective D

The student opens, closes, and uses a wheelchair.

General Information   When wheelchairs are prescribed by the medical team, they should be measured for their durability, strength, size, and weight. Additionally, they should fold easily and have replaceable parts and accessories (Figure 15). The earliest age at which a child may be placed in a wheelchair varies. A child's wheelchair should be used with the upholstery and seat of the wheelchair built up when the child is very young.

There are three major attachments to the wheelchair: heel straps, to help the student rest his feet more securely on the footrest; contoured wedge cushions, usually made of foam rubber to allow for maximum comfort of the student; and trays, attached to the wheelchair with C clamps or other connecting devices to provide a working or eating surface for the student.

Functional Settings and Suggested Instructional Activities

School

1. First practice by yourself how to open and close a wheelchair. Try various types of wheelchairs until you become proficient with the different makes. Show the student how to open a folded wheelchair. Practice.

2. Show the student how to close the wheelchair. First check to see if the arms (if removable) are locked. Fold up the footrests. Make a fold in the seat from above or below. If above, pull up, closing the chair. Assist the student in carrying out each of the steps. Practice.

3. Show the student how to use his wheelchair seat belt. Practice.

4. Ask the student in a wheelchair to wheel the chair a very short distance. Show the student how to lock and unlock the brakes of an empty chair, demonstrating how movement can be stopped or started. Assist him in doing so. Practice.

5. Call to the student to move toward you. Remind him to unlock his brakes and apply his hands to the hand rims only without touching the tires. Tell him to grasp the handrim as far back as is possible and comfortable and turn it forward. Encourage him to release his grasp and repeat the operation.

6. Stand behind the student and call to him to come to you in a backward movement. Backward wheeling is the reverse process of forward wheeling; the student should place his hands as far forward as possible on the handrim and then turn them backward. Tell him to repeat the activity until he reaches you.

7. Show the student how to make turns in his wheelchair. Assist him in putting his hand on the left handrim and in turning it in a forward direction (wheelchair will turn right). Next assist him in putting his hand on the right handrim and in turning it backward. The wheelchair will again turn toward the right, but this time in a backward direction.

8. Take the student who is in a wheelchair to a threshold. Demonstrate how a forward jerk on the handrims, without leaning forward, raises the front of the chair. Assist him in navigating the threshold using this procedure. Practice.

9. Show the student how to transfer from his wheelchair to a chair. Assist the student in placing the right front wheel of his wheelchair against the left front leg of the chair. Then assist him in placing his right knee close to the chair's right front leg. Require the student to lock his brakes, put his footplates up, and put his left hand on the left armrest of the wheelchair. Next tell him to put his right hand on the seat of the other chair. Assist him in pushing up and sliding from the wheelchair to the seat of the other chair.

10. For the student who is in bed and wants to transfer to his wheelchair, supervision is again required. Assist the student in removing the arms of his wheelchair (if possible), making sure his bed and wheelchair are on a horizontal plane whenever possible. Tie a rope to the front of the bed. Help the student pull himself up to a sitting position by using the rope. Assist him in sliding over to the chair.

11. Help the student transfer to a toilet by first removing the appropriate arm(s) of his wheelchair (if possible). Assist him in wheeling into the bath-

room and holding onto the L-shaped bar placed there for handicapped persons. Show him how to lift up and transfer to the toilet seat using the L bar as a support. Practice.

Community

1. Take a student or students in wheelchairs to a department store that has an elevator. Point out the grooves in the front of the elevator doors. Using a student as model, tell him to approach the elevator at a right angle and from a short distance. Make sure the student enters the elevator backward, so the larger back wheels will not get caught in the door grooves.
2. When working with a student who has the ability and perseverance to use his wheelchair on steps and high curbs, consult professionals certified in this area. Climbing small elevations can be taught using the right angle–short distance–back wheels first procedure discussed in Activity 1.
3. Park a car into which the student can transfer as close to the curb as possible. Whenever possible, transfer is handled best when the level of the wheelchair and the car seat are the same. Assist the student in standing up, supported by his right hand, right armrest, and right foot. Turn the student a little to the right and then tell him to support himself with his right hand on the left armrest of the wheelchair or the car door frame. The student can now do a pushup and carry himself over to the car seat.

Functional Emphases In designing your own instructional activities and plans, emphasize the following elements:

1. Development of skill in opening, closing, and transporting a wheelchair.
2. Movement of a wheelchair over various surfaces.
3. Movement of a wheelchair over various terrains.
4. Development of skill in transferring to a chair, toilet, and car.
5. Development of skill in transferring from a bed to a wheelchair.

General Objective III

The student will be able to move or walk, with or without assistive devices, to a degree that will allow him to function optimally in diverse settings.

Specific Objectives

(*Note:* The specific objectives that follow include activities for nonambulatory students as well as those who are ambulatory. Activities have been selected to reflect how a student moves or walks in his living and learning areas, how he travels within the community, and how he uses public or private transportation.) The student:

A. walks or moves in a wheelchair on a flat surface, including sidewalks.
B. walks or moves in a wheelchair over thresholds and up and down curbs.
C. walks or moves in a wheelchair through doorways.
D. walks or moves in a wheelchair in a line.
E. avoids ruts, holes, and other uneven surfaces.
F. walks or moves in a wheelchair up and down hills, inclines, and ramps.
G. walks or moves in a wheelchair in aisles and around stationary objects and other obstacles.
H. walks or moves in a wheelchair safely on icy surfaces in inclement weather.
I. turns corners when walking or using a wheelchair.
J. follows routing and detour symbols when walking or using a wheelchair.
K. crosses streets when walking or using a wheelchair.
L. walks or moves in a wheelchair into and out of home and public toilets.
M. steps or moves in a wheelchair into and out of elevators.
N. gets into and out of cars or transfers into and out of cars from his wheelchair.
O. walks up and down stairways.
P. steps on and off buses, trains, planes, and other public transportation vehicles.

Specific Objective A

The student walks or moves in a wheelchair on a flat surface, including sidewalks.

Functional Settings and Suggested Instructional Activities

School

1. Play Follow the Leader and tell the leader to do things that require the student to move in his wheelchair around the room or on a hard-topped playground.
2. Tape cutouts of feet on the floor, making various pathways. Tell the student to follow the footprints to a hidden prize or favorite object.
3. Play Musical Chairs using very slow music. Wheelchair students may claim a seat by placing their hand on the back or seat of the chair.

Home and Community

1. Ask the parents to assist their child if he has difficulty walking on a flat surface. Suggest that they tell him to hold onto them for support, and

encourage him to let go and to try a few steps on his own. Tell them to gradually increase the number of steps until he can walk independently.

2. Ask the parents to encourage their child to walk or move in his wheelchair throughout the house and community. Tell them to give him directions that require him to walk or move in the room, e.g., "John, shut the door, please." Tell them to walk beside him in case he loses his balance or the control of his wheelchair while on the street. They should tell him to walk by the walls because he may want to lean against them if he feels unsteady, loses his balance, or loses control of his wheelchair.

Functional Emphases In designing your own instructional activities and plans, emphasize the following elements:

1. Avoidance of hazards when working on a variety of flat surfaces.
2. Observation of safety rules when walking or moving in a wheelchair.
3. Experience with a variety of flat surfaces (e.g., sidewalks, blacktop, and pavement).

Specific Objective B

The student walks or moves in a wheelchair over thresholds and up and down curbs.

Functional Settings and Suggested Instructional Activities

School

1. Assist the student in walking or moving in a wheelchair over thresholds. As the student approaches a threshold, call his attention to it. Demonstrate lifting first one foot and then the other to step over the threshold. Practice and praise his efforts.
2. Construct an obstacle course. Use thresholds bought in a lumber yard or pieces of scrap wood that vary in height. Make curbs out of 2×4's. Practice moving the wheelchair over the threshold and curbs.
3. For the student who has difficulty stepping over thresholds, give additional help. Tell the student to walk up to the threshold, place his foot against the threshold, and lift or slide his foot over it. Repeat for the second foot. This often helps the student who is unsure of his balance.
4. Place threshold-height pieces of wood or blocks on the floor. Play Follow the Leader and walk over the blocks. Encourage the student to follow you. As the student becomes more sure of this activity, ask him, if he is capable, to walk backward and at an angle over the thresholds. Move backward and forward with the wheelchair-bound student over the pieces of wood or blocks.
5. Ask the student to walk out of the room and back into the room. Do this in between activities or during free time to give the student practice in

walking over thresholds. The wheelchair student may practice with his wheelchair at home or in his living quarters.

Community

1. Practice walking in and out of stores in the community that have different types of thresholds.
2. Practice walking up and down curbs while in the community when crossing streets. Also use inclined curbs that have been built for the handicapped whenever possible.

Functional Emphases In designing your own instructional activities and plans, emphasize the following elements:

1. Awareness of safety factors involved in walking or moving a wheelchair over thresholds and down curbs.
2. Calculation of heights of thresholds and curbs.
3. Experience with a variety of curbs and thresholds.
4. Awareness of hazards and traffic patterns associated with walking up and down curbs.

Specific Objective C

The student walks or moves in a wheelchair through doorways.

Functional Settings and Suggested Instructional Activities

School

1. Take the student around the building in which he is being taught. Practice walking or moving in a wheelchair through various types of doorways (single doors, double doors, swinging doors, and doors with an "in" and "out" side, such as in a cafeteria where one group is entering as another is leaving through the same doorway).
2. For the student who is having difficulty judging the width of the doorway, tell him to stand in front of the doorway and place his hands on each side of the doorway. The student on crutches should put out one hand only. Having done this, he can then lower his arms and walk through easily.
3. On the floor, place a masking tape line that passes from the room through the doorway and into the corridor. Tell the student to line up on the tape and walk or move in a wheelchair through the doorway utilizing the line as a guide.

Home and Community

1. Ask the parents to assist their child in walking or moving through doorways. As he approaches a doorway, tell them to guide him through the middle, reminding him to avoid the walls on either side of him.

2. Ask the parents to send their child on errands within the home that require him to go in and out of doorways. Examples are returning materials to another room and eating in a special area of the house.
3. Eat at restaurants in the community that are designated as accessible to the handicapped. Select ones that have doorways leading to individual dining rooms.

Functional Emphases   In designing your own instructional activities and plans, emphasize the following elements:

1. Experience with a variety of doorways through which to move.
2. Awareness of safety factors involved in walking through doorways.
3. Judgment as to the width of doorways.

Specific Objective D

The student walks or moves in a wheelchair in a line.

Functional Settings and Suggested Instructional Activities

School

1. Assist the student in walking or moving in a line. Form a line with peers who are able to walk or move in a wheelchair and ask them to demonstrate to other students.
2. For students who have trouble maintaining a line, stand them on a taped line. Ask each student to place his hand on the shoulder of the person in front of him and practice walking or moving. Encourage him to drop his hand as he becomes more sure of himself.
3. Play games in a line such as Follow the Leader or marching in line to music.
4. Ask the students to line up for daily activities such as washing hands, going to lunch, going to gym, or for dismissal.

Community

1. Go food shopping with the student. Ask him to wait in line at the checkout counter when he is through making his purchases. Assist him when necessary.
2. Plan a trip to the local movie theater. Tell the student he may have to wait in line to purchase the tickets. Assist the student if necessary. See the movie.

Functional Emphases   In designing your own instructional activities and plans, emphasize the following elements:

1. Awareness of safety factors involved in walking or moving in a wheelchair in a line.

2. Experience with a variety of activities and situations that require walking or moving in a line (e.g., lining up for school activities, waiting in a line for a movie, and waiting in a store's checkout line).

Specific Objective E

The student avoids ruts, holes, and other uneven surfaces.

Functional Settings and Suggested Instructional Activities

School

1. In the classroom, construct uneven surfaces. Place mats on the floor and put balls or blocks of wood under them to produce uneven surfaces. Also, place boxes or large pieces of wood on top of mats. Lead the student over the mats. Encourage him to step or move over small bumps or uneven areas and around larger uneven areas. Ask the student to practice traveling over the mats independently. Explain that, when he is outdoors in the community, he should avoid similar uneven surfaces.
2. Get large sheets of foam rubber and place them in the classroom or on the playground. Cut holes and large ridges in the foam rubber to simulate potholes and ruts. Demonstrate stepping or moving over holes and ridges and avoiding them. Help the student to walk or move over the foam rubber with you. Encourage the student to practice walking or moving over the foam rubber independently. Explain that, while walking, moving, or playing outside, he should avoid similar ruts and holes.

Community

1. Assist the student in avoiding ruts, holes, and other uneven surfaces. Take the student along sidewalks to a park or playground in the neighborhood. Call the student's attention to curbs, holes, and ruts in the dirt on the playground. Demonstrate stepping over small curbs, ruts, or holes, and going around larger ones to avoid stepping into them and falling or tripping. Assist the student in doing the same.
2. When possible, take the student to a sandy area. Dig holes in the sand and assist the student as he practices avoiding them. Encourage the student to move first slowly, then quickly around the holes (the latter to simulate when he is in a hurry and might forget where he is walking).

Functional Emphases

1. Awareness of hazards when walking on uneven surfaces.
2. Knowledge of safety factors associated with avoiding ruts, holes, and other uneven surfaces.
3. Judgment as to how to avoid ruts and holes.
4. Estimation of distances before holes and ruts.

5. Estimation of size and depth of holes and ruts.
6. Attention to people and traffic patterns around and/or near ruts and holes.

Specific Objective F

The student walks or moves in a wheelchair up and down hills, inclines, and ramps.

Functional Settings and Suggested Instructional Activities

School

1. Construct or borrow ramps for short stairways (2 or 3 steps) or place wide, heavy pieces of ½-inch plywood (4 × 8 feet) over the stairs. If necessary, place two wooden poles or rails at each end of the ramp. String clothesline rope between the rails to make a rope railing. Demonstrate how to walk or move over the ramp. Encourage the student to practice walking or moving up and down the ramp. Use ramps to enter and leave the building, whenever possible.
2. Practice walking up and down ramps found in the school, especially those at entrances and exits.

Community

1. Assist the student in walking or moving up and down hills and inclines. Demonstrate this to the student and help him to do the same. Exercise caution. The wheelchair student must know how to use brakes as a prerequisite to this activity.
2. Take the student on a field trip to a shopping center that has ramps either between shopping levels or in the parking garage. Demonstrate to the student how to walk or move up and down ramps and inclines. Utilize railings when available. Assist the student as he walks or moves up and down with you. Encourage the student to walk or move up and down independently.
3. Take the student to a park or playground that has hilly areas. Demonstrate walking or moving up and down the hills. Show the student how to overbalance, i.e., lean forward going uphill and backward going downhill, to avoid losing his balance.
4. Take a hike in the woods or a similar place. Try to walk or move in areas having hills, ruts, holes, and uneven surfaces. Check to see how well the student avoids these obstacles during the hike.
5. If you are near a beach, take the student there. Demonstrate and then practice walking up and down sand hills.

Functional Emphases In designing your own instructional activities and plans, emphasize the following elements:

1. Awareness of safety factors and hazards involved in navigating hills, inclines, and ramps.
2. Use of a variety of ramps and inclines typically found in the community.
3. Calculation of height of ramps and inclines.
4. Judgment as to appropriate speed needed to navigate ramps, inclines, and hills when using a wheelchair.

Specific Objective G

The student walks or moves in a wheelchair in aisles and around stationary objects and other obstacles.

Functional Settings and Suggested Instructional Activities

School

1. Arrange classroom furniture in aisles. Assist the student in walking or moving in aisles, between furniture, and around stationary objects.
2. Tell the student to stand or sit in his wheelchair behind you. Ask the student to follow you as you walk up and down the classroom aisles. As he feels more confident about negotiating the aisles, ask him to walk or move in his wheelchair up and down the aisles independently.
3. In the cafeteria, require the student to get his tray and return it when he is finished with his lunch. Remind the student to avoid the cafeteria tables, benches, large trash cans, etc. Reward him.
4. In the gym, place mats and other large physical education equipment (trampoline, medicine balls, volleyball nets) in various places around the gym. Play a game of Follow the Leader, and tell the leader to go around each obstacle and reward the other students for following.

Home and Community

1. Ask the parents to rearrange the furniture at home or in the living quarters periodically, and require their child to walk or move in a wheelchair around the pieces of furniture.
2. Go shopping with the student in stores that have aisles. Assist the student in maneuvering in and out of aisles when necessary.
3. Find a community area where construction work is being started. Point out to the student areas that need to be avoided. Assist him in maneuvering around these areas.

Functional Emphases In designing your own instructional activities and plans, emphasize the following elements:

1. Awareness of situations where navigation in aisles or around objects is required, i.e., in stores, movies, and churches and synagogues.

2. Awareness of safety factors involved in walking or using a wheelchair to move around stationary objects and other obstacles.
3. Estimation of distances between obstacles and stationary objects.

Specific Objective H

The student walks or moves in a wheelchair safely on icy surfaces in inclement weather.

Functional Settings and Suggested Instructional Activities

School

1. Demonstrate the slippery characteristic of ice by using ice cubes. Tell the student to run his fingers over ice cubes and feel how slippery they are. Then wrap the student's finger in different materials (velvet or sandpaper) or put on a rubber finger and ask him to note how some materials slide smoothly over the ice and others seem to grip it. Explain that rubber, as found on rubber-soled shoes or rubber boots, helps to resist the slipperiness. Explain also that sandpaper has this same effect and that is why we throw sand on icy ground or roads.
2. Discuss safety on ice. Explain to the student that he should never go on frozen ponds or rivers unless he has been told by his parents or park police that it is safe. Stress that he should always be accompanied by a responsible adult (i.e., a parent and/or teacher).

Community

1. Assist the student in walking or moving on ice. Take him to the playground when ice has formed. (You may make icy surfaces by pouring water on the ground in freezing weather.) Take the student to a skating pond that is safely frozen (the wheelchair student should not be allowed on frozen ponds) or to an indoor skating rink that may be used year round. Show the student how to move or walk on ice with regular shoes and then with boots or rubber-soled shoes. Explain that rubber-soled shoes or boots grip the ice and make walking on icy surfaces safer and easier. Demonstrate the technique of placing the entire bottom of the foot on the ice rather than the ordinary toe-heel manner of walking. Practice walking or moving on icy surfaces. (For crutch and cane adaptations for use on ice, see Specific Objectives IIB and IIC.)
2. In wintertime, take the student on field trips where she will encounter icy ground. Practice walking or moving safely on the ice.

Functional Emphases   In designing your own instructional activities and plans, emphasize the following elements:

1. Awareness of safety factors involved in walking or using a wheelchair on ice.
2. Identification of situations in which *not* to walk or move on ice (i.e., on semifrozen ponds and lakes).
3. Avoidance of areas that present hazards because of icy surfaces.

Specific Objective I

The student turns corners when walking or using a wheelchair.

Functional Settings and Suggested Instructional Activities

School

1. Assist the student in turning corners when walking or using a wheelchair. Tell the student to walk or use a wheelchair to go down the hallways of the school. As he approaches a corner, demonstrate turning the corner. Ask the student to follow you. The student who has trouble turning the corner may need additional practice.
2. Play Follow the Leader. Ask the leader to lead students, both walking and in their wheelchairs, around corners. This game may be played indoors or out.
3. Construct a maze using large portable blackboards, desks, tables, and other large pieces of furniture. Be sure maze corridors are wide enough to accommodate wheelchairs. Tell the student to move through the maze, turning the various corners.

Home and Community

1. Ask the parents to send their child on errands throughout the home. Tell them to go with him for the first time or two to make sure he is going to the correct areas and turning the corners correctly.
2. Tell the parents to clear aisles and passageways in the home so the child can move his wheelchair freely in these areas. Ask them to tell him at different times of the day or evening to do specific chores. Ask them to observe if he is moving around corners appropriately. They should provide assistance when necessary.
3. Take the student grocery shopping. Go up and down each aisle so that the student will have to turn corners at each end.
4. Take the student to a neighborhood museum that is at his interest level. Assist him in walking around and browsing, turning corners as he goes. Check to see that the museum or gallery is easily accessible to wheelchairs.

Functional Emphases In designing your own instructional activities and plans, emphasize the following elements:

1. Awareness of safety factors involved in turning corners while using a wheelchair.
2. Use of a variety of areas within the home, school, and community that require walking or moving in wheelchairs around corners.
3. Awareness of hazards and traffic patterns associated with walking around corners.

Specific Objective J

The student follows routing and detour symbols when walking or using a wheelchair.

Functional Settings and Suggested Instructional Activities

School

1. In the hallways of the school, use directional arrows to indicate the way to the cafeteria, playground, and other special areas. Place a representative picture next to the directional arrow. Explain to the student that the sign means that the direction of the arrow leads to the place portrayed by the picture.
2. Show the student pictures or cutouts of various safety signs, including detour signs. Ask the student to identify the signs and what each one means.
3. Construct an obstacle course on the playground or in the classroom. Place detour signs at various places along the course. Walk through the course with the student, stopping at each sign. Ask the student to show you where the sign is telling him to go. Offer help if he needs it. Tell the student to use the obstacle course to practice following the detour signs. Explain to him that he should also follow detour signs in the community.

Community

1. Assist the student in following detours. Take the student on a field trip to an area where there is construction. Show the student a detour sign, and explain that the arrow tells which way to go. Demonstrate following the direction of the arrow on the detour sign. Ask the student to follow you.
2. Take the student on a field trip within the neighborhood. Point out crosswalks. Explain that they are used by pedestrians to guide them across the street. Assist the student in using the crosswalks to cross the street, but only after she has stopped, looked, listened, and ascertained that it is safe to do so.

Functional Emphases In designing your own instructional activities and plans, emphasize the following elements:

1. Interpretation of routing and detour signs.

2. Use of a variety of systems (i.e., signs, symbols, pictures, and rebuses) that indicate the need to take a detour.
3. Judgment as to when a detour should be followed.
4. Awareness of hazards and/or traffic patterns associated with detours.

Specific Objective K

The student crosses streets when walking or using a wheelchair.

Functional Settings and Suggested Instructional Activities

School

1. Make signs saying "Walk" and "Don't Walk" or obtain those that are made commercially. Drill the student until he does what the signs are telling him to do. Stress that even when he sees a "Walk" sign, he should still stop, look, and listen before crossing the street.
2. Within the school building, set up "streets" made of sheets of heavy paper or gym mats. Mark crosswalks, and construct "Walk" and "Don't Walk" signs (a volleyball net post with the sign stuck on it is an easy way to do this, allowing the sign to be easily changed). Tell the student to practice crossing within the crosswalks and obeying the signs. Encourage the student to use the streets when changing positions between activities or as a separate activity.
3. Tape or purchase a record of traffic sounds. Play this for the student and encourage him to identify the sounds. Discuss how these sounds would affect the student preparing to cross the street. Perhaps a horn would cause the student to look and see if the horn were warning him not to cross, a siren would warn the student to step back on the curb and wait until the fire engine or ambulance has passed, and a policeman's whistle would tell the student to obey the policeman, regardless of the lights.

Community

1. Assist the student in crossing streets when walking or using a wheelchair. Take the student to a street that is not very heavily traveled. Discuss the safety involved in crossing streets independently. Tell the student always to stop before stepping off the curbs, look all around and both ways to be sure the street is clear, and listen for the sound of cars or sirens. Tell the student to cross the street when it is safe.
2. Take the student on a field trip within the neighborhood. Point out "Walk" and "Don't Walk" signs. Tell the student to cross streets by himself using the signs as a guide.

Functional Emphases In designing your own instructional activities and plans, emphasize the following elements:

1. Awareness of hazards and traffic patterns when crossing streets.
2. Comprehension of signals and signs when crossing streets.
3. Avoidance of crossing streets in dimly lit and unsafe areas.
4. Utilization of crosswalks and crossing areas.
5. Recognition of the sounds of traffic.
6. Attention to verbal commands made by crossing guards and police officers.
7. Recognition of vehicular patterns that countermand obeying traffic signals.

Specific Objective L

The student walks or moves in a wheelchair into and out of home and public toilets.

Functional Settings and Suggested Instructional Activities

Home and Community

1. Ask the parents to assist their child in using the toilets in his home. Tell them to praise him when he uses them appropriately.
2. Tell the parents to provide opportunities for their child to use relatives' bathrooms during times they are visiting. Suggest that they visit the bathrooms beforehand to make sure they are accessible.
3. Assist the student in walking or moving in a wheelchair into and out of coin-operated toilets. Take the student to a store or building that has coin-operated toilets (you may want to secure permission from the store personnel first). Show the door to the student and note the amount of money needed. Put the correct coin(s) into the slot. Turn the door latch and push in. Go into the toilet and close the door behind you. Next open the door and take the student into the stall. Show him the knob to turn to lock the door and how to release it to unlock it. Give the student an opportunity to practice turning the knob. Exercise caution because some students cannot handle the locking of doors and should use the other toileting facilities.
4. Give the student a purse with coins in it. Ask the student to choose the appropriate coin(s), put it (them) into the slot, turn the door latch, and push in the door. Tell the student to walk into the stall. You may wish to go in with him until you feel he is able to handle the knobs on the inside of the door. Instruct the student to open the door and walk out of the stall. Practice.
5. For the student in a wheelchair, look for toilet stalls that have a wheelchair insignia on the door. If there is no insignia, the wheelchair will not fit inside the stall with the door closed. If facilities for wheelchairs are available, see Specific Objective IID for more information on maneuvering in wheelchairs.

Functional Emphases In designing your own instructional activities and plans, emphasize the following elements:

1. Use of a variety of public toilets.
2. Awareness of a toilet's sanitary condition.
3. Development of motor skills necessary to walk or wheel into and out of public toilets.
4. Identification of handicapped insignias on public toilets.
5. Development of motor skills necessary to open, close, lock, and unlock toilet doors.

Specific Objective M

The student steps or moves in a wheelchair into and out of elevators.

Functional Settings and Suggested Instructional Activities

Community

1. Assist the student as he steps into elevators. Take the student to a building that has elevators (you may want to contact the building superintendent to obtain permission to use the elevators for practice and to find out when the elevators are least busy). Engage the switch or button that stops the elevator at your floor and lock it on stop or hold so that it will not leave the floor while you are practicing. Show the student that the doors are open and that the elevator is level with the floor. Make sure the student looks for these two things before entering the elevator. Demonstrate stepping into the elevator by stepping over the grooves where the doors slide open and shut. Place your hand on the door jamb so that it will not accidently close. Do this two or three times so that the student sees what you are doing. Take the student by the hand and walk him into the elevator. Ask him to enter the elevator independently. Practice.

2. Assist the student in stepping out of elevators. Ask the student to stand in the elevator with you. Close the elevator doors and have them open again. Place the elevator button on hold or stop. Position the student so that he is facing the doors. Once they are open, step out of the elevator over the grooves where the doors slide. As you step out, place your hand against the door jamb so that the doors will not close as you walk through. Demonstrate this two or three times so that the student can see what you are doing. Point out the rubber padding on the door jamb. Take the student by the hand and walk him out of the elevator. Encourage the student to leave the elevator independently and practice stepping out of the elevator.

3. Tell the student why he should step over the grooves (so that his shoes will not get caught or he will not trip over the grooves), and why he should put his hand against the door jamb (because the doors, during normal use, could begin to close as he walks through). Explain that his hand can make the door reopen if the door begins to close too soon.

4. Take the student to a building with elevators. Show the student how to enter and leave the elevators. If the elevators are crowded, make sure the student faces the doors, says "Excuse me," when entering and leaving, and keeps his hands by his sides to avoid touching others in the elevator. Remind the student never to use elevators in case of fire.

Functional Emphases   In designing your own instructional activities and plans, emphasize the following elements:

1. Use of a variety of elevators, including those found in buildings, stores, and schools.
2. Awareness of the safety factors involved in going into and out of elevators.
3. Recognition of "Out of Order" signs, "No Smoking" signs, and special regulations placed on and inside elevators.
4. Selection of the correct button to push when going to a specific floor.
5. Estimation of the space available in an elevator when it appears full or crowded.
6. Avoidance of elevators during fires or fire drills.
7. Identification of procedures to follow when an elevator stops between floors or when the elevator door does not open to let one out.

Specific Objective N

The student gets into and out of cars or transfers into and out of cars from his wheelchair.

Functional Settings and Suggested Instructional Activities

School

1. In the classroom, encourage the student to practice getting into and out of a car by pretending chairs are car seats.
2. Set up four or six chairs as seats in a car and label the appropriate chair as the driver's seat. Tell the student to sit on a chair, using the steps in Activity 1. Tell him to take turns being the driver. Encourage him to pretend he is on a trip and to get into and out of his car to go shopping or stop for lunch or sightseeing.

Community

1. Assist the student as he gets into and out of cars. Take the student to the school parking lot or the parking area where he can use a car to practice getting in and out. Open the car door. Demonstrate to the student how to sit sideways on the seat and then to swing his legs into the car. Do this two or more times until the student is familiar with the actions involved. Get out of the car by swinging your legs out with your feet flat on the ground

outside the car. Get into and out of the car, telling the student what you are doing. Ask the student to get into and out of the car. Practice.

2. Stress safety rules: (1) never get into a stranger's car; (2) do not practice getting into and out of cars unless you have permission and supervision; and (3) do not put your hands on the car door jamb for support as you get into the car because you may get your hand caught.

Functional Emphases In designing your own instructional activities and plans, emphasize the following elements:

1. Development of motor skills necessary to transfer into and out of a car.
2. Use of a variety of cars in which to practice transferring.
3. Awareness of safety skills necessary in transferring into and out of a car.

Specific Objective O

The student walks up and down stairways. (*Note:* For the student using crutches, consult medical personnel for instructions.)

Functional Settings and Suggested Instructional Activities

School

1. Using flashcards, drill the student until he identifies the words *stairs* and *stairway*. These are necessary survival words to enable the student to find the stairs in public buildings easily.
2. If the school has stairways, practice using them during times of low traffic.

Home and Community

1. Ask the parents to allow their child to use the stairways whenever appropriate. Tell them to carefully monitor this activity because of the dangers that can quickly arise.
2. Take the student to a ball game or other recreational event that requires walking up stairs to enter the facility. You may wish to arrive early if the student has difficulty with walking up and down stairs.

Functional Emphases In designing your own instructional activities and plans, emphasize the following elements:

1. Development of motor skills necessary for ascending and descending steps.
2. Use of a variety of stairways and numbers of steps.
3. Awareness of safety factors involved in walking up and down steps.
4. Modification of stairs, when necessary, to make them less slippery and more accessible (e.g., use of rubber stair treads).
5. Avoidance of stairs that are dimly lit or in unsafe places or areas.
6. Calculation of stair height when walking up and down.
7. Use of stair rails when available.

Specific Objective P

The student steps on and off buses, trains, planes, and other public transportation vehicles.

Functional Settings and Suggested Instructional Activities

School

1. Assist the student in stepping on and off buses. Ask the individual in charge of transportation for your school if you may borrow a bus for a short period of time. Perhaps arrange for the bus to come to school an hour before departure time. Take the student to the bus and point out the steps and their height, handrails, and folding bus doors. Ask the bus driver to open the door. Demonstrate stepping onto the bus steps and grasping the handrail at the same time. Tell the student what you are doing as you do it slowly. When you reach the top of the bus steps (usually two steps), turn around and, grasping the handrail, step down the bus steps.
2. Ask the student to imitate your actions as described in Activity 1. If the student is having difficulty stepping on and off the bus, take him by the hand and walk him through the activity. Once he has developed a degree of confidence, encourage him to practice stepping on and off the bus.

Community

1. Take the student on a field trip involving transportation. Many shopping centers, museums, parks, and athletic stadiums are on or near bus lines. Require the student to step on and off the bus as independently as possible.
2. If there is a train station in your town, arrange a field trip to the train station. (If your town has no train station, you will have to use stepping on and off buses as a substitute for trains.) Ask the trainmaster to arrange for your student to practice stepping on and off trains that are not being used. Show the student the train car and point out the various parts, including steps, wheels, and door. Demonstrate grasping the handrail and stepping onto the train steps and into the train car. Once in the train car, turn around and step down the train steps and out of the train. Explain to the student what you are doing as you do it.
3. If there is a commuter train in your community, take the student on a train trip to a nearby town. Go out for lunch or a visit and then return home on the train.
4. Assist the student in stepping on and off airplanes. If there is an airport in your community, call and ask if you may come to the airport and take a tour of the airport, including stepping on and off a plane. Once at the airport, take the student onto the airfield and show him the plane, the boarding steps, the door, and other parts of the plane. Demonstrate walking up the boarding steps by holding the handrail and carefully climbing the boarding steps. Once at the top of the steps, step into the plane, turn

around, and descend the steps, grasping the handrail and walking down the boarding steps slowly and carefully.

Functional Emphases   In designing your own instructional activities and plans, emphasize the following elements:

1. Use of a variety of public transportation vehicles.
2. Avoidance of public transportation vehicles that appear unsafe or poorly maintained.
3. Awareness of safety procedures needed to step on and off public transportation.
4. Use of safety devices (rails, handles, and seat belts) commonly found on public transportation.
5. Comprehension of arrival and departure schedules of public transportation.

General Objective IV

The student will acquire those gross motor skills that are an integral part of recreational activities.

Specific Objectives

(*Note:* Whenever possible, nonambulatory students should be encouraged to participate in recreational activities with materials modified or adapted to their individual needs.) The student:

A. pulls a wagon or pull toy.
B. throws balls, beanbags, Frisbees, and other recreational equipment.
C. hits appropriate recreational equipment.
D. catches objects used during recreation.
E. balances his body as he participates in recreational activities.
F. marches.
G. runs.
H. gallops.
I. slides.
J. hops.
K. jumps.
L. skips.
M. dances.
N. climbs.
O. rides Big Wheels, tricycles, and bicycles.

Specific Objective A

The student pulls a wagon or pull toy.

Functional Settings and Suggested Instructional Activities

School

1. Arrange for relay races using wagons and blocks. Divide the students into teams. Establish a race course, and place half of each team at each end of the course. At each end, place a block for each member of the team. Ask one student to pull a wagon from one end of the course to the other and place a block in the wagon. Then the next student pulls the wagon to the other end of the course. That student places a block in the wagon, and the next student takes over. This is repeated until each member of the team has a turn. The first team to finish is the winner.
2. Set up a seated towel pull. Seat two students on the floor or in wheelchairs (with brakes set) facing each other. The students seated on the floor pull a towel in an alternating pattern, lifting and then lowering each other to and from the floor. Students in wheelchairs pull back and forth, causing each other to lean forward and balance in their wheelchairs. Exercise caution in this activity.

Home

1. Ask the parents to assist their child as he pulls a wagon or pull toy. Ask them to demonstrate grasping the handle or string and pulling the wagon or toy. Tell them to ask the child to imitate their actions and practice pulling the toy or wagon.
2. Tell the parents to ask their child to pull a wagon and place some toys into it at toy cleanup time. Ask them to tell him to return the toys to their proper place.

Functional Emphases In designing your own instructional activities and plans, emphasize the following elements:

1. Use of a variety of pull toys and wagons to pull.
2. Selection of toys that are safe and nontoxic.
3. Avoidance of toys that are very small in size and have a large number of parts.
4. Movement of pull toys and wagons on different surfaces.

Specific Objective B

The student throws balls, beanbags, Frisbees, and other recreational equipment.

Functional Settings and Suggested Instructional Activities

School and Community

1. Arrange for a game of beanbag throw. Place a tire on the floor. Ask the student to stand up or to sit in his wheelchair and toss beanbags into the tire. Encourage the student to practice throwing beanbags overhand and underhand into the tire. Scores can be kept, or successful throws can be rewarded.
2. Play "Paper Shot Put" by crumpling pieces of scrap paper and using these as simulated shot puts. Ask the student to throw the paper as far as he can. Mark the distance with a piece of tape on which the student's name or a color has been written.
3. Form two teams. Place two tires on the floor, and ask each member of the two teams to throw beanbags into the tire designated as belonging to his team. Each student throws three beanbags and scores one point for his team each time his beanbag lands within the tire.
4. Start a game of Nerf basketball. Ask the student to practice throwing or "shooting" the Nerf basketball into a wastebasket or plastic laundry basket. Once the student is used to the Nerf basketball, form teams, make rules, and allow the students to play Nerf basketball during free time or rainy day recess. The physical education teacher may want to help you establish or modify rules for the game.
5. At recess, give the student a Frisbee. Demonstrate how to throw and catch it. Encourage the student and his peers to use the Frisbee on the playground.
6. Show the student how to play horseshoes. For the younger student, a plastic set of horseshoes may be used. Schedule a tournament that will allow the student to compete, individually or in teams, with his peers.

Home

1. Ask the parents to assist their child in throwing balls, beanbags, Frisbees, and other recreational training equipment in an area that has been cleared of breakable objects. Tell them to show him the above-mentioned equipment and demonstrate the appropriate use of each. Tell them to give him time to practice with each one.
2. Ask the parents to play catch with their child using a variety of balls. They may want to start with soft rubber or tennis balls and eventually use a softball or baseball.

Functional Emphases   In designing your own instructional activities and plans, emphasize the following elements:

1. Selection of a variety of recreational equipment.
2. Use of recreational equipment that is safe and nontoxic.
3. Avoidance of recreational areas that are hazardous, poorly lit, unventilated, or unsafe.

4. Use of motor skills necessary to participate in recreational activities.
5. Estimation of distances when throwing Frisbees and other recreational objects.

Specific Objective C

The student hits appropriate recreational equipment.

Functional Settings and Suggested Instructional Activities

School and Community

1. Make a Paddle Ball game and set it up within the classroom. This game consists of a baseball-size Wiffle ball hanging from the ceiling on a thin piece of cord. The student holds a short plastic bat in his hand and attempts to hit the hanging ball with a plastic bat.
2. Get tennis racquets and balls. Show the student how to practice hitting balls against the gym wall or against an outdoor wall with no windows. Set up a net and demonstrate how to use the equipment. Show the student how to hit balls back and forth over the net on the playground or the sidewalk around the playground. Tell the student to imitate your actions. Practice.
3. Demonstrate and assist the student as he hits appropriate recreational equipment (e.g., hitting a ball with a bat or tennis racquet). Set aside time for the student to practice these activities.
4. Set up a badminton game and encourage the students to play together at recess, either outdoors or in the gym.
5. Set up a croquet game on the playground. Demonstrate how to play the game, emphasizing how sometimes it is important to hit the ball very gently. Tell the student to imitate your actions. Schedule a tournament, allowing for team and individual play.
6. For the student who is having difficulty in hitting a ball with a bat, play a modified version of baseball using a bat and a volleyball. This can be fun for all students and will encourage those having difficulty hitting smaller balls.
7. Get a Wiffle baseball and bat. Demonstrate their use and ask the students to work in groups of three, hitting, throwing, and catching the ball. Rotate positions so that each student has a turn at each activity. Form teams to see who hits the most Wiffle baseballs. The students may use softballs and regular bats once you feel they are ready for them.

Functional Emphases   In designing your own instructional activities and plans, emphasize the following elements:

1. Selection of recreational equipment that is safe.
2. Facilitation of appropriate motor skills.

3. Knowledge of rules for using specific recreational equipment.
4. Modification of recreational equipment when necessary.

Specific Objective D

The student catches objects used during recreation.

Functional Settings and Suggested Instructional Activities

School and Community

1. Using the Time Bomb toy, encourage the students to pass it back and forth to each other. When the bomb goes off, the student holding it is eliminated from the game.
2. Seat two students on the floor facing each other. Ask one student to roll the ball and the other to catch it. Tell them to take turns rolling and catching the ball.
3. Place the students on a large circle marked with masking tape (indoors) or marking chalk (outdoors). Stand in the center of the circle and bounce the ball to each student. Tell each student to catch it and return it to you. Do this until everyone has had a turn. If the student is just learning to catch, you may want to call his name before you bounce the ball to him. Once the student is better at catching, surprise him by throwing the ball randomly without calling his name. This can make the game more fun.
4. Play a game of Hot Potato. Seat or stand the students on a marked circle. Pass a ball from one student to the next proceeding around the circle. Play music as the students pass the ball. Stop the music randomly. The student holding the ball when the music stops is eliminated. Do this until one student is left as the winner.
5. Assist the student in catching a ball, beanbag, Frisbee, or other recreational equipment. Play catch with the various recreational objects. Demonstrate ways to catch: with two hands, with one hand, or by trapping the object against the body. Encourage the student to practice throwing and catching balls, beanbags, Frisbees, and other recreational equipment at appropriate times.

Home

1. Ask the parents to demonstrate bouncing a large ball and catching it. Ask them to encourage their child to practice bouncing and catching. The child should begin by using two hands to bounce and catch, and gradually switch to one hand as he becomes more skillful in catching the ball.
2. Ask the parents to demonstrate bouncing balls in time to music. Tell them to have their child stand in a large marked circle. Tell them to play popular music, marches, or familiar tunes and ask him to bounce a ball to the beat of the music. Suggest that the parents stand at the center of the circle

and demonstrate bouncing a ball to establish a rhythm to the bouncing and to provide a model.

Functional Emphases In designing your own instructional activities and plans, emphasize the following elements:

1. Development of motor skills necessary for catching objects.
2. Selection of safe recreational equipment.
3. Estimation of space needed in which to catch an object.
4. Knowledge of rules used in recreational activities involving the catching of objects.

Specific Objective E

The student balances his body as he participates in recreational activities.

Functional Settings and Suggested Instructional Activities

School

1. Assist the student in maintaining his balance during recreational activities. Demonstrate balancing using arms, hands, and upper body as well as legs and feet. Ask the student to imitate your actions and practice balancing.
2. Do balancing activities to music. Ask the student to balance on one foot with his eyes closed, on his tiptoes, on his tiptoes with his eyes closed, and with his arms extended in various directions.
3. Play Simon Says. Include commands requiring the student to balance (e.g., "Simon says, 'hop on one foot'").
4. Play Follow the Leader. Engage in activities requiring the student to balance, such as walking on a balance beam or a line that has been chalked on the floor.
5. Mark out a hopscotch court on the floor with masking tape (indoors) or marking chalk (outdoors). Give the student a beanbag as a marker. After he has thrown it, tell him to pick up the beanbag while balancing on one foot.

Home

1. Ask the parents to do exercises as part of their child's daily schedule. Tell them to include things such as hopping or standing on one foot and bending forward, backward, and sideways from the waist. Be sure to include upper body exercises that would be suitable for students in wheelchairs.
2. Ask the parents to construct a Twister game by pasting cutout footprints on an old shower curtain. Ask them to show their child how to play Twister by placing his feet on the footprints. Tell them to supervise closely because this type of balancing activity may be difficult.

Functional Emphases In designing your own instructional activities and plans, emphasize the following elements:

1. Development of motor skills necessary for balancing.
2. Awareness of safety factors involved in balancing.
3. Use of a variety of games and activities that require balancing.
4. Modification of balance games and activities when appropriate.

Specific Objective F

The student marches.

Functional Settings and Suggested Instructional Activities

School

1. Play marching music. Ask the student to join you as you march to the music.
2. Beat a drum or tom-tom and ask the student to march to the beat of the instrument.
3. Play Follow the Leader and tell the student to march. Encourage her to pantomime such things as "beat your drum" and "blow your horn" as she marches.
4. Give the student rhythm band instruments. Play marching music and encourage the student to march as she plays her rhythm band instrument.
5. Ask the student to clap her hands and march to a marching rhythm.
6. Chant a cadence and ask the student to march to it.

Community

1. Take the student on a field trip to see a parade. There are often parades on various holidays or half-time shows at football games that the student might enjoy.
2. Make arrangements to watch a school or other marching band practice.

Functional Emphases In designing your own instructional activities and plans, emphasize the following elements:

1. Use of a variety of music for marching.
2. Identification of events or activities that utilize marching.
3. Development of motor skills necessary for marching.
4. Identification of the child's left and right feet.
5. Development of diverse marching movements.
6. Comprehension of marching instructions, especially those involving directions.

Specific Objective G

The student runs.

Functional Settings and Suggested Instructional Activities

School

1. During physical exercise, model running in place and ask the student to imitate you.
2. Play Follow the Leader. Tell the leader to run and periodically change speed.
3. Ask the student to run short sprints. Time him and chart his time.
4. Arrange for in-class competitions. Organize a field day where students in various classes compete against each other for fun.
5. Form a race course with tires as markers so the student can run around the tires and back in a figure 8. Divide the students into teams; the first team to complete the race is the winner.

Home

1. Ask the parents to assist the child as he runs. Tell them to demonstrate running and encourage him to imitate their actions. Suggest that they walk with him, gradually go faster until he is running, and say, "Now we are running!"
2. Tell the parent to include running as part of the child's daily exercise during good weather.

Functional Emphases In designing your own instructional activities and plans, emphasize the following elements:

1. Development of motor skills necessary for running.
2. Judgment as to when and where to run.
3. Determination of lanes or boundaries in which to run.
4. Identification of safe places in which to run.
5. Awareness of proper foot care before and after running.
6. Awareness of proper footwear for running.

Specific Objective H

The student gallops.

Functional Settings and Suggested Instructional Activities

School

1. Assist the student in galloping. Demonstrate galloping and ask the student to imitate your actions. Practice.

2. Play the *William Tell* Overture and ask the student to gallop to the music.
3. Beat a galloping rhythm with wooden blocks. Ask the student to gallop to the rhythm. Change the tempo and ask the student to adjust his galloping to match the change in the tempo.
4. Play "Pony Express." Divide the students into teams. Assign each team a toy horse on a stick. Mark out a start and finish line. The first team member gallops to the finish line and back to the starting line, and then gives his horse to the second team member. Repeat this until each team member has a turn. The first team to finish is the winner.

Functional Emphases   In designing your own instructional activities and plans, emphasize the following elements:

1. Development of motor skills necessary for galloping.
2. Judgment as to when and where to gallop.
3. Avoidance of galloping games or activities that appear unsafe.

Specific Objective I

The student slides.

Functional Settings and Suggested Instructional Activities

School

1. Show the child how to do some simple square dancing that requires him to slide (the "Virginia Reel" is a good one). You may wish to modify the difficulty and number of steps involved to suit the student's abilities.
2. Place large gym mats on the floor. Ask the student to remove his shoes and to run and slide on the mat.

Community

1. Demonstrate how to slide into a base during a baseball game. You may want the physical education teacher to help show the student the safest way to do this correctly. Once the student has been shown, encourage him to practice sliding under supervision.
2. Take the student to a square dance in which he may have the opportunity to slide during the dance routine.

Functional Emphases   In designing your own instructional activities and plans, emphasize the following elements:

1. Development of motor skills necessary for sliding.
2. Awareness of times when it is safe to slide.
3. Avoidance of sliding activities or games that appear unsafe.
4. Use of sliding equipment that is safe and supervised.
5. Identification of sports in which sliding is part of the game (e.g., baseball).

Specific Objective J

The student hops.

Functional Settings and Suggested Instructional Activities

School

1. Assist the student as he hops. Demonstrate hopping and encourage the student to imitate your actions. Practice.
2. Play a game of "Hop Tag." Use the same rules as tag, instructing the students to hop rather than run.
3. Play the music for the "Bunny Hop." Demonstrate and ask the student to join you in doing the "Bunny Hop."
4. Play Simon Says. As one of the commands, say "Simon says, 'Hop on one foot.'"

Home

1. Ask the parents to read their child a story about rabbits (*Peter Rabbit, Peter Cottontail*). Tell them to ask the child to pretend he is a rabbit and hop around the room. Tell the parents to make sure this activity is age appropriate.
2. Ask the parents to use masking tape (indoors) or marking chalk (outdoors) and mark out a hopscotch court. Tell them to show their child how to play hopscotch.

Functional Emphases   In designing your own instructional activities and plans, emphasize the following elements:

1. Development of motor skills necessary for hopping.
2. Avoidance of hopping games or activities that appear unsafe.
3. Development of ability to hop on both the left and right feet.
4. Use of a variety of games or activities that usually require hopping (e.g., Simon Says and "Hop Tag").

Specific Objective K

The student jumps.

Functional Settings and Suggested Instructional Activities

School

1. Assist the student as he jumps. Demonstrate jumping and encourage the student to imitate your actions.
2. Place gym mats on the floor. Place a low object as an obstacle in the middle of the mat. Encourage the student to jump over the obstacle.

3. Place a box with low sides on the floor. Show the student how to jump into and out of the box. Assist him in doing so.
4. Do the standing broad jump. Assist the student in doing a broad jump. Measure and chart the student's distance. Encourage the student to practice and try to improve his jumps.
5. During exercise periods, demonstrate and assist the student in doing jumping jacks.
6. Show the student how to jump over a rope. Ask two students to hold the ends of the rope. Start with the rope flat on the floor. Tell the student to jump over it; then raise it a little. Raise it gradually so that the student must jump a little higher at each turn. Be sure there are mats under the rope.
7. Play jump rope with the student. Show him how to jump rope with others holding the rope and also to jump while holding the rope himself.

Functional Emphases In designing your own instructional activities and plans, emphasize the following elements:

1. Development of motor skills necessary for jumping.
2. Estimation of distance or height needed to jump.
3. Awareness of safety factors involved in jumping.
4. Selection of a variety of equipment used in jumping (e.g., ropes and high bar).
5. Avoidance of some jumping equipment (e.g., a trampoline that is rated unsafe or is poorly made).

Specific Objective L

The student skips.

Functional Settings and Suggested Instructional Activities

School

1. Demonstrate skipping and encourage the student to imitate your actions. Practice.
2. Play slow music. Ask the student to skip slowly to get the rhythm of skipping. Once the student becomes somewhat skilled, play livelier music and ask the student to skip to it.
3. Ask the student to choose a partner. Play some music and tell the students to hold hands and skip together to the music.
4. Ask the students to remove their shoes. Divide the students into two teams and place their shoes in a pile. Have each student skip to his shoes, put them on, and skip back to his team. Upon the return of the student, the next person on the team does the same. The first team to finish is the winner.

5. Play "A Tisket, A Tasket" and ask the student to skip as she acts out the song. One student can carry a letter or object. The other sutdents sit on the floor in a large circle. The student with the letter or object skips around the circle and drops it behind one person. That person picks it up, skips after the other student, and tries to catch her before she gets to the other student's place in the circle.
6. Play "Skip To My Lou" and other folk dances that require or suggest skipping.

Community

1. Take the students to a grassy area of the schoolyard or to a park. Ask the students to skip in the grass. Check to be sure the grass is clear of glass and other sharp or dangerous objects.
2. Take the students to a beach or park with large sandy areas. Ask the students to take off their shoes and skip through the sand.

Functional Emphases   In designing your own instructional activities and plans, emphasize the following elements:

1. Development of motor skills necessary for skipping.
2. Awareness of left and right parts of the body.
3. Use of a variety of games and activities that involve skipping.
4. Experiences with a variety of surfaces on which to skip.
5. Awareness of safety factors to be observed when skipping.

Specific Objective M

The student dances.

Functional Settings and Suggested Instructional Activities

School

1. Plan a dance. Invite another class or group of students and ask them to dance to popular music.
2. Teach the students some simple square dances. Take the students individually and in twos through the steps. Do the dances to spoken commands before using the music. The physical education teacher may want to recommend some simple dances to begin with. Once the students learn a dance or two, arrange for them to perform for others or demonstrate to other classes.
3. Do folk dances, perhaps ethnic ones that would be of interest to the students. Show the students pictures of the kinds of native costumes worn for folk dancing.
4. Learn the current dances. Show the student how to do them.

Home and Community

1. Ask the parents to assist their child in learning to dance. Tell them to demonstrate different types of dancing.
2. Ask the parents to play classical music such as the *Nutcracker* Suite and encourage their child to dance to the music.
3. Attend a dance recital or performance.
4. Take the student to a school or community dance.

Functional Emphases   In designing your own instructional activities and plans, emphasize the following elements:

1. Development of motor skills necessary for dancing.
2. Selection of a variety of music used for dancing.
3. Identification of different events that have dancing (e.g., school dances, weddings, and birthday parties).
4. Identification of and experience with different types of dances, including ethnic dances.
5. Knowledge of dancing etiquette and rules (e.g., when to switch partners and how to ask someone for a dance).

Specific Objective N

The student climbs.

Functional Settings and Suggested Instructional Activities

School

1. Construct an obstacle course. Include obstacles that may be climbed over. As the student goes through the obstacle course, make sure she climbs over things whenever possible.
2. Take the student to the gym. Demonstrate climbing up a knotted rope. Help the student climb up the rope. Be sure to use mats and spotters for safety during this activity.
3. Take the student to the school playground and practice climbing (e.g., climbing on a jungle gym).

Home and Community

1. Ask the parents to tell or read their child a story with climbing in it (e.g., *Rapunzel*). When the characters in a story climb, the parents should encourage the child to pretend by pantomiming climbing.
2. Take the student to a playground or neighborhood park. Assist the student in climbing on play equipment. Tell him to climb up the steps to the slide and slide down. Join in climbing with the student on the jungle gym.

Functional Emphases In designing your own instructional activities and plans, emphasize the following elements:

1. Development of motor skills necessary for climbing.
2. Awareness of safety factors involved in climbing.
3. Selection of a variety of activities that require supervised climbing.
4. Selection of a variety of safe equipment on which to climb (e.g., jungle gyms and sturdy ladders).
5. Experience with climbing on a kitchen stepstool.

Specific Objective O

The student rides Big Wheels, tricycles, and bicycles.

Functional Settings and Suggested Instructional Activities

School

1. Seat the student on a Big Wheel, tricycle, or bicycle. Place his feet on the pedals and secure them with pedal straps. Move the student's legs in a pedaling motion. Encourage the student to pedal independently. For the student who has difficulty reaching the pedals, construct wooden blocks to affix to the pedals.
2. Place brightly colored tape on the floor to form a path. Encourage the student to follow the path on his tricycle.
3. Show the student how to pedal backward and forward.
4. Show the student how to turn corners.
5. Make Big Wheels, tricycles, and bicycles available during free time and encourage the student to ride them in activities such as "Follow the Leader."

Home and Community

1. Ask the parents to assist their child in riding Big Wheels, tricycles, and bicycles. Tell them to let the child get on a Big Wheel, tricycle, or bicycle and then gently move it until he feels safe on the moving vehicle.
2. Ask the parents to seat their child on a Big Wheel, tricycle, or bicycle. Tell them to show him how to hold the handlebars and steer the vehicle. Suggest that they also show him how to move the vehicle with his feet on the floor rather than on the pedals.
3. Place obstacles on a bike path and show the student how to maneuver around them while on his Big Wheel, tricycle, or bicycle.

Functional Emphases In designing your own instructional activities and plans, emphasize the following elements:

1. Development of motor skills necessary for riding Big Wheels, tricycles, and bicycles.

2. Use of age-appropriate recreational equipment.
3. Awareness of safety factors involved in riding recreational equipment.
4. Selection of a variety of recreational equipment suitable for riding.
5. Avoidance of recreational riding equipment that is of the incorrect size or is poorly constructed.
6. Use of modifications to recreational riding equipment when necessary.
7. Awareness of times when it is safe to participate in riding activities.
8. Selection of safe areas in which to ride.

Special Materials List

Books

Peter Rabbit
Peter Cottontail
Rapunzel

Kits

Peabody Language Development Kit. American Guidance Service, Publishers Building, Circle Pines, MN 55014.

Records

Nutcracker Suite
William Tell Overture

Equipment

Junior Walker with Saddle Seat. Kaplan School Supply Co., 600 Jonestown Road, Winston-Salem, NC 27103.

Suggested Readings/References

Angney, A., & Hanley, E. M. (1979). A parent-implemented shaping procedure to develop independent walking of a Down's syndrome child: A case study. *Education and Treatment of Children, 2,* 311–315.

Bergen, A. (1974). *Selected equipment for pediatric rehabilitation.* Valhalla, NY: Blythedale Children's Hospital.

Beter, T. R., Cragin, W. E., & Drury, F. D. (1972). *The mentally retarded child and his motor behavior.* Springfield, IL: Charles C Thomas.

Bobath, B., & Bobath, K. (1975). *Motor development in the different types of cerebral palsy.* London: Heineman Medical.

Cipani, E., Augustine, A., & Blomgren, E. (1980). Teaching the severely and profoundly retarded to open doors: Assessment and training. *Journal of Special Education Technology, 3,* 42–46.

Cipani, E., Augustine, A., & Blomgren, E. (1982). Teaching profoundly retarded adults to ascend stairs safely. *Education and Training of the Mentally Retarded, 17,* 51–54.

Colvin, N. R., & Finholt, J. M. (1981). *Guidelines for physical educators of mentally handicapped youth: Curriculum, assessment, IEP's.* Springfield, IL: Charles C Thomas.

Cratty, B. J. (1975). *Remedial motor activity for children.* Philadelphia: Lea & Febiger.

Finnie, N. R. (1975). *Handling the young cerebral palsied child at home.* New York: Dutton.

Folding electric wheelchairs: A new dimension in mobility. (1976). Torrence, CA: A-BEC.

Fraser, B. A., Galka, G., & Hensinger, R. N. (1980). *Gross motor management of severely multiply impaired students, Vol. I: Evaluation guide.* Austin: PRO-ED.

Galka, G., Fraser, B. A., & Hensinger, R. N. (1980). *Gross motor management of severely multiply impaired students, Vol. II: Curriculum model.* Austin: PRO-ED.

Geddes, D. (1974). *Physical activities for individuals with handicapping conditions.* St. Louis: Mosby.

Gruber, B., Reeser, R., & Reid, D. H. (1979). Providing a less restrictive environment for profoundly retarded persons by teaching independent walking skills. *Journal of Applied Behavior Analysis, 12,* 285–297.

Hughes, J., & Riley, A. (1981). Basic gross motor assessment: Tool for use with children having minor motor dysfunction. *Physical Therapy, 61,* 502–511.

I Can: Physical education program field service unit for physical education and recreation for the handicapped. (1976). Department of Health, Physical Education and Recreation, Michigan State University. Northbrook, IL: Hubbard.

Jenkins, J. R., Fewell, R., & Harris, S. R. (1983). Comparison of sensory integrative therapy and motor programming. *American Journal of Mental Deficiency, 88,* 221–224.

Millen, H. M. (1974). *Body mechanics and safe transfer techniques.* Detroit: Aronsson Printing.

Mullins, J. (1979). *A teacher's guide to management of physically handicapped students.* Springfield, IL: Charles C Thomas.

Ottenbacher, K., Short, M. A., & Watson, P. J. (1981). The effects of a clinically applied program of vestibular stimulation on the neuromotor performance of children with severe developmental disability. *Physical and Occupational Therapy in Pediatrics, 1,* 1–11.

Pearson, P., & Williams, C. (Eds.). (1972). *Physical therapy services in the developmental disabilities.* Springfield, IL: Charles C Thomas.

Presland, J. (1982). *Paths to mobility in "special care": A guide to teaching gross motor skills to very handicapped children.* Kidderminster, Worcestershire, England: BIMH Publications.

Rarick, G. L., & Dobbins, D. A. (1972). *Basic components in the motor performance of educable mentally retarded children: Implications for curriculum development.* Berkeley, CA: University of California.

Riani, R. M., & McNeny, R. (1981). Wheelchair clinic: A better way to prescribe. *Clinical Management in Physical Therapy, 1,* 18–19.

Robinault, L. P. (1973). *Functional aid for the multiply handicapped.* Evanston, IL: Harper & Row.

Schmidt, R. A. (1975). *Motor skills.* New York: Harper & Row.

Sellick, K. J., & Over, R. (1980). Effects of vestibular stimulation on motor development of cerebral palsied children. *Developmental Medicine and Child Neurology, 22,* 476–483.

Sherrill, C. (1980). Posture training as a means of normalization. *Mental Retardation, 18,* 135–138.

Stainback, S., Stainback, W., Wehman, P., & Spangiers, L. (1983). Acquisition and generalization of physical fitness exercises in three profoundly retarded adults. *Journal of The Association of the Severely Handicapped, 8,* 47–55.

Stein, J. U. (1977). Physical education, recreation and sports for special populations. *Education and Training of the Mentally Retarded, 12,* 4–13.

Stephens, B., Baumgartner, B. B., Smeets, P. M., & Wolfinger, W. (1976). Promoting motor development in young retarded children. In R. Anderson & J. Greer (Eds.), *Educating the severely and profoundly retarded.* Baltimore: University Park Press.

Stone, C. (1977). Motor skills. In N. Haring (Ed.), *Developing effective individualized education programs for severely handicapped children and youth.* Washington, DC: Bureau of Education for the Handicapped.

Vannier, M. (1977). *Physical activities for the handicapped.* Englewood Cliffs, NJ: Prentice-Hall.

Wehman, P., & Marchant, J. (1977). Development of gross motor recreation skills in children with severe behavioral handicaps. *Therapeutic Recreation Journal, 11,* 48-54.

Wheeler, R. H., & Hooley, A. M. (1976). *Physical education for the handicapped.* Philadelphia: Lea & Febiger.

Wilson, V., & Parks, R. (1976). Promoting ambulation in the severely retarded child. In R. Anderson & J. Greer (Eds.), *Educating the severely and profoundly retarded.* Baltimore: University Park Press.

4 | Fine Motor and Prevocational Skills

Proficiency in the use of the hands, arms, and upper torso is vital to progress in most activities of daily life. Foremost among these skills are those involved in activities that enable people to care for themselves in their environment. Self-care development, including eating and dressing, manipulation of toys and other playthings, and the use of utensils and other tools, is largely dependent upon growth in fine motor skills (Edgar, Maser, & Haring, 1977; Sternlicht & Hurwitz, 1981). The intent of this chapter is to provide the reader with instructional objectives and activities that highlight the acquisition of functionally relevant fine motor and prevocational skills. Prevocational skills have been included to stress their great dependence upon facilitation of proficiency in the area of fine motor skills. However, this emphasis is not meant to minimize the critical role of cognitive and affective skills in vocational adjustment.

The objectives for initial, and therefore fundamental, manipulative skills, including grasping, releasing, touching, and passing objects, were developed from a review of professional literature (Banus, Kent, Norton, Sukiennicki, & Becker, 1979; Bunker, 1978; Copeland, Ford, & Solon, 1976) and following consultation with occupational therapists, developmental pediatricians, nurses, and other professionals who work in early childhood programs for the handicapped, especially those programs that serve youngsters with severe physical handicaps (Healy & Stainback, 1980; Mullins, 1979).

The fine motor skills involved in dressing and undressing are included in both the Self-Care and Fine Motor sections of this curriculum because these skills have been designated as priority needs of moderately and severely handicapped students by occupational therapists, special educators, and parents. The emphasis in the self-care experiences is on achieving the task. The goal of the fine motor unit activities is to use the task as a means of enhancing fine motor skills (Adelson & Sandow, 1978; Edgar et al., 1977; Kramer & Whitehurst, 1981).

Leisure-time activities also should be employed as a means of encouraging fine motor development because almost all toys and games require the use of the hands and arms, especially the toys and games of young children. Parents in home and community leisure activities have a singular opportunity not only to instruct their children in the appropriate utilization of leisure time but also to simultaneously develop the fine motor skills necessary for so many of life's activities.

Although the use of the upper extremities in operating simple appliances, objects, conveniences, and home accessories also involves the development of fine motor skills, the discussion of these skills is not presented here. Chapter 5 ("Household Management and Living Skills") contains the functional settings and suggested instructional activities for these skills.

Prevocational skills pertinent to the fine motor area are focused on because of the important role that these specific skills play in the development of meaningful IEPs and because they lead to the development of many of the motoric competencies for functioning as an adult in the demanding world of work. Vocational activities are not the subject of this curriculum but may be found in numerous other sources.

The Suggested Readings and Special Materials List at the end of this chapter provide information on the fine motor skill areas discussed within this section. The reader should decide which materials and information are applicable to a specific student or students being taught. Toys or games mentioned in the chapter can be found in local toy stores or can be ordered through educational catalogs.

General Objectives of the Unit

   I. The student will acquire those initial manipulative skills that will facilitate the development of more advanced fine motor skills and the functional use of the upper extremities.
  II. The student will undress and dress using those fine motor skills that will allow him to function as optimally as possible.
 III. The student will engage in leisure-time activities involving the use of the upper extremities and will do so using those fine motor skills that will allow him to function optimally.
  IV. The student will acquire those fine motor skills that will allow him to use his upper extremities optimally in operating simple appliances, objects, conveniences, and home accessories.[3]
   V. The student will acquire those fine motor skills that will enable him to use his upper extremities optimally in prevocational activities.

---

[3] See Chapter 5 for suggested instructional activities and functional emphases in this area.

General Objective I

The student will acquire those initial manipulative skills that will facilitate the development of more advanced fine motor skills and the functional use of the upper extremities.

Specific Objectives

The student:

A. touches and holds objects, toys, and playthings.
B. reaches for and grasps objects.
C. releases small objects, toys, and playthings.
D. picks up objects, materials, and playthings.
E. passes objects, materials, and playthings.
F. places objects, materials, and playthings into appropriate forms.

Specific Objective A

The student touches and holds objects, toys, and playthings.

Functional Settings and Suggested Instructional Activities

School

1. Place a board covered with various materials in front of the student. Include sandpaper, felt, silk, leather, and wood. Tell the student to touch different parts of the board, or touch one yourself and urge the student to imitate your behavior.
2. If there is a juice and snack time or time when materials are to be passed out to other students in the room, give the student the material or containers of juice to hold for you. Point out to the student that he is holding the juice or other materials, and thank him for being a good helper. Practice this activity daily.

Home and Community

1. Ask the parents to demonstrate touching and feeling different common objects. Tell them to have their child touch soft items such as pillows or felt and hard objects such as appliances and furniture.
2. Visit a neighborhood playground during play time. Give the student several pieces of play equipment to hold. When other students need the equip-

ment, tell him to give it to them. Rotate this job among the other students so that all students will have an opportunity to hold specific equipment.

Functional Emphases In designing your own instructional activities and plans, emphasize the following elements:

1. Identification of light and heavy objects.
2. Selection of objects that can be easily held.
3. Judgment as to whether or not toys are safe.
4. Identification of objects and things that should never be touched.
5. Identification of objects that should not be touched under certain circumstances.

Specific Objective B

The student reaches for and grasps objects.

Functional Settings and Suggested Instructional Activities

School

1. Show the student how to play a game with miniature objects. Place several objects in front of him, and tell him that he is to pick one up and hide it in his hand while you look away. Then you guess what he has in his hand.
2. Take the student out to the playground where there is a chinning bar. Lift the student up (make sure that safety precautions are observed), and tell him to grasp the bar. Reinforce the student by saying, "Good job," if he has done it appropriately. Tell the student to practice his chinning during his free time if he feels like doing so.

Home and Community

1. Ask the parents to place a small object such as a toy in front of their child. Ask them to demonstrate reaching for the object and bringing it close to them. Ask them to tell the child to imitate their actions by reaching for the object in front of him. They should reinforce this activity by saying, "Good job." If he reaches for the object. If he reaches for the object, he should be allowed to play with it.
2. Take the student to a mailbox on the street. Tell the student you want him to mail a letter, and that first he has to grasp the handle of the mailbox and pull it down. Demonstrate grasping the handle, and tell the student to imitate your actions. Tell the student to mail the letter if he grasps the handle of the mailbox.

Functional Emphases In designing your own instructional activities and plans, emphasize the following elements:

1. Avoidance of objects that are difficult to grasp.

2. Modification of objects (e.g., eating utensils) when necessary.
3. Judgment as to whether or not objects can be grasped.
4. Observance of safety procedures when reaching for an object.
5. Experience with a variety of objects that require grasping (e.g., salt and pepper shakers, articles of clothing, and toys).

Specific Objective C

The student releases small objects, toys, and playthings.

Functional Settings and Suggested Instructional Activities

School

1. As part of a leisure activity, play the game Blockhead, in which the student has to pile, balance, and release blocks. Emphasize the words "Let go" to the student as he withdraws his hand from a block that has just been balanced.
2. Ask the student to pass out small paper plates and paper cups during a party. Praise him if he releases the plates and cups correctly.

Home and Community

1. Ask the parents to play with their child when he is playing with his toys. Ask them to tell him to pass toys to them and praise him if he releases them at the appropriate time. Ask them to practice this activity with him.
2. Take the student to a mailbox on the corner. Tell the student to place several letters in the mailbox opening. Tell him to release the letters once they clear the opening. If the student brings any of the letters back, tell him he did not let go of them, and he must go back and do it over again. Practice this activity with a toy mailbox and sample letters in the learning area or at home.

Functional Emphases In designing your own instructional activities and plans, emphasize the following elements:

1. Identification of objects that can be easily released once they are held.
2. Modification of objects so they can be held and released easily.
3. Judgment as to when objects should be released.
4. Experience with a variety of objects, toys, and playthings.

Specific Objective D

The student picks up objects, materials, and playthings.

Functional Settings and Suggested Instructional Activities

School

1. Play a matching game in which you place a set of objects in front of you and a duplicate set in front of the student. You pick up and hold up an object, and he must pick his duplicate object and hold it up. He then goes first, and you continue taking turns.
2. During a leisure activity, play games that involve picking up playing objects (e.g., dominoes, bingo space markers, checkers, and marbles).

Home and Community

1. Ask the parents to demonstrate putting their thumbs and forefingers together in a pincer grasp. Tell them to pick up several small objects such as paper clips or rubber bands that have been placed in front of their child. Ask them to encourage the child to imitate their actions.
2. Take the students to a field where there are flowers that may be picked. Tell the student to pick as many flowers as he can and bring back a bouquet. Reward the student for doing a good job by tying a bow around the bouquet and asking him to whom he would like to give the flowers.

Functional Emphases In designing your own instructional activities and plans, emphasize the following elements:

1. Identification of different objects that can be picked up.
2. Avoidance of objects that should not be picked up.
3. Selection of appropriate times to pick up something.
4. Modification of objects that may be difficult to pick up.

Specific Objective E

The student passes objects, materials, and playthings.

Functional Settings and Suggested Instructional Activities

School

1. At the end of the day, tell the student to help you pass out papers or clothing to the other students. Give the student a pile of papers that are to be sent home, and tell him to pass one paper to each student.
2. Play recreational games that require the passing of an object. As an example, place the students in a circle and give one student a bean bag. Tell the students to pass the bean bag as long as they hear music playing in the background. When the music stops, the one holding the bean bag has to sit down. The student who is left is the winner. Similar games such as Time Bomb can be played.
3. Set up a relay game where the student has to pass an object or stick to another student during the race.

Home and Community

1. Ask the parents to request certain condiments to be passed during a meal. Ask them to praise their child if he passes them appropriately.
2. While on the playground or at a recreational center, ask the student to pass you some sporting equipment. Praise him if he does it correctly and tell him to play or participate in games as a reward.

Functional Emphases In designing your own instructional activities and plans, emphasize the following elements:

1. Judgment as to whether objects are too heavy to be passed.
2. Modification of toys or playthings so they can be easily passed.
3. Observance of appropriate safety procedures for passing different types of objects.
4. Discretion as to when objects should or should not be passed.

Specific Objective F

The student places objects, materials, and playthings into appropriate forms.

Functional Settings and Suggested Instructional Activities

School

1. During leisure time, present the student with many toys that require the placing of one part on or into another. Present games to the student such as Lego, Rig-a-Jig, Lincoln Logs, Tinker Toys, and erector sets.
2. If the student uses a lunch box, observe if he puts away his thermos after eating. If he needs help, assist him in putting away his thermos in its lunch box holder correctly.

Home

1. Ask the parents to demonstrate the placing of puzzle parts into their corresponding forms. Ask them to tell their child to imitate what they have done, and give him a simple four- or five-piece wooden puzzle.
2. At the time of a birthday or when candles are part of holiday celebrations or decorations, ask the parents as part of a home leisure activity to place candle holders in front of their child and tell him to place candles in them. If he does it correctly, they should tell him that he may put the birthday candle holders on the cake or help with the holiday decorations.

Functional Emphases In designing your own instructional activities and plans, emphasize the following elements:

1. Judgment as to whether certain objects fit into corresponding forms.
2. Selection of appropriate objects that must be put away in forms.

3. Use of safety procedures when placing materials in forms (e.g., not forcing an object into a form).

General Objective II

The student will undress and dress using those fine motor skills that will allow him to function as optimally as possible.

Specific Objectives

The student:

A. opens and closes zippers.
B. opens and closes Velcro.
C. unbuttons and buttons clothing.
D. opens and closes snaps.
E. hooks and unhooks hooks and eyes.
F. laces and ties a bowknot.

Specific Objective A

The student opens and closes zippers.

Functional Settings and Suggested Instructional Activities

School

1. Show the student how to zip and unzip boots and shoes with zippers. Assist him in doing so during actual dressing and undressing times.
2. Tell the student to dress in front of a mirror and to check his movements as he zips and unzips during dressing and undressing. Help the female student to reach behind her back to zip and unzip dresses and blouses.
3. When both opening and closing zippers have been mastered, show the student how to dress in clothes such as jackets or car coats with zippers that need to be started on their track by the wearer. Demonstrate how to line up the two sides of the zipper and then insert the right prong into the zipper track casing. Once the student masters this operation and has practiced sufficiently, show him how to complete the zipping and unzipping

processes. (*Note:* Whenever possible, avoid the purchase of articles of clothing that require starting zippers on a track.)

Home

1. Ask the parents to show their child how to open and close nonclothing items such as carrying cases, pillow cases, and shaving kits. Tell them to show him how to use his thumb and index finger in opposition to hold the zipper tag. Tell them to use an oversized tag if necessary, especially during the beginning stages.
2. Ask the parents to then proceed to opening and closing zippers on clothing items (male—pants; female—dresses, pants, and skirts).

Functional Emphases In designing your own instructional activities and plans, emphasize the following elements:

1. Avoidance of zippers that are extremely small or poorly made.
2. Selection of clothing with zippers that work easily.
3. Modification of zippers when necessary (i.e., putting a ring on the zipper tag).
4. Observance of safety procedures in zippering clothing and outer wear.
5. Instruction and practice in the motor skills necessary to open and close a zipper.

Specific Objective B

The student opens and closes Velcro.

Functional Settings and Suggested Instructional Activities

School

1. Plan a Halloween party where the student dresses up. Provide costumes that use Velcro fasteners. Praise the student if he puts on and uses the Velcro fasteners correctly.
2. Plan an exhibit or demonstration of the different types or ways clothing can be fastened (i.e., buttons, zippers, snaps, and Velcro). Point out the Velcro fasteners and encourage the student to use them.

Home

1. Ask the parents to sew Velcro fasteners on clothing that their child has difficulty in opening or closing. Ask them to practice the making of these fasteners with him.
2. Ask the parents to include clothing with Velcro fasteners as part of their child's wardrobe at appropriate times (going shopping, to school, or running an errand). Ask them to tell the child to select clothing with these fasteners. They should praise him if he uses the fasteners correctly.

Functional Emphases In designing your own instructional activities and plans, emphasize the following elements:

1. Judgment as to when to use Velcro rather than other fasteners.
2. Selection of clothing that is adaptable for Velcro fasteners.
3. Modification, when appropriate, of Velcro in size and length.

Specific Objective C

The student unbuttons and buttons clothing.

Functional Settings and Suggested Instructional Activities

School

1. Play dress-up in parents' clothes, costumes, or oversize clothes for Halloween, Thanksgiving, and other holiday parties. Tell the student to select garments that have buttons.
2. Once the student has shown some skill in buttoning, show him how to unbutton. Demonstrate how to use the thumb and index finger of one hand to pull the cloth over the button while pushing it through the hole with the other hand. It may be necessary to use large-size buttons and oversize clothing in the beginning.

Home and Community

1. Ask the parents to assist their child in buttoning his clothing during actual dressing times. Tell them to establish a buttoning pattern (e.g., top to bottom).
2. Ask the parents to engage in unbuttoning activities with their child during actual undressing times such as toileting, before showers and baths, before changing clothes for recreational and work activities, and before bedtime.
3. Participate in a sporting or recreational event that requires the student to change clothes (e.g., racquetball, tennis, or swimming). Praise the student if he unbuttons and/or buttons his clothing correctly when he is undressing and dressing.

Functional Emphases In designing your own instructional activities and plans, emphasize the following elements:

1. Selection of a variety of buttons used as fasteners.
2. Use of buttoning aids when appropriate.
3. Instruction and practice in the motor skills necessary for buttoning and unbuttoning.
4. Avoidance of buttons that are poorly made, too small, or nonfunctional.
5. Experience with various sizes and shapes of buttons.

Specific Objective D

The student opens and closes snaps.

Functional Settings and Suggested Instructional Activities

School

1. During leisure time, demonstrate to the student how to snap wooden and plastic snap toys together by inserting the snap part into its holding receptacle. Assist him in connecting these toys together. Once the student succeeds in snapping these toys together, show him how to slip his thumb-tip under the snap and pull it open with his index fingertip and thumbtip acting in opposition.
2. For the student who appears to be having difficulty with snapping, demonstrate these movements on a snapping frame. Assist the student in doing so. Place an interesting picture behind the snapped-shut material as a reward for the student.

Home

1. Ask the parents to tell their child to practice snapping and unsnapping on Dapper Dan and/or Dressie Bessie dolls during his or her play time.
2. Ask the parents to then proceed to snapping and unsnapping clothing during dressing and undressing situations. Suggest that they use oversize clothing with oversize snaps in the beginning and gradually reduce the size of the clothing and snaps.

Functional Emphases In designing your own instructional activities and plans, emphasize the following elements:

1. Selection of a variety of snaps used as fasteners.
2. Instruction and practice in the motor skills necessary for snapping and unsnapping.
3. Avoidance of snaps that are poorly made, too small, and/or decorative.

Specific Objective E

The student hooks and unhooks hooks and eyes.

Functional Settings and Suggested Instructional Activities

School

1. Show the student how to use the thumb and index finger of one hand to hold the eye in place and the other hand's thumb and index finger to guide the hook into the eye. Begin by using an appropriate hook-and-eye board. Assist the student in modeling and practicing your actions.

2. During dressing activities, practice with the student putting on a skirt or dress or pants with hooks and eyes. Assist the student if necessary.
3. Assist the female student in unhooking and hooking the eye(s) and hook(s) on her bra. (*Note:* For this activity male teachers should ask a female aide, a class mother, a female teacher, or a female student to assist the student.)

Home

1. Ask the mother to encourage her daughter to practice hooking and unhooking a dress or bra with a hook and eye in the back. Tell her to remind her daughter to use a mirror to help her find the hook and eye. Also remind her to tell her daughter to feel with her fingers to find the hook and eye. The daughter should also close her eyes and practice relying on touch alone.
2. It may be necessary for the father to assist his son in using the modified hook and eye often found at the top of a pair of pants. This hook and eye is a sort of sliding hook that slips into a channel. Tell the father that he should assist his son in hooking and unhooking this modified hook and eye whenever he is dressing and undressing until he does it independently.

Functional Emphases In designing your own instructional activities and plans, emphasize the following elements:

1. Selection of a variety of hooks and eyes to use as fasteners.
2. Instruction and practice in the motor skills necessary for using hooks and eyes.
3. Avoidance of hooks and eyes that are poorly made, too small, or serve only a decorative function.

Specific Objective F

The student laces and ties a bowknot.

Functional Settings and Suggested Instructional Activities

School

1. Show the student how to tie and knot shoelaces used during recreational activities (on sneakers, bowling shoes, roller and ice skates, and tennis shoes). Assist him in doing so during recreational pursuits. Lacing shoes in order to participate in an athletic event or to be part of a team may provide the motivation that will assist the student in simple shoelace tying.
2. During leisure time, show the student how to lace a lace card. Assist him in lacing. Most lacing cards come with patterns; therefore, help the student follow the pattern. Begin with simple patterns and work up to those that are increasingly more difficult.

Home

1. Ask the parents to show their child how to tie a shoelace in a bowknot. (*Note:* It may be more practical to buy only loafers for the child if there is inordinate difficulty in learning to tie a shoelace.)
2. Tell the parents to show their daughter how to tie a bowknot on the top of nightgowns, some blouses, and capes. Tell them to assist her in doing so and reward her for dressing neatly.

Functional Emphases In designing your own instructional activities and plans, emphasize the following elements:

1. Instruction and practice in the motor skills necessary for lacing and tying a bowknot.
2. Selection of clothing, shoes, and other wearing apparel that requires the lacing and tying of a bowknot.
3. A decision as to whether or not to purchase clothes that require lacing and/or tying a bowknot.

General Objective III

The student will engage in leisure-time activities involving the use of the upper extremities and will do so using those fine motor skills that will allow him to function optimally.

Specific Objectives

The student:

A. holds, picks up, and plays with small toys and playthings such as noise-makers, clothespins, pot covers, and boxes.
B. passes small toys and playthings to a peer or significant adult.
C. builds with blocks and other playthings.
D. sifts, shapes, pours, and builds with sand.
E. fills containers, pours, and otherwise engages in play with water.
F. strings beads, spools, and other playthings.
G. finger paints.
H. fits pieces of puzzles, pegs, and other playthings into their corresponding forms.
I. pastes paper and objects onto paper.

J. colors with crayons on paper or in a coloring book.

K. molds and shapes clay, Play Doh, and plasticene and makes objects with these materials.

L. bends and shapes pipe cleaners.

M. weaves using simple forms.

N. folds and constructs out of paper and cardboard.

O. spins wheels and dials and also throws dice in table games.

P. cuts with scissors.

Q. shuffles, deals, and performs other tasks involved in playing simple card games.

R. sketches and draws simple objects with crayons, colored pencils, charcoal, and/or colored chalk.

S. draws and paints wtih a brush and paints.

T. sews and makes simple clothing out of fabric.

U. constructs using one medium such as wood or other natural materials.

V. constructs using several media, including paper, wood, fabric, leather, cord, yarn, and natural materials (shells, grass, rice, beans, and macaroni).

W. embroiders, crochets, knits, and does needlepoint and macramé.

Specific Objective A

The student holds, picks up, and plays with small toys and playthings such as noisemakers, clothespins, pot covers, and boxes.

Functional Settings and Suggested Instructional Activities

School

1. During play time, give the student clay or Play Doh balls that he can hold and squeeze. Show him how to hold and play with it. Use a Nerf ball for variety.

2. Place in front of the student a colorful stuffed animal, doll, or other soft toy such as a squeeze toy with a noisemaker. Demonstrate how to pick up the object by using the thumb in opposition to all of the fingers. Encourage him to model your behavior and assist him if necessary. A squeeze toy with a noisemaker is often reinforcing.

3. Place a variety of objects in front of the student. Play the game of "Show and Tell," in which you name an object and the student picks it up and shows you the object named.

Home

1. Ask the parents to find toys and other playthings that interest their child. Ask them to offer each object in turn to him. If he opens his hand, they should place the object between the opened fingers. If not, they should

assist him in opening his fingers, and then place the object between the opened fingers. If necessary, they may have to take his fingers and close them around the object. They should then indicate through words and/or gestures that he is to hold the object, and should encourage him to hold the object for increasingly longer periods of time.

2. Ask the parents to observe young children at play as they explore their world with their hands. Ask them to make an inventory of objects that fascinate their child. Remind them that nontoys are often more intriguing to children than commercial products, and they should provide the opportunity for their child to play with both.

3. Ask the parents to play games that include picking up small objects, such as checkers, dominoes, bingo, and pick-up sticks.

Functional Emphases In designing your own instructional activities and plans, emphasize the following elements:

1. Avoidance of objects with sharp points, sharp edges, and that can be easily swallowed.

2. Avoidance of using small objects and toys with students who put objects into their mouths, noses, eyes, or ears.

3. Selection of toys and objects that are well constructed and have a minimum of parts.

4. Modification of toys or objects so they can be easily held.

5. Use of age-appropriate toys and playthings.

Specific Objective B

The student passes small toys and playthings to a peer or significant adult.

Functional Settings and Suggested Instructional Activities

School

1. Play the "Hidden Object" game. Hide a favored toy in your hand. Encourage the student to find the hand in which it is hidden. When the student does so, pass the object to him. Then reverse roles; encourage him to hide the object and to pass it to you when you guess the hand in which it is hidden.

2. Simulate a tea party and ask the student to pass the sugar, lemon, milk, or biscuits.

3. Arrange the students in a circle and play a game of passing objects. Use a bean bag, ball, or stuffed toy. Play music for a variation and tell the students to stop passing the object when the music stops and to start passing it again when the music starts.

Home

1. Ask the parents to play games with their child that involve passing small toys to each other (e.g., miniature furniture to be placed in a dollhouse).
2. Ask the parents to carry out an assembly task while the child passes them needed objects (e.g., a toy nut to be attached to a toy bolt).

Functional Emphases In designing your own instructional activities and plans, emphasize the following elements:

1. Avoidance of objects with sharp points, sharp edges, and that can be easily swallowed.
2. Avoidance of using small objects and toys with students who put objects into their mouths, noses, eyes, or ears.
3. Selection of toys and objects that are well constructed and have a minimum of parts.
4. Modification of toys or objects so they can be easily held.
5. Use of age-appropriate toys and playthings.

Specific Objective C

The student builds with blocks and other playthings.

Functional Settings and Suggested Instructional Activities

School

1. Give the student, during play time, two 3×3-inch blocks, and take two for yourself. With your pair of blocks, stack one on top of each other. Indicate to the student in some way that he is to construct a building just like yours. Assist him if necessary. If the student is successful, give him three, then four, then five blocks and indicate in some way that he is to build a taller building each time. For variety, use paper cups, poker chips, books, and boxes. Encourage the student to construct tall houses and buildings. Assist him when necessary.
2. Give the student a collection of cartons of varying sizes, and encourage him to build various structures. Assist him when necessary.

Home

1. Ask the parents to use large wooden blocks constructed by makers of educational toys and games to build roads, platforms, bridges, and tunnels. Tell them to encourage their child to build similar structures. Tell them to start with large blocks and then build small towns and cities with standard-size blocks.

2. Ask the parents to give their child a collection of nontoys (e.g., pudding boxes and cans) and encourage him to build various structures.

Functional Emphases In designing your own instructional activities and plans, emphasize the following elements:

1. Avoidance of objects with sharp points, sharp edges, and that can be easily swallowed.
2. Avoidance of using small objects and toys with students who put objects into their mouths, noses, eyes, or ears.
3. Selection of toys and objects that are well constructed and have a minimum of parts.
4. Modification of toys or objects so they can be easily held.
5. Use of age-appropriate toys and playthings.

Specific Objective D

The student sifts, shapes, pours, and builds with sand.

Functional Settings and Suggested Instructional Activities

School

1. Supply the student with a sand pail and shovel. Show him how to fill the pail with sand. Assist him in doing so.
2. Show the student how to pour sand from a pail back into the sandbox or sand table. Assist him in doing so.
3. Show the student how to pour sand from a pail into another container in the sandbox or on the sand table. Assist him, if necessary, when he does it.
4. Show the student how to build sand pies by filling a pail with slightly wet sand, turning the filled pail over, and tapping the bottom of the pail until the sand comes loose. Assist him in carrying out each of the steps in the sequence. Use containers of different sizes and shapes to make different cakes and pies.
5. Show the student how to dig holes for tunnels and valleys and how to mold and pack slightly wet sand to make mountains, buildings, and castles. Assist him in creating his own castles in the sand. Reward him for a job well done.

Community

1. Take the student to a playground where there is a sandbox. Join him in playing with the sand.
2. If possible, take the student to a beach. Join him in building sand castles.

Functional Emphases In designing your own instructional activities and plans, emphasize the following elements:

1. Use of a variety of containers for holding and sifting sand.
2. Use of a variety of sand ranging from coarse to fine beach sand.
3. Safety factors involved in playing with sand (i.e., avoiding getting it in one's eyes or in open cuts).
4. Avoidance of using sand that is contaminated with glass, debris, or other foreign substances.
5. Awareness of the need to clean up an area after playing with sand.

Specific Objective E

The student fills containers, pours, and otherwise engages in play with water.

Functional Settings and Suggested Instructional Activities

School

1. Show the student how to fill various containers with water at a water table. Assist him in doing so.
2. Show the student how to pour water from one container to another while playing at a water table. Assist him in doing so and give him containers of various sizes.
3. Show the student how to pour water through a sieve and to feel the water as it comes out. Assist him in doing so.
4. Show the student how to fill plastic detergent bottles with water, put on a perforated cap, and squirt water out into the water table. Use a little detergent to make bubbles. Assist the student in doing so.
5. Show the student how to float plastic containers such as margarine tubs and then to sink them by putting in weights. Assist him in doing so.

Home

1. Ask the parents to give their child plastic toy dishes, toy pots and pans, a dishrag, and soap. Ask them to show him how to scrape, wash, and rinse the dishes and pots, and assist him in doing so.
2. Ask the parents to place their child in a tub of water. Tell them to give him a Busy Bath Toy and demonstrate how to play with it.

Functional Emphases In designing your own instructional activities and plans, emphasize the following elements:

1. Use of a variety of toys and playthings for water play.

2. Avoidance during water play of detergents, perfumes, or water coloring that may cause skin reactions.
3. Awareness of water temperature.
4. Recognition of safety factors to consider when engaging in water play (e.g., spilling water on the floor, forgetting to shut off the sink or tub, and using toys or playthings that are easily broken).

Specific Objective F

The student strings beads, spools, and other playthings.

Functional Settings and Suggested Instructional Activities

School

1. Tie knots at the ends of two pieces of shoelace or heavy string. Give the student one of the strings or laces and several spools. Take your own lace and string several spools on it. While doing this, explain your actions. Then ask the student to make a chain like yours. Assist him if necessary. When completed, tie the two ends together and make a bracelet or necklace to put on a doll, stuffed toy, the student, or yourself.
2. Repeat Activity 1; this time use wooden beads of different sizes and shapes. String in any pattern; disregard color and shape.
3. Use macaroni that has been dyed various colors by using food dyes. Collect pasta of various shapes. Show the student how to create single-strand bracelets, necklaces, belts, and headbands. Show the student how to create simple designs by alternating various macaroni shapes and colors. For variety, add beads and/or spools. Give the student the finished product and ask him to make one just like yours. Assist him if necessary. If he is successful, ask him to make his own necklace, bracelet, headband, etc. Encourage him to make these items as gifts for special occasions.
4. Show the student how to string wooden beads by shape. At first use one color and shape, and then make designs using various shapes and colors. Encourage the student to copy your designs and then to create color and shape designs of his own. Assist him when needed.
5. Show the student how to string buttons using a needle and thread. Begin by using large buttons. Encourage him to copy your design. If necessary, thread the needle and knot the thread for him. Challenge him to create his own designs. Reward him for creating interesting designs and jewelry.
6. Show the student how to string cranberries and popcorn to make party and holiday decorations. Encourage him to copy your designs and to create designs of his own. Reward the student for making his contribution to the party and to future occasions.

Home

1. Ask the parents to show their child how to string wooden beads in different color patterns and shapes.
2. Ask the parents to show their child how to string buttons into different patterns.

Functional Emphases In designing your own instructional activities and plans, emphasize the following elements:

1. Avoidance of small objects that can be swallowed or put in eyes, ears, or other body openings.
2. Selection of beads, spools, and other playthings that are painted with non-toxic colors.
3. Development of cognitive skills in developing stringing patterns.
4. Use of a variety of stringing materials, including natural materials (cranberries and popcorn) and those that are commercially made.

Specific Objective G

The student finger paints.

Functional Settings and Suggested Instructional Activities

School

1. Show the student how to use all parts of his hands, such as the fingertips, fingernails, knuckles, palms, sides, and heels, to create linear shapes and patterns with finger paints. At first, use only one color and then gradually add one or two more. Encourage the student to make designs of his own. (It is important to establish procedures for working to minimize problems with keeping clothes and the learning area as clean as possible.)
2. Make a finger paint picture and then cover the finished painting with a clean sheet of paper and rub evenly. Lift the print off by pulling evenly from one side to the other. Hang the print up to dry. Show the student how to make his own print. Remind him to wash his hands completely before making the print. Display the print on the classroom bulletin board and in building display cases and bulletin boards.

Home

1. Ask the parents to join their child in finger painting as a leisure activity.
2. Ask the parents to display their child's finger paintings in a suitable place in the house.

Functional Emphases In designing your own instructional activities and plans, emphasize the following elements:

1. Selection of a variety of colors of finger paints.
2. Use of finger paints that are nontoxic.
3. Awareness of the need to clean up after finger painting.
4. Development of skill in safely opening finger paint bottle covers that are stuck.

Specific Objective H

The student fits pieces of puzzles, pegs, and other playthings into their corresponding forms.

Functional Settings and Suggested Instructional Activities

School

1. Show the student a form board with simple geometric shapes. Show the student how to match the shape of the wooden insert with its embedded form. Show the student how to line it up with the background. Encourage him to model your actions and to work the form board himself.
2. Give the student a form board with different-size cutouts of the same basic geometric shape. Show the student how to match the individual pieces to their corresponding backgrounds. Assist him in completing the form board.

Home

1. Ask the parents to obtain simple wooden puzzles of two or three pieces. Tell them to show their child how to study the puzzle, remove the pieces (one at a time or by turning the board over), and pick up the pieces of the puzzle and put them back into the form board. (*Note:* Children who have difficulty picking up pieces of puzzles should be given Simplex type puzzles with knobs on each piece or should be taught to slide pieces of puzzles off the table into their hands.)
2. Ask the parents to show their child how to form shapes and simple constructions by putting together pieces of Lego, Rig-a-Jig, Lincoln Logs, Tinker Toys, and erector sets. (*Note:* Encourage the child to copy the designs provided with the instructions and to create his own patterns.)

Functional Emphases In designing your own instructional activities and plans, emphasize the following elements:

1. Selection of a variety of puzzles according to the child's functioning level, age, and interests.
2. Selection of puzzles that are painted with nontoxic paints.

3. Use of safety procedures in putting a puzzle together (e.g., not forcing pieces into a form).
4. Modification of puzzles and/or pieces so that they can be more easily picked up and fitted into a form.
5. Application of strategies for completing a puzzle (e.g., working down the border first or looking for color cues).

Specific Objective I

The student pastes paper and objects onto paper.

Functional Settings and Suggested Instructional Activities

School

1. Show the student how to create a collage by pasting and overlapping pictures taken from picture magazines. Assist him in making his collage.
2. Show the student how to create a collage out of various colored papers, including tissue paper, crêpe paper, cellophane, construction paper, wrapping paper, and foils. Assist him in creating his own collage.
3. Make a mosaic of colored strips of paper. Show the student how to create his own. Assist him if necessary.
4. Show the student how to make an assemblage by gluing objects on a piece of cardboard. Use natural objects such as bark of trees, leaves, small twigs, stones, pebbles, weeds, flowers, pine cones, berries, acorns, or sea shells that have been collected on trips. Encourage the student to touch and examine the objects before making his own collage.
5. Make mosaic-type designs by pasting seeds, beans, berries, rice, and pasta on tagboard, wood, or cardboard. Encourage the student to create his own mosaics.

Home

1. Ask the parents to cut interesting pictures out of picture magazines. Tell them to assist their child in pasting pictures on colored construction paper. Tell them to make a scrapbook of pictures and use the scrapbook to develop communication skills.
2. Ask the parents to make an assemblage of leaves, tissue paper, and yarn. Tell them to assist their child in making his own collage of organic materials such as leaves, various fabrics, and papers.
3. Ask the parents to collect yarn, sticks, stones, leaves, gravel, and twigs. Tell them to make a bas-relief by pasting the materials on cardboard. Tell them to show their child how to overlap items to create interesting shapes. They should assist him in collecting materials and in creating his own bas-relief.

Functional Emphases In designing your own instructional activities and plans, emphasize the following elements:

1. Selection of a variety of pastes, paper, and objects.
2. Use of paste that is nontoxic and washable.
3. Development of cognitive abilities in designing pasting projects and pasting patterns.
4. Awareness of procedures for cleaning up after pasting projects.
5. Modifications of pasting applicators for students who may have difficulty holding a pasting stick or brush.
6. Awareness of safety factors in opening dried or infrequently used paste jars.

Specific Objective J

The student colors with crayons on paper or in a coloring book.

Functional Settings and Suggested Instructional Activities

School

1. Give the student a large crayon and a piece of paper. Show him how to hold the crayon so that he can easily make marks on the piece of paper. Place the crayon in his hand so that it rests on the third finger. Assist him in holding it in place with the thumb held in opposition to the index finger. After the crayon is positioned properly, hold it in the student's hand, guide his hand, and help him to make marks on the paper. Remove your hand and encourage him to scribble on his own. Reward him for any attempts as well as for successes.
2. Give the student different-color crayons and repeat Activity 1. Scribble vertical and horizontal lines. Encourage the student to imitate your movements and to create similar "pictures" on his paper.
3. Scribble circles, loops, semicircles, and other curvilinear shapes. Encourage the student to imitate your movements and to create similar "pictures" on his paper.
4. Using a magic marker, outline shapes on a piece of paper and encourage the student to scribble or color within the lines. Play music and encourage the student to color with a crayon as she listens to the music.

Home

1. Ask the parents to find pages in a coloring book of animals, people, and scenes that interest their child. Tell them to help the child select different colors for different parts of the picture. They should remind him to stay within the bounderies while coloring.
2. Ask the parents to take walks around the community with their child and point out the colors of objects in the environment. Tell them to take a box

of crayons with them and ask the child to match the correct color of crayon with the real color.

Functional Emphases In designing your own instructional activities and plans, emphasize the following elements:

1. Selection of a variety of sizes and colors of crayons.
2. Use of a variety of materials to color, including pictures in coloring books, ditto color sheets, and pictures drawn by the student or others.
3. Use of crayons that are nontoxic.
4. Development of cognitive skills to color within boundaries and in specific picture areas.
5. Modification of crayons (wrapping tape or clay around them) when necessary.
6. Avoidance of crayons that stain clothing or cannot be easily removed from apparel.

Specific Objective K

The student molds and shapes clay, Play Doh, and plasticene and makes objects with these materials.

Functional Settings and Suggested Instructional Activities

School

1. Show the student how to roll clay, Play Doh, and plasticene between his fingers to make long, snakelike coils of clay. Assist the student in making his own lengths of clay.
2. Give the student a large ball of clay, Play Doh, or plasticene. Show him how to pinch, pull, pound, and dig with his fingertips, and to squeeze this ball into a variety of shapes. Assist him in creating new shapes.
3. Give the student a large ball of clay, Play Doh, or plasticene. Show the student how to separate the ball of clay into new sections and to create different shapes by forming and molding these pieces.

Home

1. Ask the parents to engage their child in leisure experiences using clay to create simple objects (e.g., fruit and foods).
2. Ask the parents to join their child in making clay figures and animals.

Functional Emphases In designing your own instructional activities and plans, emphasize the following elements:

1. Use of a variety of clay, plasticene, and Play Doh.
2. Selection of clay, plasticene, and Play Doh that are nontoxic.
3. Development of fine motor skills necessary for shaping and making objects.

4. Implementation of the steps required to protect furniture and floors before beginning a clay, plasticene, or Play Doh project.
5. Recognition of the need to clean up after playing with clay, plasticene, and Play Doh.

Specific Objective L

The student bends and shapes pipe cleaners.

Functional Settings and Suggested Instructional Activities

School

1. Bend and shape pipe cleaners into interesting shapes. Give the student a pipe cleaner and show him how to bend and shape it. Use colored pipe cleaners for variety.
2. Show the student how to bend and shape pipe cleaners into simple figures by using more than one pipe cleaner. For example, a simple human figure can be made with three pipe cleaners.

Home

1. Ask the parents to join their child in creating interesting shapes with pipe cleaners.
2. Ask the parents to purchase different-color pipe cleaners, and encourage their child to use them during free play or quiet activities.

Functional Emphases In designing your own instructional activities and plans, emphasize the following elements:

1. Awareness of safety factors involved in using pipe cleaners.
2. Selection of a variety of sizes and colors of pipe cleaners.
3. Development of fine motor skills necessary to bend and shape pipe cleaners.
4. Avoidance of pipe cleaners with sharp edges or points.
5. Avoidance of pipe cleaners that are fragile from overuse or have been used for other purposes (e.g., cleaning a pipe).

Specific Objective M

The student weaves using simple forms.

Functional Settings and Suggested Instructional Activities

School

1. Show the student how to weave sticks through slits in oilcloth. Assist him in doing so.
2. Show the student how to create an alternating pattern of weaving sticks under and over slits of oilcloth. Use colored sticks for variety.
3. Using a small weaving frame and colored yarn, demonstrate how to weave squares. The squares may then be sewn together.
4. Using a large blunt needle with yarn, weave rows in varied colors in a dishcloth.

Home

1. Ask the parents to show their child how to weave sticks through slits in oilcloth.
2. Ask the parents to show their child how to weave colored paper into slits made in paper. Tell the parents to assist him if necessary.

Functional Emphases   In designing your own instructional activities and plans, emphasize the following elements:

1. Use of a variety of materials for weaving.
2. Development of fine motor skills necessary for weaving.
3. Identification of weaving aids and frames.
4. Recognition of weaving patterns.
5. Consideration of safety factors when using weaving materials that have sharp points.

Specific Objective N

The student folds and constructs out of paper and cardboard.

Functional Settings and Suggested Instructional Activities

School

1. Show the student how to fold paper in half horizontally and vertically. Assist him in doing so.
2. Show the student how to make an old-fashioned fan with pleats. Use heavy and colorful wrapping paper. Fold the paper in folds of about ½ inch. To form the handle, glue together a section of the fan. Assist the student in making his own fan.
3. Show the student how to make a Yankee Doodle hat from a piece of rectangular paper. Fold the paper horizontally. Fold down the two sides at the center of the fold and then fold the botton strips on both sides of the triangle. Assist the student in creating her own triangular hat.
4. Show the student how to make snowflakes and other decorations by folding and cutting paper. Make a circle of 6 to 8 inches by drawing around the

edge of an overturned dish or saucer. Cut the circle out of the paper, fold it in half, in half again, and in half two more times. Cut pieces out of the sides and the base of the paper. Assist the student in making his own decorative doilies and other decorations.

5. Show the student how to make a single decorative paper chain by cutting strips of colored paper, pasting the first strip in a circle, slipping the next strip through the circle and pasting the ends of that strip together, and so on. Assist the student in making colorful chains. Suggest different color patterns.

Home

1. Ask the parents to show their child how to fold paper into different shapes.
2. Ask the parents to show their child how to fold paper napkins for setting a table. Tell them to show him how to fold the napkins in half and in a triangular pattern.

Functional Emphases   In designing your own instructional activities and plans, emphasize the following elements:

1. Use of a variety of paper and cardboard.
2. Development of fine motor skills necessary for folding and constructing.
3. Awareness of safety considerations when using scissors.
4. Development of cognitive abilities involved in planning and then folding paper for a project.
5. Use of related materials (e.g., glue, paint, and crayons) that are nontoxic.

Specific Objective O

The student spins wheels and dials and also throws dice in table games.

Functional Settings and Suggested Instructional Activities

School

1. Collect table games such as Fat Cat that require the spinning of a wheel by snapping the index finger against the thumb and into the wheel before moving a marker on the game board. Show the student how to start the wheel moving. Encourage him to spin the wheel himself. Assist him if necessary; play the game.
2. Collect table games such as Monopoly, Scooby Doo, and Which Witch that require the rolling of dice before moving a marker on the game board. Show the student how to pick up the dice, enclose them in his hand, shake them, and roll them on a surface. Ask him to imitate you and assist him if necessary. Play the games.

Home

1. Ask the parents to engage their child in playing various table games involving the rolling of dice (e.g., Yahtzee and Candy Land).
2. Ask the parents to join the child in playing games involving spinning a wheel (e.g., roulette).

Functional Emphases   In designing your own instructional activities and plans, emphasize the following elements:

1. Selection of a variety of games that use wheels, dice, and dials.
2. Awareness of motor skills necessary to play table games.
3. Selection of age-appropriate table games.
4. Awareness of cognitive strategies needed for specific table games.
5. Awareness of counting and color skills needed to participate in table games.

Specific Objective P

The student cuts with scissors.

Functional Settings and Suggested Instructional Activities

School

1. Using teaching (double-handled) scissors, show the student how to cut paper.
2. Once the student has developed skill in picking up scissors and moving them in the cutting movement, show him how to use the scissors to cut paper into strips. These strips may be used for a meaningful follow-up project such as weaving. It will probably be necessary in the beginning to make cutting lines with a black crayon or a felt pen. Show the student how to guide the tips of the scissors and the blades along the marked lines.
3. Draw various sizes of straight-line geometric shapes, including squares, rectangles, and triangles, on several pieces of construction paper. Show the student how to cut out these shapes with a pair of scissors. Ask him to cut out the shapes on his piece of construction paper. Assist him if necessary and practice.
4. Draw circles of various sizes on several pieces of construction paper. Show the student how to use the scissors to cut out the circles. Encourage him to cut the circles on his piece of construction paper. Assist him if necessary and practice.
5. Show the student how to cut out a picture with straight-line borders from an old magazine. Give the student the picture when you have cut three of the four sides and ask him to complete the job. Then give him his own picture to cut out of a magazine. Ask him to cut this picture out and use it later in a scrapbook or mount it for display on the bulletin board.

6. Show the student how to trim a picture with straight-line borders that have not been carefully cut out. Give him a picture of his own to trim. Assist him if necessary.

7. Show the student how to cut out of paper simple shapes such as pumpkins, candy canes, eggs, trees, or silhouettes of famous people for bulletin board display and decorations for holidays and other special events. Encourage him to join his peers in making the decorations for the learning area.

Home

1. Ask the parents to show their child how to cut out clothing for a paper doll.

2. Ask the parents to show their child how to cut pictures out of magazines as part of making collages or a picture scrapbook.

Functional Emphases   In designing your own instructional activities and plans, emphasize the following elements:

1. Awareness of safety factors involved in using scissors.

2. Use of a variety of scissors according to the type of material that they are to cut.

3. Modification or selection of scissors for students who have difficulty using conventional types.

4. Avoidance of scissors that are broken, too dull, or are an incorrect size.

5. Awareness of where to store scissors after their use.

Specific Objective Q

The student shuffles, deals, and performs other tasks involved in playing simple card games.

Functional Settings and Suggested Instructional Activities

School

1. Show the student how to shuffle a deck of cards by slipping parts of the deck in and out of the pack. While you are shuffling one deck in this manner, give the student a pack to shuffle at the same time. Assist him if necessary in shuffling his own deck.

2. Show the students how to cut a deck by picking up part of the deck and placing it face down on the playing surface. Tell the student to cut a deck and assist him if necessary.

3. Show the student how to deal cards for simple two-handed games. Give the student a deck of cards and ask him to deal out a set number of cards. Assist him if necessary.

Home

1. Ask the parents to purchase some simple card games (e.g., "Fish"). Tell them to play these games with their child after explaining the rules to him.
2. Tell the parents to include a deck of cards when they pack for a trip with their child. Tell them to suggest playing card games to their child during leisure time on the trip.

Functional Emphases　In designing your own instructional activities and plans, emphasize the following elements:

1. Selection of card games that are age appropriate.
2. Development of fine motor skills necessary for playing cards.
3. Use of strategies involved in specific card games.
4. Modification of cards (e.g., putting them on large pieces of cardboard) for students who have difficulty in handling conventional cards.
5. Development of academic skills required in certain card games (e.g., adding and subtracting scores and/or points).

Specific Objective R

The student sketches and draws simple objects with crayons, colored pencils, charcoal, and/or colored chalk.

Functional Settings and Suggested Instructional Activities

School

1. Place a common everyday object on a table. Use objects with simple shapes such as an apple, block, can, bottle, banana, or book. Use a crayon to sketch and then color the object drawn. Encourage the student to make a drawing also. Show him how to select appropriate colors. Assist him if necessary.
2. Once the student has mastered drawing some simple objects, ask him to draw and color more complex everyday objects such as a flower, clock, radio, chair, lamp, telephone, sink, or refrigerator. Assist him if necessary.
3. If the student is successful in drawing various single common objects, place common objects in a still life arrangement, and encourage the student to draw them. Assist him if necessary.
4. After the student has demonstrated competency with crayons, introduce him to the use of colored pencils, charcoal, and colored chalk.

Home and Community

1. Tell the parents to include a sketch pad, colored pencils, and colored chalk as part of any gifts they purchase for their child at holiday or birthday times. Tell them to engage him in using these materials.

2. If the student shows skill in drawing common objects, encourage him to draw scenes (without people) of the school, the hospital, the community, and the playground. Assist him if necessary. Display his work prominently.

Functional Emphases   In designing your own instructional activities and plans, emphasize the following elements:

1. Use of a variety of sketching and drawing materials.
2. Use of sketching and drawing materials that are nontoxic.
3. Awareness of the need to clean up an area after drawing and put pencils, crayons, and chalk away.

Specific Objective S

The student draws and paints with a brush and paints.

Functional Settings and Suggested Instructional Activities

School

1. Set up a paint area with paint pans, brushes, and water containers. Put a file of pictures in this learning station. Encourage the student to use this paint area when he has free time and feels like painting.
2. Show the student how to paint a picture on a rock using a brush and tempera paints.
3. Show the student how to make a leaf painting. Show him how to paint the veined surface of various sizes and shapes of leaves and then place the leaf, paint side down, on paper and gently press it. Assist him in collecting his own leaves and in making his own leaf print.
4. Show the student how to print with plasticene. Demonstrate how to use pencils, nails, sticks, and scissors to create texture on a flattened piece of plasticene. Then paint the hardened plasticene with thick tempera paint and press it on a variety of different textured papers. Encourage the student to make his own plasticene print. Display his work and keep a folder of it.

Home

1. Ask the parents to purchase a paint set for their child. Tell them to model its use as a leisure activity.
2. Ask the parents to introduce their child to different colors by painting natural objects in their natural colors.

Functional Emphases   In designing your own instructional activities and plans, emphasize the following elements:

1. Use of a variety of sizes of brushes and a variety of colors of paints.
2. Use of paints that are nontoxic.

3. Awareness of the types of paint thinners and brush cleaners.
4. Development of the fine motor skills necessary for painting.
5. Modifications of paint brushes when necessary.

Specific Objective T

The student sews and makes simple clothing out of fabric.

Functional Settings and Suggested Instructional Activities

School

1. Show the student how to cut fabric to make a scarf or handkerchief. Show the student how to thread the needle and to make a knot at the end of the thread. If he is unable to thread the needle, do it for him. Demonstrate how to fold back the material along the edges to make a narrow hem.
2. Show the student how to sew an apron. A student might enjoy sewing a shop apron with pockets for tools. Purchase a simple pattern for a work apron.
3. Show the student how to attach simple appliqué designs out of felt, denim, or other heavy fabric. Show the student how to sketch the design, cut it out, and sew it on a garment.
4. Show the student how to trace simple figures and designs on iron-on tape. Assist him in cutting out and placing these designs on garments.

Home

1. Ask the parents to show their child how to replace a missing button.
2. Ask the parents to show their child how to sew a simple hem.

Functional Emphases　In designing your own instructional activities and plans, emphasize the following elements:

1. Use of a variety of materials and cloth for sewing.
2. Selection of the appropriate-size needle and thread.
3. Selection of appropriate color of thread and/or fabric.
4. Safe use of scissors when cutting material.
5. Safe use of pins and needles when making clothing.
6. Use of patterns when designing and making clothing.
7. Safe use of dyes and any chemicals used to change material colors.

Specific Objective U

The student constructs using one medium such as wood or other natural materials.

Functional Settings and Suggested Instructional Activities

School

1. Show the student how to make a clay figure by using the pinch and pull method. Make sure that the figure is able to stand alone by making a solid base.
2. Show the student how to make a clay figure by using the solid construction approach. This approach involves shaping the various parts of the figure and then joining them together by using a mixture of clay and water that has been formed into a thick paste called slip. Assist the student in creating his own sculpture. After drying, fire the completed work and arrange for its exhibition.
3. Show the student how to make clay pottery by using the coil method (i.e., roll out clay and then wind it in coils around a jar or bottle). Attach this to a flat base of clay that you have shaped with your hands. Remove the jar or bottle and complete the top of the piece. Allow the clay to dry, then fire it in a kiln.
4. Show the student how to make pinch-pot ash trays, flower pots, or decorative pieces of pottery. Shape clay into a ball (the size depends upon the size of the desired object) and make a dent in the middle of the ball with your thumb. Then widen the dent by pinching the clay outward between your thumb and fingers. Shape the final piece and add details; dry, fire, glaze, and fire once again. Then assist the student in creating his own pinch-pot pottery.
5. Collect a series of boxes of various sizes and shapes. Arrange these boxes in various ways to create different sculptured effects. Ask the student to join you in rearranging the boxes to form a new design. Encourage the student to form his own pattern. The student's final design may be sealed together by using rubber cement (use caution because of dangerous fumes). Paint the boxes or cover them with wrapping paper or foil to create different effects.
6. Collect scrap wood. From the various pieces, select ones that resemble objects. Use a rasp if necessary to help shape the wood to create the desired sculpture. Sand. Use felt pens or poster paints to add details. Use thumbtacks to add other features.
7. Show the student how to make popsicle stick and tongue depressor sculptures or functional pieces such as a mat to go under a flower pot. Create a design, and then glue the sticks together. Assist the student in creating his own sculptures and functional pieces.

Home

1. Ask the parents to show their child how to build a city or town with building blocks.
2. Ask the parents to show their child how to use empty boxes to build a city or town or to make rhythm instruments.

Functional Emphases In designing your own instructional activities and plans, emphasize the following elements:

1. Use of a variety of materials that are easily obtained and are nontoxic.
2. Development of motor skills necessary for constructing projects.
3. Use of a variety of tools in constructing projects.
4. Awareness of safety rules involved in using tools.
5. Use of a variety of paints, stains, and glues.
6. Awareness of precautions to be taken relevant to dangerous fumes and/or odors.
7. Avoidance of materials that have sharp edges or points or that splinter easily.

Specific Objective V

The student constructs using several media, including paper, wood, fabric, leather, cord, yarn, and natural materials (shells, grass, rice, beans, and macaroni).

Functional Settings and Suggested Instructional Activities

School

1. Make a wire sculpture and mount it on a piece of wood. Drill or punch a hole in a flat piece of wood and sand it smooth. Put glue in the hole and insert a dowel. Coil, twist, bend, shape, and wrap wire to form a sculpture. Attach the wire to the dowel. Assist the student in creating his own wire stabile. As a variation, ask the student to make a human figure, animal, or insect sculpture.
2. Construct a sculpture out of junk. Arrange the pieces of junk and attach the parts together to form the whole unit. Assist the student in finding suitable discarded objects and in creating his own sculptured piece.
3. Show the student how to make a mobile using cutout shapes from several different lightweight media such as soft wood (balsa), cork, cardboard, paper, and wire. Assist the student in creating his own multimedia mobile. Hang it in the room.
4. Show the student how to create a multimedia picture using such things as colored chalk, colored paper, scraps of material, sandpaper, foil, feathers, wax, and tempera paints. Use a variety of tools including brushes, felt pens, tooth and nail brushes, sponges, and wire screens. Assist the student in creating his own picture.
5. Show the student how to make people and animals from plastic bottles. Attach facial features cut from tagboard to the bottle using masking tape. Wrap the bottle with newspaper strips, and use kitchen paper toweling for the last layer. Use tissue paper, yarn, beads, and fabric to decorate.

Home

1. Ask the parents to purchase magazines that have instructions for creating craft objects out of scrap and junk material. Tell them to select appropriate activities and join their child in their execution.
2. Ask the parents to use natural materials found in the home or in the neighborhood to create collages, dioramas, or table displays.

Functional Emphases In designing your own instructional activities and plans, emphasize the following elements:

1. Use of a variety of materials that are easily obtained and are nontoxic.
2. Development of motor skills necessary for construction projects.
3. Use of a variety of tools in construction projects.
4. Awareness of safety rules involved in using tools.
5. Use of a variety of paints, stains, and glues.
6. Awareness of precautions to be taken relevant to dangerous fumes and/or odors.
7. Avoidance of materials that have sharp edges or points or that splinter easily.

Specific Objective W

The student embroiders, crochets, knits, and does needlepoint and macramé.

Functional Settings and Suggested Instructional Activities

School

1. Show the student how to make an embroidery sampler.
2. Buy a needlepoint kit with a simple pattern. Show the student how to thread the needle with the yarn. Read the directions in the kit. Teach the basic horizontal continental stitch and assist the student in completing the design.
3. Crochet simple articles such as pot holders or squares for an afghan. Use a fairly large crochet hook and knitting worsted weight yarn.
4. Knit simple articles such as pot holders, squares for an afghan, or a straight scarf. Use the garter stitch.
5. Macramé a simple article such as a belt or wall hanging. Use heavy cord or string.

Home

1. Ask the parents to determine which thread or yarn skill would be appropriately selected for their child in terms of skills and interests.
2. Ask the parents to teach the simplest needlework skills to their child and to gradually increase the complexity of the task until the child is able to produce something of functional value.

Functional Emphases In designing your own instructional activities and plans, emphasize the following elements:

1. Use of a variety of materials for embroidery, crocheting, knitting, and doing needlepoint and macramé.
2. Observation of safety procedures when using needles, hooks, and other small tools.
3. Implementation of patterns that are laid out as well as the creation of one's own patterns.
4. Selection of templates or plans (i.e., for knitting and crocheting).
5. Selection of kits that have all materials needed for a specific project.
6. Development of motor skills necessary for embroidery, crocheting, knitting, and doing needlepoint and macramé.

General Objective IV

The student will acquire those fine motor skills that will allow him to use his upper extremities optimally in operating simple appliances, objects, conveniences, and home accessories.[4]

General Objective V

The student will acquire those fine motor skills that will enable him to use his upper extremities optimally in prevocational activities.

Specific Objectives

The student:

A. picks up and holds simple tools.
B. assembles parts of an object to make the whole object.
C. assembles parts of an object to make a section of the object.
D. disassembles small units of two or more parts.

---

[4]See Chapter 5 for suggested instructional activities and functional emphases in this area.

E. separates continuous rolls of paper, plastic sheeting, cloth, and bagging material into measured parts.

F. sorts by type of object.

G. sorts by size of object.

H. sorts by shape of object.

I. sorts by color of object.

J. inserts literature into envelopes for mailing.

K. inserts objects into corresponding forms.

L. inserts objects into envelopes.

M. inserts objects into boxes.

N. inserts and packs assorted objects into a package.

O. wraps objects in paper and inserts them into containers.

P. seals clasp-type envelopes.

Q. seals packages and cartons using tape.

R. wraps and ties packages of various shapes and sizes.

S. pastes and sticks labels on containers.

T. sorts small objects using tweezers.

U. uses a stapler.

V. uses scissors.

W. uses stencils.

X. uses a hammer.

Y. uses a screwdriver.

Z. uses pliers.

AA. uses a standard and an adjustable wrench.

BB. uses hand and electric drills.

CC. uses a soldering iron, pencil, or gun.

DD. uses sandpaper.

EE. paints and stains wood.

FF. inspects objects by manipulating and using them.

GG. maintains grounds.

Specific Objective A

The student picks up and holds simple tools.

Functional Settings and Suggested Instructional Activities

School

1. Place several different-size screwdrivers on a table near the student. Obtain a board 1 inch thick, 3 inches wide, and 8 inches long. Drill four holes at equal intervals in the board. Place four different-size screws in the holes and tell the student that each one requires a different-size screwdriver. Tell the student to hold the different screwdrivers and give them to you when you ask for them.

2. Place different-weight hammers on a table (8, 12, and 16 ounce). Tell the student to pick up each hammer, hold it, and then put it down.

Home

1. If there is a home workshop or tools are available, ask the parents to place a screwdriver, hammer, and pair of pliers on a table. Tell them to ask their child to pick up the hammer by its handle and, after a few seconds, tell him to put the hammer down. Tell them to repeat this activity with the screwdriver and pliers. Ask them to emphasize putting tools down gently so that they will not mark surfaces.
2. Tell the parents to hammer a nail into a piece of wood while their child is watching. Tell them to give the child the hammer and tell him to hold it for them while they are lining up another nail to hammer. Repeat this activity with a screw and screwdriver and then with a nut and bolt and a pair of pliers.

Functional Emphases   In designing your own instructional activities and plans, emphasize the following elements:

1. Identification of a variety of simple tools.
2. Use of simple tools that are safe and easily handled.
3. Knowledge of the types of tools in a specific category. (e.g., types of screwdrivers such as regular or Phillips).
4. Avoidance of simple tools that are poorly made and/or easily broken.
5. Judgment of when to use a specific tool for a specific job.

Specific Objective B

The student assembles parts of an object to make the whole object.

Functional Settings and Suggested Instructional Activities

School

1. Tell the student to bring in a jigsaw puzzle from home or provide him with one. Set up the puzzle on a table in the corner of the room. At certain times of the day, ask the student to go to the table and work on the jigsaw puzzle.
2. Place on a table a large ball (4 to 6 inches) of Play Doh or clay. Tell the student to flatten the ball with his hands until it is the shape of a flat circle. Cut the flat shape into four parts with a butter knife. Separate the pieces and rearrange them so the pointed ends and corners are not in the correct position. Tell the student to put the pieces back together so that they form the flat circle.

Home

1. Ask the parents to give their child a three-dimensional, three- to four-piece puzzle commensurate with his mental age. Tell them to separate the three or four pieces that make up the puzzle and place them on a desk or table-top and tell him to put the pieces of the puzzle together to form a picture.
2. Tell the parents to place several empty jars of different sizes and shapes on a table in front of their child while placing the lids of these jars in a separate pile. Ask them to tell the child to put each jar lid on the appropriate jar.

Functional Emphases   In designing your own instructional activities and plans, emphasize the following elements:

1. Selection of a variety of objects that come in parts to assemble.
2. Avoidance of objects that have very small parts and/or fragile parts that are poorly made.
3. Knowledge of how parts fit together to form a whole object.

Specific Objective C

The student assembles parts of an object to make a section of the object.

Functional Settings and Suggested Instructional Activities

School

1. Draw an 8-foot square with chalk (or use masking tape) on the floor or outside on the playground. Give the student enough 12×12-inch floor tiles to cover half of the 8-foot area. Tell the student to fill in half of that particular area.
2. Place parts of a large model airplane or car kit in front of the student. Tell the student to put together pieces of a specified section, such as the tail assembly or part of the frame. After that is completed, tell the student to prepare another section and put it to one side.

Home

1. Tell the parents to set up a table with strings and large beads on it. Tell them to place at the front of the table, as a model, a string with two beads that have been strung on it. (Remind them to make sure that there is a knot in the end of the string.) Tell them to give the child a pile of beads and several strings and ask him to string two beads on each string just as in the model.
2. Tell the parents to give their child a four- to eight-piece puzzle. Ask them to tell him to complete half of the puzzle and pass it to them. For the child who might not understand the concept of halves, the pieces can be color

coded and the child requested to complete all the blue pieces or all the red ones.

Functional Emphases In designing your own instructional activities and plans, emphasize the following elements:

1. Selection of a variety of objects that require the assembling of several parts.
2. Use of parts of an object that are well made, safe and nontoxic.
3. Use of plans, pictorials, schematics, and drawings to aid in assembling parts of an object.

Specific Objective D

The student disassembles small units of two or more parts.

Functional Settings and Suggested Instructional Activities

School

1. Obtain large toy plastic nuts, washers, and bolts that come in various colors. Place several nuts and washers on the large bolts, and tell the student to take them apart. Provide the student with a box full of such parts and instruct him to take them apart.
2. Give a metal coffee pot to the student. Tell him to take the basket and other removable parts out of the coffee pot. Select various types of coffee pots for variety.

Home

1. Ask the parents to show their child a toy stacking ring (a dowel rod with rings on it). Tell them to require the child to remove just two of the rings. They can then vary the activity by increasing or reducing the number of rings they want him to remove.
2. Tell the parents to give their child a take-apart toy airplane already put together (Fisher-Price toy airplane). Tell them to point out to him that the airplane comes apart in sections. Ask them to tell him to take apart the entire airplane (four to six pieces) when it is ready to be put away.

Functional Emphases In designing your own instructional activities and plans, emphasize the following elements:

1. Selection of a variety of units or toys that require disassembling.
2. Selection of materials that are well made, safe, and nontoxic.
3. Use of plans and instructions to aid in the disassembling process.
4. Use of tools to aid in the disassembling process.

Specific Objective E

The student separates continuous rolls of paper, plastic sheeting, cloth, and bagging material into measured parts.

Functional Settings and Suggested Instructional Activities

School

1. Place a roll of aluminum foil in its box on a table with a piece of foil partially rolled out. Place a piece of masking tape on the desk marking out a specified interval, such as 8 inches. Tell the student to hold the box, pull out the aluminum foil until it reaches the masking tape mark, and then tear off the foil. Tell the student to practice this activity until he provides the required amount.
2. Place a large box of plastic trash bags (20-gallon capacity) on a table. Give the student dry garbage and/or raked leaves. Assist him in tearing off the plastic bags and filling them with the garbage or leaves.
3. Set up a table with various size rolls of plastic tape in tape holders. In front of each holder, lay out a premeasured length of tape. Tell the student to unroll the same lengths of tape that are displayed in front of the tape holder. Repeat the activity using different tapes. Use the cut tape for some purpose such as sealing packages.

Home

1. Ask the parents to take their child to the bathroom. Tell them to point out the toilet paper on the toilet paper holder and demonstrate removing five or six sections. Ask them to demonstrate how toilet paper comes in sections that can easily be separated and tell the child to either count or use a measuring aid (a stick that measures out pieces of paper) to tear off the required amount.
2. Ask the parents to take their child into the kitchen. Tell them to point out the paper towel holder and the paper towels on it. Ask them to give the child one paper towel torn off the roll and, using that piece as a model, tell him to tear off a specific number of towels needed for a project.

Functional Emphases In designing your own instructional activities and plans, emphasize the following elements:

1. Whenever possible, selection of material that is safe, nontoxic, and flame resistant.
2. Calculation of how much material is required for a specific job, activity, or time.
3. Avoidance of material that requires special handling precautions or safety clothing, unless it is part of a job.
4. Use of rolls of material that are easily handled.

5. Calculation of cost of materials (i.e., is it cheaper to purchase a large roll or material in bulk?).

Specific Objective F

The student sorts by type of object.

Functional Settings and Suggested Instructional Activities

School

1. Lay out on a table a plastic box with six or more compartments (these boxes are usually used for holding such objects as fishing gear). In a large cardboard box mix a variety of paper clips, buttons, rubber bands, beads, etc. Seat the student in front of the cardboard box and the plastic compartmentalized container, and instruct him to sort the objects by placing a different object in each compartment of the plastic container. Continually check to make sure the student is sorting the objects correctly.
2. Obtain a grab bag of electrical parts such as resistors, capacitors, and diodes. Discontinued models of such parts can be purchased cheaply from electronics firms or from stores such as Radio Shack. Lay out on the table five 12-inch squares of masking tape. Put one type of electronic component in each square and tell the student to sort through the box and place the objects he finds in the appropriate square. Use the parts for a class project.

Home

1. Tell the parents to give their child a box with different types of beads during playtime. Tell them to place in front of him five different strings, each one with a different type of bead on it. Ask them to tell him to look through the box and place in front of him the beads that he finds that match the beads on the strings. Remind them to tell him to place the matching beads next to the correct string.
2. Ask the parents to obtain a box full of plastic silverware (knives, forks, and spoons). Tell them to place three large plastic glasses or other containers in front of the box. Tell them to ask the child to place all the forks in one glass, all the spoons in another glass, and all the knives in the third glass.

Functional Emphases   In designing your own instructional activities and plans, emphasize the following elements:

1. Selection of a variety of objects to sort.
2. Use of objects that are safe and nontoxic.
3. Identification of different shapes, colors, and sizes of objects to sort.
4. Calculation of quantities required to be sorted (e.g., putting 10 plastic knives or forks in a package).

Specific Objective G

The student sorts by size of object.

Functional Settings and Suggested Instructional Activities

School

1. Obtain from a hardware store one pound each of six-penny, eight-penny, ten-penny, and twelve-penny nails. Mix them together and place them in the middle of the table. Tell the student to sort the nails and put them back into their original boxes. Tell him to sort this way whenever he has nails that are mixed together.
2. Give the student a bowl full of various-size paper clips. Place the appropriate number of empty envelopes in front of the student, and tell him to put a different size of clip into each envelope and then continue sorting the clips this way until the bowl is empty. Use the clips when appropriate.

Home

1. Ask the parents to obtain a bushel basket of fruit or vegetables appropriate to the season. Tell them to make sure that there are various sizes in the basket. Ask them to tell the child to sort the different-size fruit or vegetables from the biggest to the smallest size.
2. Tell the parents to place a bowl containing a single type of nut in front of their child. They should make sure the nuts are in various sizes ranging from jumbo to small. Tell them to ask the child to place the nuts into plastic bags according to size. The plastic bags can be Baggies or bags obtained from candy companies. Eat the nuts for snacks.

Functional Emphases   In designing your own instructional activities and plans, emphasize the following elements:

1. Use of a variety of sizes of objects to sort.
2. Selection of objects that are safe and nontoxic.
3. Calculation of different sizes of objects, how to sort them, and where to place them.
4. Avoidance of objects, unless precautions are taken, that have sharp edges or are dangerous to handle.

Specific Objective H

The student sorts by shape of object.

Functional Settings and Suggested Instructional Activities

School

1. Place a shape box in front of the student (these toys usually require triangles, circles, or squares to be pushed through holes of the same shape). Mix up the shapes that go into the box and place them in a stack in front of the student. Tell the student to push the shapes through the appropriate-shape holes into the box.
2. During playtime, give the student a mailbox (Play Skool) with openings of various sizes and shapes. Mix up the shapes that come with the mailbox, and tell the student to sort and place each one into the appropriate opening in the mailbox.

Home

1. Tell the parents to have their child sort his toys by shape and put them in different containers or compartments of his toy chest. Tell them to urge him to practice this activity when he has to clean up his toys in his room.
2. Ask the parents to obtain a box of various shapes of wood scraps. Tell them to show their child the different shapes of wood that are in the scrap box, and ask him to sort them according to their shapes as part of a play activity. When possible, build a project with them.

Functional Emphases   In designing your own instructional activities and plans, emphasize the following elements:

1. Use of a variety of shapes of objects to sort.
2. Selection of objects that are safe and nontoxic.
3. Calculation of different shapes of objects, how to sort them, and where to place them.
4. Avoidance of objects whose shapes include sharp edges that may be dangerous to handle.

Specific Objective I

The student sorts by color of object.

Functional Settings and Suggested Instructional Activities

School

1. Place a small box of assorted poker chips in front of the student. Place three plastic boxes, one for each color, in front of the student. Tell the student that you want him to place a different color into each of the containers.
2. Construct a spool holder by gluing ¼ × 8-inch dowels onto a piece of wood. Make sure the dowels are evenly spaced and can accommodate various size spools of thread. Give the student a large box containing spools of assorted

colors of thread. Tell the student to put all the spools of one color on a single dowel until the dowel is filled. Stress that the spools will be going into a package marked to be a specific color, and they should not be mixed up.

Home

1. Tell the parents to give their child three large-size packages of assorted colored construction paper, and tell her that they want her to pick out all the papers of certain colors so they can be used for holiday decorations (e.g., orange and black for Halloween). Ask them to tell the child to place the papers into separate piles according to color.
2. Ask the parents to give their child a large box of mixed crayons that have been accumulated during the year. The child is to sort the crayons by colors and place them in empty crayon boxes labeled by colors.

Functional Emphases In designing your own instructional activities and plans, emphasize the following elements:

1. Use of objects that include a variety of colors.
2. Identification of primary and secondary colors.

Specific Objective J

The student inserts literature into envelopes for mailing.

Functional Settings and Suggested Instructional Activities

School

1. Contact a service station or stationery store for free or inexpensive calendars. Select an appropriate-size envelope for these calendars, and tell the student to put one calendar into each envelope. Emphasize that this job must be done neatly and that it is important that the calendars do not become wrinkled or bent while they are being inserted into the envelopes. Send the calendars to friends as gifts.
2. Plan a party by writing invitations on different-size index cards. Obtain the appropriate-size envelopes for them. Set up two or three piles of different-size cards with their appropriate envelopes in front of the student. Seat the student close to the work, and point out the different types of cards and their envelopes. Tell him to insert the cards into the envelopes until all of the cards or envelopes are used up.

Home

1. Tell the parents to arrange for their child to complete a mailing project (e.g., party invitations). Tell them to assist him in completing the mailing, and reward him for a job well done.

2. Tell the parents to enlist the help of their child in inserting and sending out brochures and literature as part of a charity activity. The Heart Fund and similar organizations are often looking for people to perform this activity.

Functional Emphases In designing your own instructional activities and plans, emphasize the following elements:

1. Use of a variety of sizes and types of literature for insertion into envelopes.
2. Use of a variety of sizes and types of envelopes, including those that need to be moistened as well as those that are self-sticking.

Specific Objective K

The student inserts objects into corresponding forms.

Functional Settings and Suggested Instructional Activities

School

1. In preparation for a job, obtain from a food market or grocery store the Styrofoam or plastic forms used to ship apples, pears, plums, eggs, etc. Take the student to the grocery store to show him how the produce is packed, pointing out the particular type of containers and their forms. Set up a production line where the student is required to take, for example, an apple and put it in the form. Repeat this activity until the form is filled. Then tell the student to pass the completed form down to the end of the table.
2. Purchase or obtain thumbtacks by the gross or in bulk quantity. Construct cards of old parts of corrugated cardboard cut to the desired size to hold the thumbtacks. Place pencil dots at equal intervals on the card to indicate where you want the thumbtacks placed. Show the student a completed card, and tell him to fill in the pile of cards that are placed in front of him in exactly the same way. Be sure to tell the student that he must exercise caution because thumbtacks are sharp and can be dangerous. Use the thumbtacks when needed.

Home

1. Ask the parents to put a large pile of common pins in front of their child. In another pile, place paper or cloth forms in which the pins will be placed. Tell the parents to complete a card and show it to the child. They should then tell the child to complete a card, with assistance from the parents if necessary. Caution should be emphasized, especially in retrieving the pins from the pile.
2. Ask the parents to gather a collection of lightbulbs that do not have containers. Tell them to place the bulbs on a table covered with a scatter rug or other nonslip surface. Obtain appropriate-size cardboard containers,

and place them right next to the pile of bulbs. Tell the parents to ask the child to put each bulb in a cardboard container and then place it in a third pile. Once proficiency is gained in this task, the parents should ask the child to place the completed packages into a large carton to hold them for future use.

Functional Emphases In designing your own instructional activities and plans, emphasize the following elements:

1. Use of a variety of objects that require insertion into their corresponding forms.
2. Avoidance of objects that are dangerous or have sharp points or edges unless special precautions are taken.
3. Awareness of how objects are to be placed or fitted into forms.

Specific Objective L

The student inserts objects into envelopes.

Functional Settings and Suggested Instructional Activities

School

1. Simulate the mailing out of samples. Stack 20 bars of soap into several piles. Tell the student to put one bar of soap into each of the envelopes provided next to the pile. Tell him to do so as quickly as he can. Caution the student to be careful not to damage the soap by dropping it or putting it into the envelope too quickly. Repeat the activity. This time, vary the amount of time you allow the student to complete the task. As an example, tell the student, "You have 5 minutes (or 10 or 15 minutes) to complete this activity." At intervals, give him warnings that there are only 4 minutes left, 2 minutes left, and so on.
2. Obtain pipe cleaners in bulk quantities (many distributors will sell them to you by the thousands). Purchase or construct rectangular envelopes that can accept the pipe cleaners. Set up piles of pipe cleaners according to how many will fit into an envelope, such as 25, 50, or 100. Tell the student to put the pipe cleaners into appropriate-size envelopes. Caution the student that he is not to bend the cleaners or stretch them out of shape. Require the student to hold the first one he completes in front of him so that you can examine it.

Home

1. Tell the parents to monitor how their child cleans up small parts from toys like Lego or an erector set. If he is having difficulty, tell them to provide him with envelopes so he can insert the small parts in them and keep them all together.

2. Tell the parents to demonstrate to their child as part of a hobby activity how to keep stamps, coins, or similar type items together by inserting them into envelopes. Tell the parents to participate with him in this activity and provide encouragement and guidance.

Functional Emphases   In designing your own instructional activities and plans, emphasize the following elements:

1. Use a variety of envelopes and objects that require insertion into envelopes (e.g., coins or stamps).
2. Recognition of the most appropriate or best-size envelope(s) to use for specific projects or activities.
3. Observation of appropriate safety procedures when inserting objects into envelopes.

Specific Objective M

The student inserts objects into boxes.

Functional Settings and Suggested Instructional Activities

School

1. Place a large pile of paper clips in the middle of a table. Obtain the appropriate-size box into which these specific clips can be placed. Show the student how to place paper clips into the box until it is filled. Tell her to fill as many boxes as possible within a predetermined amount of time and then place the boxes in a third pile.
2. Place a pile of $3\frac{3}{4} \times 1\frac{1}{2}$-inch gum labels in front of the student. Next to the labels, place the box in which they are to be packed. Demonstrate packing the labels in the bottom part of the package and then covering or closing it by having a sleeve slide over it. Tell the student to pack as many labels in a package as possible. If the student has difficulty placing the sleeve on the package, check to see if she has placed too many labels in it. Take out some of them if necessary. Practice this activity.

Home

1. Tell the parents to demonstrate to their child how to put away fragile items such as jewelry into their respective boxes. Tell them to praise her when she does it appropriately.
2. Tell the parents to ask their child for help when they are storing objects that will not be used for a long time (e.g., Christmas decorations). Tell them to demonstrate how to safely insert the objects into their boxes.

Functional Emphases   In designing your own instructional activities and plans, emphasize the following elements:

1. Use of a variety of objects and boxes.
2. Awareness of safety procedures to use when inserting various-size objects into boxes.
3. Comprehension of what size of object should go into what size of box.

Specific Objective N

The student inserts and packs assorted objects into a package.

Functional Settings and Suggested Instructional Activities

School

1. When appropriate, ask the student to bring his lunchbox to school. Remove the sandwiches, desserts, etc., from the lunchbox and place them in front of the student. Tell the student to repack his lunchbox in a way that will allow everything to fit and not be crushed. As part of a follow-up activity, arrange for the student to make and pack his own lunch on the following day.
2. Make first aid kits. Obtain quantities of Bandaids, mercurochrome, burn ointment, gauze, and adhesive tape from a drug store or a drug supply company. Set up piles of the various items. Obtain the appropriate-size cardboard or plastic containers into which these materials will be inserted. Tell the student to insert the various components of a first aid kit into the plastic containers and then pack them into a carton that has been placed on the floor next to the student.

Home

1. Tell the parents, as a part of a leisure activity, to purchase in bulk form assorted fishing material such as lures, anchors, and flies. Tell them to obtain plastic compartmentalized containers, and place them in a pile next to these materials. Ask them to place one of each object into each of the compartments, and to tell their child to complete the package by inserting a specific number of objects into each of its appropriate compartments and then closing the lid. The parents should take the student fishing and use the materials that were packaged.
2. Tell the parents to obtain several large empty boxes used for holding crayons. These specific boxes usually have a compartment for large crayons and one for middle-size crayons in the same container. Tell them to place a large bowl of their child's assorted crayons in front of him and ask him to begin putting the appropriate-size crayons into the compartments in a crayon box, and close the flap of the box. The child is to practice this activity until the boxes are filled.

Functional Emphases In designing your own instructional activities and plans, emphasize the following elements:

1. Use of a variety of objects.
2. Avoidance of objects that are dangerous and so brittle that they require special handling and packing (materials requiring special handling can be used at a later time after proper instruction as to how they should be packed).
3. Selection of the right package according to strength and size.

Specific Objective O

The student wraps objects in paper and inserts them into containers.

Functional Settings and Suggested Instructional Activities

School

1. Purchase a large quantity of small bars of soap such as those found in motel or hotel rooms. The soap should be unwrapped if possible, or, if bought wrapped, the wrapper should carefully be taken off and used to form a second pile. A third pile should include a rectangular or square box to hold the wrapped soap. First demonstrate, then tell the student to wrap each individual bar of soap in its paper and insert it into the box.
2. Collect articles and canned goods as part of a charity drive. When the student comes across a fragile item, tell him to wrap it in paper and then insert it in a package, box, or container that is available. Tell him that this will protect the item from breaking or being damaged.

Home

1. Tell the parents to place a pile of plastic plates, a pile of heavy packaging paper, and a pile of large cartons into which the packaged plates are to be vertically inserted and packed in front of the child. Tell them to demonstrate wrapping a plate and inserting it into the carton. Tell them to ask him to wrap each plate individually and then place it in the carton. The child who is successful in wrapping plastic or Melmac plates may proceed to the wrapping of china and glass plates. Suggest that she use this activity to help someone move.
2. Tell the parents to place a pile of jewelry, such as small tie clasps and rings, on a table. Ask them to obtain an appropriate quantity of small plastic boxes into which these materials can be placed and to obtain some tissue paper that is used to wrap jewelry. Tell them to demonstrate to their child how to wrap a piece of jewelry and place it into a container. Ask them to tell the child to imitate their actions and wrap the remaining jewelry.

Functional Emphases In designing your own instructional activities and plans, emphasize the following elements:

1. Avoidance of objects that are so fragile that wrapping them requires special procedures or handling.
2. Selection of appropriate containers in which to place wrapped objects.
3. Avoidance of objects that have sharp edges (e.g., knives, cutting instruments, and blades of tools) unless special wrapping materials or procedures are used.

Specific Objective P

The student seals clasp-type envelopes.

Functional Settings and Suggested Instructional Activities

School

1. Obtain a large supply of calendars and envelopes and place them in two piles in front of the student. Tell the student to place each of these calendars in its appropriate-size envelope, make sure it fits securely, and then seal it. Point out that some types of calendars have spiral bindings, and it is important that these do not stick out or rip any part of the envelope before sealing. It is important to emphasize to the student that he must seal these envelopes carefully and that he is not to bang the flap or clasp down if the envelope is bulky. Send the calendars to friends as gifts.
2. As part of a class project, ask the student to collect proof-of-purchase seals from grocery store products. After an adequate supply has been collected, encourage the student to place them in a mailing envelope with the appropriate information required by the company. Tell him to seal the envelope using the gummed flap and the clasp. Inspect the finished project and point out, when appropriate, what a good job he has done.
3. Tell the student to bring in a picture he would like mailed to someone. Tell the student to insert the picture into an envelope and seal it. Point out that he must be careful because roughness may scratch the picture inside.

Home

1. Tell the parents to allow their child to seal clasp-type envelopes whenever they have to mail one. Practice when necessary.
2. Ask the parents to buy a large greeting card that requires a clasp-type envelope at holidays or birthdays. Ask them to tell their child to seal and mail it to a special person.

Functional Emphases In designing your own instructional activities and plans, emphasize the following elements:

1. Awareness of the different sizes of clasp-type envelopes that are available.
2. Avoidance of clasp-type envelopes that are broken and/or have a sharp edge.
3. Selection of the appropriate-size envelope for the job.
4. Knowledge of when and when not to use a clasp-type envelope, taking into consideration cost as well as need.

Specific Objective Q

The student seals packages and cartons using tape.

Functional Settings and Suggested Instructional Activities

School

1. Tell the student to bring in an empty box. Tell him that he is going to make a grab box. Place an object or a toy in the student's grab box. Assist the student in wrapping his box and then tell him to seal the package using tape provided in a dispenser.
2. Give the student shoeboxes of several sizes and ask him to place some favored objects that he would like to have mailed home in a box. Simulate or actually carry out the activity.

Home

1. Tell the parents to obtain a package that needs to be sealed. Tell them to demonstrate how to measure a length of packaging or masking tape approximately 6 to 8 inches longer than the flap to be sealed and tear it off. Ask them to tell their child to watch as they place the tape on the two flaps that meet, securing them in place, and then to rub his hands over the tape gently, forming a tight seal.
2. Ask the parents to plan a birthday party or select someone in the family or in their child's school to whom the child would like to give a gift. Tell them to place a roll of cellophane tape in its appropriate holder and a gift that has been wrapped in paper but needs to be sealed in front of the child. Ask them to tell him to tear off some of the cellophane tape and secure the ends of the package. The parents should monitor this activity to ensure that he conserves tape and does a neat job. They should also check throughout this activity because the child may have difficulty with tape sticking to his fingers.

Functional Emphases In designing your own instructional activities and plans, emphasize the following elements:

1. Selection of a variety of types of tape to use for sealing packages and cartons.

2. Avoidance of tapes that are of such poor quality that they are difficult to start or continually rip as they are being removed from their roll.
3. Determination of what type and size of tape to use for a specific package (e.g., masking tape, mailing tape, or gum tape).
4. Use of safety procedures when using the tearing edge on tapes that come in their own dispenser.

Specific Objective R

The student wraps and ties packages of various shapes and sizes.

Functional Settings and Suggested Instructional Activities

School

1. Supply the student with two shoeboxes, one placed on top of the other. Demonstrate to the student how to wrap the shoeboxes in brown or decorative paper. Make sure they are securely wrapped. Take a length of string and tell the student to wrap it around the boxes horizontally two or three times. Next, tell him to wrap the boxes vertically two or three times. Demonstrate slowly so that the student can see how you change the direction of the string without losing its tension. Tell the student to watch you as you make a knot with the ends of the string and encourage him to imitate your actions. Give him other packages and tell him to practice wrapping them. It may be necessary first to have the student practice tying knots and bows with scrap material. When this is necessary, ask the student to first tie pieces of yarn, then rope, and then string together. By using thick tying material, it will be easier for the student to see the knot taking form.
2. Place several stacks of books on a table in front of the student. Each stack should consist of three or four books. Then give the student wrapping paper and precut lengths of string. Demonstrate the wrapping and tying of books. Tell the student to imitate your actions and to make as many packages as there are stacks available.

Home

1. Ask the parents to plan with their child to send clothes to a charity such as Goodwill or the Salvation Army. Tell them to place a large pile of clothes that are to be donated on a piece of brown paper in the middle of the floor. Ask them to tell the child to wrap the clothes as best as he can and then to tie them into a bundle. Tell the parents to closely monitor this activity and practice often.
2. Repeat the above activity using plastic bags that require the use of a variety of ties for closing.

Functional Emphases In designing your own instructional activities and plans, emphasize the following elements:

1. Calculation of how much paper is needed to wrap a package.
2. Knowledge of how to tie packages of various sizes and weights.
3. Use of a variety of paper (e.g., Christmas wrapping, birthday wrapping, or tissue paper to fit the occasion).
4. Knowledge of the type of tape and tying material acceptable for mailing by the post office.

Specific Objective S

The student pastes and sticks labels on containers.

Functional Settings and Suggested Instructional Activities

School

1. Demonstrate placing the student's name label on a mailbox, his closet, and his other belongings located in the classroom. Tell him to label other appropriate articles.
2. Demonstrate how to use a plastic label-maker machine. Place on a table in front of the student a strip of plastic labels that you have already punched. Simple words or letters may be used to paste on objects. For the student who is unable to read or decode simple sight words, obtain labels in a variety of colors. These labels can be found in colors ranging from very bright shades to pastels. They also come in various widths. You may want the student to select a color of his own, such as red, and to place a red label on all of the materials in his learning area. Demonstrate how to pull the backing off the label and press it on an object. Encourage the student to imitate this activity, labeling all appropriate objects.

Home

1. Ask the parents to obtain Mr. Yuk labels from the poison control center of their state. Ask them to give their child a roll of Mr. Yuk labels and a supply of spray cans or bottles that need such a label pasted on them. Ask them to tell him to paste one label on each bottle and to return the bottles to their appropriate storage place.
2. Ask the parents to obtain cloth labels that can be applied by pressing on clothing. Ask them to put their child's name, assigned color clue, or rebus clue on the label and place a pile of these in front of him. Tell them to demonstrate to the child how to paste or stick these labels on parts of his clothing where they will not be seen when the clothes are worn. They should also point out the labels that are already there. Ask them to encourage the child to apply the labels to his clothes.

Functional Emphases   In designing your own instructional activities and plans, emphasize the following elements:

1. Decision as to what type and size of label to use.
2. Modification (cutting to size) of labels when necessary.
3. Avoidance of labels that are so poorly made that they rip easily or fail to stick.
4. Use of labels that are self-sticking or pressure sensitive.

Specific Objective T

The student sorts small objects using tweezers.

Functional Settings and Suggested Instructional Activities

School

1. Demonstrate the use of tweezers to the student. Assist him in holding a pair of large tweezers, gently pressing the points together, and then releasing them. Place a small object such as a pin on the table in front of the student and assist him in picking it up. Place several pins in front of the student and tell him to pick them up and place them in a small container that has been placed next to him.
2. Obtain from an electronics supply house or a store such as Radio Shack an assortment of small electronic parts (many of these can be bought as part of a grab bag promotion and are very inexpensive). Place these small objects in a pile in front of the student and give him a pair of tweezers. Tell him to use the tweezers to sort the parts that are in front of him into piles. Provide tweezers of various sizes for the student, and tell him to try each type of tweezer to find out which one is best for a given job.
3. Present the student with a grab box full of small machine screws (these can be obtained from most hardware stores and from distributors of machine screws and bolts). Tell the student to sort the screws according to size using tweezers. Repeat this activity with needles of various sizes, making sure to point out the dangers involved in working with needles. Point out that tweezers are used with needles because they are safer and prevent a person from getting stuck.

Home

1. Ask the parents to obtain a boxful of stamps as part of a leisure activity. Tell them to give their child a pile of stamps and ask him to use tweezers to sort the stamps by color, the number written on them, or size. Tell the parents to point out that stamps are easily ripped or damaged unless they are handled carefully.

2. Tell the parents to ask their child to sort seashells, beads, or buttons using tweezers during his free time or hobby time. Ask the parents to tell him to sort these materials and to place them in appropriate containers so that they may be ready for use in other activities.

Functional Emphases In designing your own instructional activities and plans, emphasize the following elements:

1. Use of a variety of tweezers to pick up a variety of objects.
2. Selection of tweezers that are well made and of the appropriate size for the specific job.
3. Awareness that some tweezers are made of a nonmetallic and/or non-magnetic material for working with special objects that require such tools.

Specific Objective U

The student uses a stapler.

Functional Settings and Suggested Instructional Activities

School The activities listed below can also be done at home.

1. Demonstrate how to use a stapler. Next, assist the student in stapling. Tell him to place a piece of folded paper in the stapler and then to press down with a quick thrust on top of the stapler, completing the stapling action. Caution the student to make sure his fingers do not go near the stapler's opening. Tell him to practice this activity as you supervise.
2. Give the student a pile of plastic bags (Baggies) in which small objects of varying sizes have been placed. First demonstrate and then tell the student to staple the tops of the bags closed and place them in a pile. Practice this activity until the required amount of bags have been stapled.
3. Tell the student you would like him to help you construct a bulletin board by stapling up the background material. Give the student a pack of the same color construction paper and show him how to staple each piece on the bulletin board. Closely monitor this activity until the complete background of the bulletin board has been stapled. Check to see that the entire board is covered.

Functional Emphases In designing your own instructional activities and plans, emphasize the following elements:

1. Awareness of the different varieties of staplers.
2. Selection of the right size of staples for a specific job.
3. Observation of safety procedures when using a stapler.

4. Decision as to how much paper is appropriate to staple.
5. Knowledge of how to fill a stapler with staples.
6. Knowledge of how to manipulate or modify certain staplers so they can be used to tack up materials.

Specific Objective V

The student uses scissors.

Functional Settings and Suggested Instructional Activities

School   The activities listed below can also be done at home.

1. On a large piece of construction paper, draw parallel lines in various widths with a crayon. Give this paper to the student and tell him to cut the construction paper into strips following the lines on the paper. When he is done, tell him to cut the strips into smaller pieces and to place them in a pile. Repeat this activity with a different colored piece of construction paper and then a third one. Again repeat cutting these pieces up into smaller pieces. When this has been completed, mix all of the small pieces together to make confetti. Encourage the student to use the confetti during an appropriate activity, such as a simulated wedding.
2. Draw various lines (zigzag, straight, and curved) in dark magic marker on a paper. Also include circles, squares, triangles, and other shapes. Tell the student to cut out the shapes along the lines. Closely supervise this activity and assist when necessary.
3. Plan a papier mâché project. Draw lines on pieces of newspaper and ask the student to cut out long strips of the newspaper to use in making papier mâché. Encourage him to continue this activity until the desired amount of paper has been cut.
4. Provide various sizes of scissors for the student to use. Demonstrate the use of fine instrument scissors, which are used for very fine work such as cutting thread, and very large scissors such as those used in cutting wallpaper. Tell the student to practice using different types of scissors on various kinds of materials.

Functional Emphases   In designing your own instructional activities and plans, emphasize the following elements:

1. Awareness of the different varieties of scissors.
2. Selection of the most appropriate size and type of scissors for the job.
3. Knowledge of safety factors involved in using scissors.
4. Knowledge of maintenance procedures required to keep scissors sharp and effectively operating.

5. Development of motor skills necessary to use scissors.
6. Awareness of modifications that can be made to standard scissors that allow them to cut more easily.

Specific Objective W

The student uses stencils.

Functional Settings and Suggested Instructional Activities

School

1. Obtain a large stencil that forms a letter or shape that you wish to reproduce. Demonstrate to the student how the stencil is placed on the appropriate surface, then line it up according to the guide holes or place it within the area to be stenciled. Point out to the student that the stencil should be straight and held or taped firmly in place. Using paint, water color, or other media, paint over the stencil. Take the stencil off and point out to the student how the paint has come through to create the shape desired. Tell the student to make his own shape and give him the stencil.
2. Cut a stencil or purchase one corresponding to the student's first name. Point out to the student that his name will appear on an object after he places the stencil on the object and paints over it. Tell the student to bring in shoe or cardboard boxes or obtain some for him. Tell him to stencil his name on the boxes, which can then be used to hold supplies such as toothpaste and a toothbrush.

Home

1. Ask the parents to give their child a stencil toy (Spyro-Graph) that utilizes plastic-type stencils during playtime. Tell them to help him make various forms by following the plastic stencil edges and to try the different types of stencils in the toy kit.
2. Ask the parents to obtain a package of Christmas decoration stencils. Tell them to ask their child to stencil a different design on several Christmas packages that are wrapped in solid colors. Ask the parents to demonstrate how to use crayons, water color, and other available media.

Functional Emphases   In designing your own instructional activities and plans, emphasize the following elements:

1. Awareness of the different types of stencils that are available.
2. Development of motor skills necessary to use stencils.
3. Selection of the most appropriate type and size of stencil for the job.
4. Avoidance of stencils that are poorly made or cannot be reused.

Specific Objective X

The student uses a hammer.

Functional Settings and Suggested Instructional Activities

School   The activities listed below may also be done at home, provided there is adequate instruction and supervision.

1. Demonstrate to the student how to hold a real hammer by placing your hand at the end of the hammer handle and grasping it tightly. Place several sizes of hammers (8, 12, and 16 ounce) on a table in front of the student. Tell him to pick up each of the hammers and then to put each one down. Give the student a hammer with which he feels comfortable. Gently move the hammer up and down over a board in imitation of the hammering motion.
2. For the student who has difficulty in controlling the hammer, tell him to grasp the hammer at its handle with one hand. Tell him to push with his other hand from the top of the hammerhead down until his hand slides somewhere on the handle where it is more comfortable so that he can control it better. Tell him to gently tap nails into soft pine wood. Make sure that he has control of the hammer.

Home

1. Ask the parents to show their child how to use a hammering bench (Fisher-Price) to hammer nails through one side, turn it over, and then hammer them back again through the other side.
2. Tell the parents to select a place in the house where it would be appropriate to hang a picture once the child has mastered hammering. Ask them to start the nail into the wall with several swings and then give the hammer to their child and tell him to hammer it in most of the way. They should be careful to check that he does not hammer the nail in completely. When this is completed, give him a picture to hang on that nail.

Functional Emphases   In designing your own instructional activities and plans, emphasize the following elements:

1. Awareness of the different types and weights (ounces) of hammers.
2. Knowledge of the safety factors involved in using a hammer.
3. Development of motor skills necessary in using a hammer.
4. Selection of the most appropriate hammer for the job.
5. Avoidance of purchasing hammers that are poorly made or are of the bargain variety.

Specific Objective Y

The student uses a screwdriver.

Functional Settings and Suggested Instructional Activities

School   The activities listed below may also be done at home provided there is adequate instruction and supervision.

1. Demonstrate the use of a screwdriver by placing its blade in a screw that has been partially started and then turning it. Tell the student to imitate your actions and hand him the screwdriver. For those students who have difficulty keeping the screwdriver blade in the groove of the screw, use screwdrivers with grippers on the side. This attachment holds the blade to the screw, and it can be found in all hardware stores.
2. Obtain large screws and place several of them into previously drilled holes in a soft pine board. Tell the student to turn each one of the screws as far down as he can. Praise the student as he is performing the activity.
3. Decrease the screw size and have the student use a screwdriver to turn screws into various types of material. First give the student a piece of balsa wood with a screw started in it, and tell him to turn the screw completely in. The student should have little trouble because balsa wood is an extremely light wood and accepts screws easily. Follow this with pine, white wood, mahogany, and then oak. Make sure that the student does not hurt his hands, because some woods, such as mahogany and oak, are quite difficult to put screws in.
4. Show the student a Phillips head screwdriver. Point out that it is not like a regular screwdriver because it has a blade in the form of an X. Place a large Phillips head screw into a soft pine board, and tell the student to turn the screw into the board. If the student experiences difficulty, substitute a screwdriver with a screw-holding attachment on it.
5. Give the student a metal plate with matching screws started in it. Give the student a jeweler's screwdriver, and ask him to turn the screws into the plate. Point out that it is important that he does not mark or mar the surface of these fine screws, so he has to turn the screwdriver slowly. Practice.

Functional Emphases   In designing your own instructional activities and plans, emphasize the following elements:

1. Awareness of the different types of screwdriver blades (e.g., regular and Phillips).
2. Knowledge of safety factors involved in using a screwdriver.
3. Awareness of modifications that can be made to a screwdriver handle that make it easier to grasp and use (e.g., wrapping tape around the handle).
4. Knowledge of modifications to screwdriver blades that allow screws to be held in place by the blade of the screwdriver and "side grippers."
5. Development of motor skills necessary to use a variety of screwdrivers.

6. Avoidance of purchasing screwdrivers that are poorly made, chip easily, or are inappropriate for the job.

Specific Objective Z

The student uses pliers.

Functional Settings and Suggested Instructional Activities

School   The activities listed below may also be done at home provided there is adequate instruction and supervision.

1. Show the student a pair of slip joint pliers. Point out that the pliers are adjustable according to the way you hold them and the way the slip joint opens. Demonstrate how to tighten a nut on a bolt with a pair of pliers. Hand him the pliers and tell him to imitate your actions.
2. Find articles around the school or home that need tightening. Tighten them using an appropriate pair of pliers.
3. Set up several dowels on a board with each having a cotter pin at its end. Demonstrate to the student how to bend the cotter pin apart by spreading it with the pliers. Tell the student to repeat this activity with the remaining cotter pins and dowels. Point out cotter pins on bicycle wheels and other objects.
4. Show the student various types of electrical or jewelers pliers, such as needlenose, diagnosis, and side cutters. Construct a bolt board that requires the use of these particular types of pliers, and tell the student to tighten the nuts on the corresponding bolts. When working with pliers such as those used in fine electrical work, be sure to emphasize to the student that he must be careful not to mar the surface of the bolt or damage the pliers.

Functional Emphases   In designing your own instructional activities and plans, emphasize the following elements:

1. Awareness of the many varieties of pliers that are available, including slip joint, adjustable, and miniature pliers.
2. Knowledge of safety factors involved in using pliers.
3. Development of motor skills necessary to use a variety of pliers.
4. Avoidance of purchasing poorly made pliers that easily break and are dangerous.
5. Knowledge of which plier to use for a specific job.
6. Awareness of when to stop tightening a nut or locking device (before it becomes damaged).

Specific Objective AA

The student uses a standard and an adjustable wrench.

Functional Settings and Suggested Instructional Activities

School

1. Show the student a standard wrench and point out that each wrench has a specific opening that fits a specific nut. Demonstrate how the wrench fits a nut by placing it over the corresponding nut and tightening it. Give the student a standard wrench and encourage him to imitate your actions. Practice.
2. Show the student an adjustable wrench and point out the adjusting knob on its side. Take the student's finger and assist him in turning the knob. Point out to him that the jaw is either opening or closing as he performs this action. Tell him to practice opening and closing the adjustable wrench.
3. Give the student an adjustable wrench and tell him to place the jaws of it on one of the nuts. If the jaws are open too far, tell him to turn the adjusting knob so that the jaws fit the nut and then tighten the nut. If the nut is too large for the wrench's jaws, have him adjust the knob in the reverse direction until the jaw opens widely and the nut fits in. Tell him to tighten the nut.
4. Construct a board or select a piece of furniture that requires the tightening of nuts. Select the equipment or construct the board in such a way that there are various shapes of nuts, such as hexagonal, square, machine-fine thread, or coarse thread. Tell the student to tighten all of the nuts with one adjustable wrench and point out to him that the wrench will have to be readjusted for each type of nut he is to tighten. Practice.

Home

1. Tell the parents to bring their child to a hardware store. While there, ask them to point out the different types of wrenches.
2. Tell the parents to select several toys that require repairing by tightening with a wrench, such as wheels on a toy bicycle or toy truck. Tell them to place the toys in a pile. Ask them to tell the child to take one and, from several wrenches, select the correct one to tighten any bolts that need tightening. Tell the parents to reinforce when appropriate, but also point out when he is not doing the activity correctly.

Functional Emphases   In designing your own instructional activities and plans, emphasize the following elements:

1. Knowledge of the different types of wrenches and their uses.
2. Awareness of safety factors involved in using standard and adjustable wrenches.

3. Development of motor skills necessary to use wrenches.
4. Identification of specific toys, objects, or equipment that require periodic tightening by wrenches.
5. Avoidance of purchasing inexpensive or poorly made wrenches.

Specific Objective BB

The student uses hand and electrical drills.

Functional Settings and Suggested Instructional Activities

School   The activities listed below may also be done at home provided there are adequate instruction and supervision and available tools or equipment.

1. Demonstrate the use of the hand drill. Be certain to point out how you hold the handle of the drill with one hand and that you turn the drill by the knob on its side with the other hand. Give the student the drill, and encourage him to imitate your actions.
2. Show the student an electric drill (a battery-powered one is preferred initially because safety hazards are minimal). Show the student how to press the trigger of the drill and point out how fast it is going. Point out the drill chuck and the key; open and close the drill jaws. Give the drill to the student, and encourage him to imitate your actions. Practice opening and closing the jaws of the drill and starting and stopping it. For the more advanced student, you may want to point out the little button next to the trigger, which keeps the drill running continuously. Supervise closely whenever the student is using electric tools.
3. Show the student a drill press. Point out the drill press wheel and turn it to adjust the height of the drill. Point out the on-off switch or treadle mechanism. Woodworking books are recommended for suggested reading if a drill press is to be incorporated into the daily activities. Wear safety glasses whenever working on the drill press.
4. Using a hand drill, place a drill bit into the chuck of the drill, and demonstrate to the student how to drill a hole in a soft pine board. Start a second hole, withdraw the drill bit and drill, and hand them to the student. Tell him to drill the hole all the way through as he has just seen you do. Practice drilling other holes. Repeat this activity with the electric drill and, when appropriate, the drill press. It is important that all activities are demonstrated first and closely supervised.

Functional Emphases   In designing your own instructional activities and plans, emphasize the following elements:

1. Awareness of the different varieties and sizes of hand and electric drills.
2. Knowledge of the safety factors involved in using drills (e.g., grounded plugs for electric drills).

3. Knowledge of how to change drill bits.
4. Selection of the right drill and bit for the job.
5. Avoidance of purchasing drills that are poorly made or appear unsafe.

Specific Objective CC

The student uses a soldering iron, pencil, or gun.

Functional Settings and Suggested Instructional Activities

School   The activities listed below may also be done at home provided there are adequate instruction and supervision and available tools or equipment.

1. Show the student a soldering iron with a long thin tip (this is usually called a soldering pencil). Emphasize safety precautions in using a tool such as this and, at all times, provide close supervision. Demonstrate how to plug the soldering iron into the wall and explain to the student that he is to wait several moments until it warms up. Remind the student that the tip is hot and that if he touches it he will burn himself.
2. Show the student some solder in a coil. (Make sure that the solder you use is rosin core, because this is used primarily for electrical work.) Demonstrate how you place a tiny bit of the coil of solder at the tip of the soldering iron and how it melts. Again stress that the solder is extremely hot and will burn him if he is not careful. Give the soldering iron and a piece of the soldering coil to the student and ask him to imitate your actions. (*Note:* This type of activity should be done on a table that is protected by a pine board or a surface that is able to withstand heat. It is further recommended that safety glasses be worn in case the solder splatters).
3. Show the student a soldering gun. Demonstrate how the pulling of the trigger of the soldering gun instantly turns the tip hot and can melt solder over the wires where they were joined. Monitor the process carefully; if the student melts too much solder, tell him so. A good soldering job will leave the finished wires bright and shiny.
4. Set up a work station where soldering will be done. Select the appropriate solder for doing jewelry work, and place a coil of it next to the soldering iron. Give the student several pieces of jewelry that require soldering on one of the clasps. Demonstrate soldering a clasp to a piece of jewelry so that the student will be able to see what you are doing. Make sure to point out that you never hold the clasp or jewelry in your hand; rather, place it in a jig or other mechanism for holding. Encourage the student to watch, imitate your actions, and practice.

Functional Emphases   In designing your own instructional activities and plans, emphasize the following elements:

1. Awareness of the wide varieties of soldering irons, pencils, or guns and their appropriateness for specific jobs.
2. Awareness of safety factors involved when using soldering equipment.
3. Awareness of the types of solder (e.g., rosin or acid core) and when each should be used.
4. Awareness of soldering aids that are available that make soldering easier and/or safer.
5. Avoidance of purchasing "bargain" soldering equipment that may be unsafe, may have a short life span, or is not Underwriters' Laboratories (UL) approved.

Specific Objective DD

The student uses sandpaper.

Functional Settings and Suggested Instructional Activities

School

1. Show the student an 8½ × 11-inch piece of medium sandpaper. Tell him to touch the sandpaper and feel how rough it is. Rub the sandpaper in a back and forth motion over a piece of wood. Show the student the sawdust that has been created and ask him to feel the wood where you have just sanded. Ask him if it is smooth.
2. Set up a soft pine board in a vise or, if the board is large enough, lay it on the table. Give the student a 3 × 4-inch piece of medium sandpaper, and tell him to place the rough side down on the board. Take the student's hand and place it on top of the sandpaper. You may also want to fold the sandpaper, making it easier to grasp. With a back and forth motion, guide the student's hand until the sawdust begins to appear. Point out the sawdust and tell the student to continue sanding the board until you tell him to stop.
3. Wrap a piece of fine sandpaper around a board 1 inch wide by 4 inches long. Place a large board in front of the student and demonstrate the back-and-forth motion of sanding. Point out that the board inside the sandpaper makes sanding easier. Tell the student to imitate your actions and sand the board. Construct a project with the board.

Home

1. Ask the parents to find objects or furniture around the home that need to be sanded (i.e., objects that do not close well or are uneven because the board has warped). Tell them to demonstrate how to sand these objects or furniture to their child. Ask them to encourage him to inspect their sanding and then ask him to sand.

2. Ask the parents to plan a simple project with their child that involves sanding. The project could be making a trivet or coasters. Tell them to monitor him as he sands.

Functional Emphases In designing your own instructional activities and plans, emphasize the following elements:

1. Awareness of the various sizes, types, and grits of sandpaper.
2. Comprehension of the classification system for grading the fineness or coarseness of sandpaper.
3. Knowledge of using the right sandpaper for the job.
4. Use of sandpaper jigs (aids) that expedite or make sanding easier.
5. Awareness of when to change sandpaper or increase or decrease the size of grit being used.

Specific Objective EE

The student paints and stains wood.

Functional Settings and Suggested Instructional Activities

School

1. Show the student a ½-pint can of water stain. Stains are usually used on new wood and can be either brushed or wiped on and then off. First, dip a ½-inch brush into the stain and spread it on the wood. Wipe it off with a cheesecloth or a soft, clean rag, Show the student the difference between the stained wood and the clean new wood.
2. Give the student a wide paint brush (1 to 1½ inches) and a 1-pint or 1-quart can of paint. Place a board that needs painting in front of him and tell him to paint the entire board using the wide brush. Carefully check the student's painting skills and point out drips or areas on the board that have either too much or too little paint. If the board is not painted in an acceptable fashion, ask the student to repeat the activity.

Home

1. Tell the parents to show their child a pint can of paint and an article that needs painting. Tell them to dip a ½-inch wide brush into the can and slowly spread the paint on a piece of wood. They should tell the child that he must not touch the paint with his hands and that he should only use the brush to spread the paint. It is suggested that latex or water-soluble paints be used before enamels because enamels are not easily removed from clothing and brushes can only be cleaned with turpentine.
2. Tell the parents to select a project or piece of wood that needs to be painted and to spread newspaper on the table where painting is to be done. Tell them to place all the materials (paint, brush, and rag) within easy

reach of their child and assist him in dipping his brush into the paint or stain and spreading it on the wood. They should make sure he only dips a small part of the brush into the paint and does not totally submerge all the bristles. Tell them to show him that the paint he is applying on the wood is covering the wood. If it is not covering the wood, they should tell him that he needs to spread more paint over the same spot. (*Note:* It is important that the child wears appropriate clothing for painting activities, that his sleeves are rolled up, and that he is under supervision.)

Functional Emphases In designing your own instructional activities and plans, emphasize the following elements:

1. Awareness of the different types, colors, and bases of paints and stains.
2. Development of motor skills necessary to paint and stain wood.
3. Use of a variety of brushes and rollers to paint or stain wood.
4. Knowledge of how to clean brushes after painting or staining.
5. Awareness of safety factors involved in using paints and stains and, when appropriate, their thinness.
6. Awareness of the different sizes of containers in which paint and stains can be purchased.
7. Comprehension of directions and warnings found on paint and stain labels.
8. Identification of appropriate areas in which to paint or stain (i.e., those with adequate ventilation and free of dust).

Specific Objective FF

The student inspects objects by manipulating and using them.

Functional Settings and Suggested Instructional Activities

School

1. Give the student a finished project such as a wall plaque that has been painted and is dry. Tell him to look at the plaque and see if the paint has covered the wood in the appropriate places. Tell him to look for places that have been missed by the painter. Encourage him to turn the board or plaque all around and to check the sides, back, and front. If the plaque requires additional painting, it can be placed in a box near other plaques the student is inspecting.
2. Give the student a box of small wooden toys, such as cars and planes, that have been constructed as part of wood projects. These toys should have movable parts such as wheels and propellers. Tell the student to inspect each toy and to turn the wheels or propellers and to make sure they move. Instruct him to place those toys with parts that do not move into a carton.

3. Give the student several piles of paper, such as notices or menus, that have been stapled in half and are going to be sent home. Tell him to look at each individual paper to make sure the staple has gone through and is holding the other side of the paper. Encourage him to separate those that are not properly stapled into a pile and bring them to you when he has completed the entire task.

Home

1. Tell the parents to encourage their child to inspect a project after completing it and tell what, if anything, could be improved. Tell them to praise him if he points out flaws or poor construction.
2. For a birthday or special occasion, ask the parents to buy a gift for their child that needs to be put together (e.g., a model, Lego, an erector set, or Capsula).

Functional Emphases In designing your own instructional activities and plans, emphasize the following elements:

1. Awareness of how to inspect a completed object or project for errors in construction, missing parts, or safety problems.
2. Utilization of checklists to analyze whether or not a completed project has all its parts and has been put together in a safe fashion.

Specific Objective GG

The student maintains grounds. (Note: These are just a few examples of the many activities that could be included under this objective.)

Functional Settings and Suggested Instructional Activities

School

1. Demonstrate the use of a nonelectric hedge trimmer and pruning device. Warn the student about the sharpness of the blades and demonstrate how to hold and use them properly. Bring the student to an area where bushes need to be pruned or clipped. Demonstrate on a small section of the bushes, and tell the student to imitate your actions.
2. Show the student (supervise closely) how to use a hand and power lawn mower. (It is recommended that a training program based upon safety and job expectations be a prerequisite before use of the lawn mower is taught.) Once the student knows how to use a lawn mower safely, assign him an area to be mowed. Tell him to inspect the area for rocks before he mows. After he has completed his job, tell him to inspect the lawn and recut parts when necessary.

3. Take the student to an area or garden where dirt needs to be shoveled. Demonstrate how to hold the shovel by grasping its handle, putting it into the dirt, and stepping on the shoulder of its blade. Ask him to dig a hole in the ground where you will be planting a small shrub or tree.

Home and Community

1. Ask the parents to connect a hose to an outside faucet and demonstrate how to turn the hose on and off by adjusting the water nozzle. Ask them to tell their child to imitate their actions and to water the flowers or grass in the immediate area.
2. Ask the parents to demonstrate to their child how to rake leaves.
3. In climates where there is snow, tell the parents to have their child help shovel the walk.
4. Tell the student, when appropriate, to look for small jobs in the community (e.g., shoveling snow, raking leaves, and/or mowing lawns). Supervise his work by making sure he does an acceptable job and follows safety rules.

Functional Emphases   In designing your own instructional activities and plans, emphasize the following elements:

1. Knowledge of the criteria needed to assess whether grounds have been well maintained.
2. Development of motor skills necessary to use groundskeeping tools.
3. Awareness of safety factors needed to use groundskeeping tools (e.g., lawn mowers, hedge trimmers, and grass clippers).
4. Awareness of the types and composition of fertilizers needed to maintain lawns.
5. Comprehension of the information on labels found on fertilizers or chemicals used in groundskeeping.
6. Awareness of warning information found on fertilizers or chemicals used in groundskeeping.
7. Knowledge of the best or most appropriate times to cut and water lawns, prune, or put down fertilizer.

Special Materials List—Prevocational Skills

Books/Pamphlets

Job Seeking Skills. Stout Vocational Rehabilitation Institute, University of Wisconsin–Stout, Menomonie, WI 54751.

General Woodworking, by Ralph J. Vernon. Steck-Vaughn Company, Box 2028, Austin, TX 78768.

Kits/Programs

Pre-Vocational Training Center. EBSCO Curriculum Materials, Box 1943, Birmingham, AL 35203.

Match-Sort-Assemble. Exceptional Education, P. O. Box 15308, Seattle, WA 98115.

Films/Filmstrips

Woodworking Trade Skills. Prentice-Hall Media, 150 White Plains Road, Tarrytown, NY 10591.

Suggested Readings/References — Fine Motor Skills

Adelson, N., & Sandow, L. (1978). Teaching buttoning to severely/profoundly multi-handicapped children. *Education and Training of the Mentally Retarded, 13,* 178–183.

Banus, B. S., Kent, C. A., Norton, Y., Sukiennicki, D. R., & Becker, M. L. (1979). *The developmental therapist.* Thorofare, NJ: Charles B. Slack.

Bayley, N. (1969). *Manual for the Bayley scales of infant development.* New York: Psychological Corporation.

Bower, T. G. R. (1977). *A primer of infant development.* San Francisco: Freeman.

Bunker, L. K. (1978). Motor skills. In M. E. Snell (Ed.), *Systematic instruction of the moderately and severely handicapped.* Columbus, OH: Charles E. Merrill.

Cipani, E., Augustine, A., & Blomgren, E. (1980). Teaching the severely and profoundly retarded to open doors: Assessment and training. *Journal of Special Education Technology, 3,* 42–46.

Copeland, M., Ford, L., & Solon, N. (1976). *Occupational therapy for mentally retarded children.* Baltimore: University Park Press.

Crnic, K. A., & Pym, H. A. (1979). Training mentally retarded adults in independent living skills. *Mental Retardation, 17,* 13–16.

Dunn, M. L. (1979). *Pre-scissor skills: Skill-starters for motor development.* Tucson, AZ: Communication Skill Builders.

Edgar, E., Maser, J. T., & Haring, N. G. (1977). Button up! A systematic approach for teaching children to fasten. *Teaching Exceptional Children, 9,* 104–105.

Ford, L. J. (1975). Teaching dressing skills to a severely retarded child. *American Journal of Occupational Therapy, 29,* 87–92.

Fulkerson, S. C., & Freeman, W. M. (1980). Perceptual-motor deficiency in autistic children. *Perceptual and Motor Skills, 50,* 331–336.

Healy, H., & Stainback, S. B. (1980). *The severely motorically impaired student: A handbook for the classroom teacher.* Springfield, IL: Charles C Thomas.

Kissinger, E. M. (1981). *A sequential curriculum for the severely and profoundly mentally retarded/multihandicapped.* Springfield, IL: Charles C Thomas.

Kramer, L., & Whitehurst, C. (1981). Effects of button features on self-dressing in young retarded children. *Education and Training of the Mentally Retarded, 16,* 277–283.

Leff, R. B. (1975). Teaching mentally retarded children and adults to dial the telephone. *Mental Retardation, 13*, 9–11.

Maynard, M. (1976). The value of creative arts for the developmentally disabled child: Implications for recreation therapists in community day service programs. *Therapeutic Recreation Journal, 10*, 10–13.

McCormick, J. E. (1977). *Motor development: Manual of alternative procedures.* Medford: Massachusetts Center for Program Development and Evaluation.

Montgomery, P., & Richter, E. (1977). Effect of sensory integrative therapy on the neuromotor development of retarded children. *Physical Therapy, 57*, 799–806.

Mori, A. A., & Masters, L. F. (1980). *Teaching the severely mentally retarded: Adaptive skills training.* Germantown, MD: Aspen Systems.

Mullins, J. (1979). *A teacher's guide to management of physically handicapped students.* Springfield, IL: Charles C. Thomas.

Robinson, C. C., & Robinson, J. H. (1978). Sensorimotor functions and cognitive development. In M. E. Snell (Ed.), *Systematic instruction of the moderately and severely handicapped.* Columbus, OH: Charles E. Merrill.

Roman, B. (1978). *Infant stimulation training skills from infancy to 36 months.* Johnston, PA: Mafex Association.

Snell, M. E. (1978). Self-care skills. In M. E. Snell (Ed.), *Systematic instruction of the moderately and severely handicapped.* Columbus, OH: Charles E. Merrill.

Sternlicht, M., & Hurwitz, R. (1981). *Games children play: Instructive and creative play activities for the mentally retarded and developmentally disabled child.* New York: Van Nostrand-Reinhold.

Task analyses and objectives for trainable mentally retarded: Communication skills, daily living skills, motor skills, and quantitative skills. (1978). Minneapolis: Minneapolis Public Schools.

Walls, R. T., Crist, K., Sienicki, D. A., & Grant, L. (1981). Prompting sequences in teaching independent living skills. *Mental Retardation, 19*, 243–246.

Whitney, P. L. (1978). Measurement for curriculum building for multiply handicapped children. *Physical Therapy, 58*, 15–20.

Suggested Readings/References — Prevocational Skills

Ackerman, A. S., Baygell, M., & Fishel, M. (1979). *It happened on the job.* New York: Globe Book Company.

Alper, S. (1981). Utilizing community jobs in developing a vocational curriculum for severely handicapped youth. *Education and Training of the Mentally Retarded, 16*, 217–221.

Becker, R. L., Soforenko, A. Z., & Widener, Q. (1979). Career education for trainable mentally retarded youth. *Education and Training of the Mentally Retarded, 14*, 101–105.

Bellamy, G. T., Sheehan, M. R., Horner, R. W., & Boles, S. M. (1980). Community programs for severely handicapped adults: An analysis of vocational opportunities. *Journal of the Association for the Severely Handicapped, 5*, 307–324.

Bellamy, G. T., Wilson, D., Adler, E., & Clark, J. (1980). A strategy for programming vocational skills for severely handicapped youth. *Exceptional Education Quarterly, 1*, 85–98.

Belmore, K., & Brown, L. (1976). A job skill inventory strategy for use in a public school vocational training program for severely handicapped potential workers. In L. Brown, N. Certo, K. Belmore, & T. Crowner (Eds.), *Papers and programs related to public school service for secondary age severely handicapped students (Vol. 6, Part 1)*. Madison, WI: Madison Metropolitan School District.

Bender, M. (1978). Teaching through imitation. Industrial education for the moderately and severely retarded. *Education and Training of the Mentally Retarded, 13*, 9–15.

Bernstein, G., & Karan, O. C. (1979). Obstacles to vocational normalization for the developmentally disabled. *Rehabilitation Literature, 40*, 66–71.

Brickey, M., Browning, L., & Campbell, K. (1982). Vocational histories of sheltered workshop employees placed in projects with industry and competitive jobs. *Mental Retardation, 20*, 52–57.

Brickey, M., & Campbell, K. (1981). Fast food employment for moderately and mildly retarded adults: The McDonald's project. *Mental Retardation, 19*, 113–116.

Brolin, D. E. (1976). *Vocational preparation of retarded citizens*. Columbus, OH: Charles E. Merrill.

Brolin, D. E., & Kobaska, L. (1979). *Career education for handicapped children and youth*. Columbus, OH: Charles E. Merrill.

Brown, L., Bellamy, T., Perlmutter, L., Sackowitz, P., & Sontag, E. (1972). The development of quality, quantity, and durability of work performance of retarded students in a public school prevocational workshop. *Training School Bulletin, 69*, 58–69.

Bucci, J. R., & Hansen, C. L. (198). A classroom based prevocational program for the severely handicapped. *Education and Training of the Mentally Retarded, 15*, 278–283.

Carlson, B. W., & Ginglend, D. R. (1977). *Ready to work: The development of occupational skills, attitudes, and behaviors with retarded persons*. Nashville, TN: Abington Press.

Christ, H. I. (1979). *The world of careers*. New York: Globe Book Company.

Clark, G. M. (1980). Career preparation for handicapped adolescents: A matter of appropriate education. *Exceptional Education Quarterly, 1*, 11–18.

Connis, R. T. (1979). The effects of sequential pictorial cues, self-recording, and praise on the job task sequencing of retarded adults. *Journal of Applied Behavior Analysis, 12*, 353–362.

Cronin, K. A., & Cuvo, A. J. (1979). Teaching mending skills to mentally retarded adolescents. *Journal of Applied Behavior Analysis, 12*, 401–406.

Dahl, P. (1978). *Mainstreaming guidebook for vocational educators—Teaching the handicapped*. Salt Lake City, UT: Olympus Publishing Company.

D'Alonzo, B. J. (1977). Trends and issues in career education for the mentally retarded. *Education and Training of the Mentally Retarded, 12*, 156–158.

David, S., & Ward, M. (1978). *Vocational education of handicapped students: A guide for policy development*. Reston, VA: The Council for Exceptional Children.

DeFazio, N., & Flexer, R. W. (1983). Organizational barriers to productivity, meaningful wages, and normalized work opportunity for mentally retarded persons. *Mental Retardation, 21*, 157–163.

Feirer, J. L. (1972). *Industrial arts woodworking*. Peoria, IL: Charles A. Bennett.

Flexer, R. W., Martin, A. S., Friedenberg, W. P., & Justice, D. (1978). Increasing the work tolerance of severely retarded persons through a work adjustment training program. *Vocational Evaluation and Work Adjustment Bulletin, 11,* 22–30.

Foss, G., & Peterson, S. (1981). Social-interpersonal skills relevant to job tenure for MR adults. *Mental Retardation, 19,* 103–106.

Gola, T. J., Holmes, P. A., & Holmes, N. K. (1982). Effectiveness of a group contingency procedure for increasing prevocational behavior of profoundly mentally retarded residents. *Mental Retardation, 20,* 26–29.

Gold, M. (1980). *Try another way training manual.* Champaign, IL: Research Press.

Halpern, A. S. (1975). Measuring social and prevocational awareness in mildly retarded adolescents. *American Journal of Mental Deficiency, 80,* 81–89.

Humm-Delgado, D. (1979). Opinions of community residence staff about their work and responsibilities. *Mental Retardation, 17,* 250–251.

Joyce, D., & McFadden, L. (1982). Adaptive industrial arts: Meeting the needs of the handicapped. *Education and Training of the Mentally Retarded, 17,* 337–339.

Kahn, C., Jew, W., & Tong, R. (1980). *My job application file: Workbook and teacher's manual.* Hayward, CA: Janus Book Publishers.

Knox, C. (1980). *Getting a job.* Baltimore: Media Materials.

Langone, J., & Westling, D. (1979). Generalization of prevocational and vocational skills: Some practical tactics. *Education and Training of the Mentally Retarded, 14,* 216–221.

Lynch, K. P. (1979). Toward a skill oriented prevocational program for trainable and severely mentally impaired students. In G. T. Bellamy, G. O'Conor, & O. C. Karan (Eds.), *Vocational rehabilitation of severely handicapped persons.* Austin: PRO-ED.

Lynch, K., Kiernan, W., & Stark, J. (Eds.). (1982). *Prevocational and vocational education for special needs youth: A blueprint for the 1980's.* Baltimore: Paul H. Brookes.

Martin, A. S., & Morris, J. L. (1980). Training a work ethic in severly mentally retarded workers—providing a context for the maintenance of skill performance. *Mental Retardation, 18,* 67-71.

National Industries for the Severely Handicapped. (1981). *Workshop inventory.* Washington, DC: author.

Parkman, H. W. (1979). Marketable skills: An art/handicraft program for trainable mentally retarded young adults. *Education and Training of the Mentally Retarded, 14,* 295–298.

Rusch, F. R., & Mithaug, D. E. (1980). *Vocational training for mentally retarded adults: A behavior analytic approach.* Champaign, IL: Research Press.

Schilit, J., & Caldwell, M. L. (1981). A word list of essential career/vocational words for mentally retarded students. *Education and Training of the Mentally Retarded, 16,* 113–117.

Schipp, S. L., Baker, R. J., & Cuvo, A. J. (1980). The relationship between attention to work task and production rate of a mentally retarded client. *Mental Retardation, 18,* 241–244.

SRA job family series. (1975). Chicago: SRA.

Thrower, R. G. (Ed.). (1974). *Industrial arts for the elementary school.* 23rd Yearbook. Bloomington, IL: American Council on Industrial Arts Teacher Education.

Walls, R. T., Haught, P., & Crist, K. (1982). Products, service contracts, operations, and tools in sheltered workshops. *Education and Training of the Mentally Retarded, 17,* 209–213.

Walls, R. T., Slenick, D. A., & Crist, K. (1981). Operations training in vocational skills. *American Journal of Mental Deficiency, 85,* 357–367.

Walls, R. T., Zane, T., & Thvedt, J. E. (1980). Trainers' personal methods compared to two structured training strategies. *American Journal of Mental Deficiency, 84,* 495–507.

Wehman, P. (1981). *Competitive employment: New horizons for severely disabled individuals.* Baltimore: Paul H. Brookes.

Wehman, P., McLaughlin, P. J., Revell, W. G., Kriloff, L. J., & Sarkees, M. D. (1980). *Vocational curriculum for developmentally disabled persons.* Austin: PRO-ED.

Weisgerber, R. A., & Smith, C. A. (1978). *Improving vocational education services for handicapped students.* Palo Alto, CA: American Institute for Research in the Behavioral Sciences.

5 Household Management and Living Skills

The ability to function successfully in a home environment is a basic skill required of all people. The skills associated with acquiring and maintaining a suitable and appropriate household must therefore be included in curriculum experiences as early as possible in the school career and then must be continually stressed into adulthood.

If home-oriented school experiences are provided in the schools, they traditionally are scheduled in the secondary years in last-minute attempts to bridge the gap between the artificiality of typical curricula and the reality of the world the soon-to-graduate student will face. However, preparation for successful functioning as a member of a household should start with the beginning school years and not just before high school commencement. School and home experiences must be coordinated in cooperative attempts by teachers and parents to provide consistency, reinforcement, and practice. The home provides a special laboratory where newly acquired skills can be practiced in vivo, thus increasing the likelihood that they will be maintained and will be expressed independently at a future time.

This chapter illuminates the need for modification in school design and equipment. To successfully program for these instructional experiences, it would be valuable to have a model living unit and to have present the furniture and appliances normally found in a home. A broom and a dustpan thus become important educational equipment equal to or surpassing the functional value of a piece of equipment more usually identified as important, such as a tape recorder.

The home provides a natural setting not only in which students may acquire the variety of skills pertinent to that setting, but also where parents may work with their children in a variety of other skills that transcend settings—for example, communication and interpersonal skills. Because of the critical role parents must play in the education of their moderately and severely handicapped children and because education for this population cannot be restricted to a 8:30-to-3 schedule, school programs must have a strong parental training program that is based on the individual assessment of parental needs and that provides continuing education for parents on how best to facilitate their child's learning (Barnard, Christopherson, & Wolf, 1977).

The myriad tasks inherent in becoming and being an integral part of a cohesive and successful household must receive the attention of curriculum planners and must be assiduously taught. These tasks include those activities of daily life that arise from planning, purchasing, storing, and preparing food (Amary, 1979; Johnson & Cuvo, 1981) and purchasing and maintaining clothes (Bender & Valletutti, 1982; Cuvo, Jacobi, & Sipko, 1981). They extend to the many activities required to satisfactorily maintain the household and its various functional and decorative equipment, appliances, and accessories (Bauman & Iwata, 1977). They encompass those competencies that make any home a satisfying and pleasurable place to live. These skills also relate to keeping a home clean, in good repair, and aesthetically pleasing so that it is a suitable and enjoyable place to live, to carry out countless household duties, to engage in various interpersonal exchanges, and to spend time in leisure activities (Stacy–Sherrer, 1981).

Designing a curriculum that proposes to prepare handicapped learners for competent participation in the life of a household demands the identification of the broad range of skills that effective, efficient, and safe household membership requires. This challenge to instructional planners at first glance seems a simple one because to appreciate the scope of the functional requirements of membership in a household, one merely must analyze the skills necessary to function in one's own household. However, to those who have already acquired the skills the automatic nature of these behaviors masks their subtle presence, interfering with the process of defining their scope and sequence.

The Suggested Readings and Special Materials List at the end of this chapter provide information on household management and living skills. The reader should decide which material and information are applicable to a specific student or students being taught.

General Objectives of the Unit

    I. The student will be functionally independent in planning meals and in purchasing, storing, and preparing food in a manner that allows him to perform optimally.

    II. The student will be functionally independent in purchasing and maintaining his clothes in a manner that allows him to perform optimally.

    III. The student will be functionally independent in caring for his living quarters, appliances, and furnishings in a manner that allows him to perform optimally.

    IV. The student will operate simple appliances, objects, conveniences, and home accessories.

General Objective I

The student will be functionally independent in planning meals and in purchasing, storing, and preparing food in a manner that allows him to perform optimally.

Specific Objectives

The student:

A. plans nutritious meals and snacks.
B. purchases the food needed for nutritious meals and snacks.
C. after shopping, stores foods in appropriate places before eating or cooking.
D. opens and closes food packages without the use of tools.
E. opens food packages using various can and bottle openers.
F. throws out food that is spoiled or contaminated.
G. effectively and safely uses kitchen utensils.
H. prepares simple, nutritious snacks or parts of meals that require no heating or cooking.
 I. effectively and safely operates major appliances, including a stove, microwave oven, and dishwasher.
J. effectively and safely operates simple appliances used in cooking.
K. prepares simple, nutritious snacks or parts of meals requiring heating or minimal cooking.
L. prepares simple, nutritious meals using cooking utensils and appliances.
M. sets the table for serving informal meals.
N. washes, dries, and stores kitchen equipment, dishes, glasses, and silverware.
O. stores unused and/or leftover food in appropriate wrappings, containers, and places.

Specific Objective A

The student plans nutritious meals and snacks.

Functional Settings and Suggested Instructional Activities

School

1. Draw a "Balanced Menu Chart" (Figure 16) for each meal as a reference guide for the student. Place pictures of nutritious foods on the chart from which he can select his meals. Color code those items that represent the

same nutritional category; for example, a red circle underneath the picture of two eggs and a red circle underneath the picture of a small bowl of cereal will show that they may be substituted for each other. Indicate to the student that he should have one red-marked food, one blue-marked food, one yellow-marked food, etc. (Geometric shapes, rebuses, or other symbols may be used as substitutes for color clues; for example, protein foods might be represented by muscles, calcium by bones, etc.) Use pictures of nutritious foods that are liked by the student.

2. Help the student to select his own daily menu from this chart. Prepare a meal. While he is eating the meal, remind him that he has selected a balanced meal.

3. Conduct a "nutritious food" tasting party for the student and his guests.

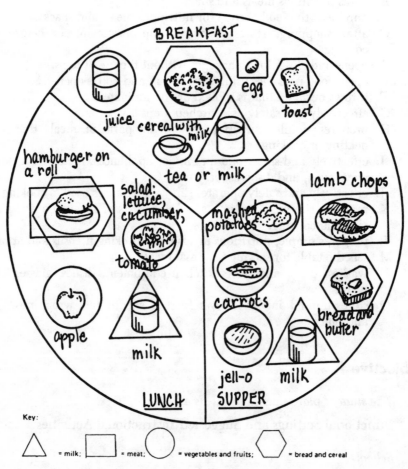

Figure 16. Balanced menu chart.

Home

1. Ask the parents to help their child plan a small breakfast, luncheon, or dinner party for his friends or classmates. After the meal planning has been completed, tell them to prepare and serve the meal to him and his guests.
2. Ask the parents to offer nutritious snacks at established times during the day (mid-morning and/or mid-afternoon). Snacks such as nuts, raisins, fruit, sliced carrots, and other raw vegetables may be used. Tell them to indicate that these are good foods to snack on between meals if you get hungry. (At all times, parents should consider the individual medical record as it relates to body weight, skin blemishes, allergies, and metabolic problems.)

Functional Emphases   In designing your own instructional activities and plans, emphasize the following elements:

1. Knowledge of ingredient information found on food labels.
2. Awareness of what constitutes different food groups.
3. Identification of places where one can purchase nutritious foods.

Specific Objective B

The student purchases the food needed for nutritious meals and snacks.

Functional Settings and Suggested Instructional Activities

School   The activities listed below can also be done at home. The parents should be urged to allow their child as much freedom as possible in implementing these critical survival activities.

1. Encourage the student to fill out a "Shopping List Form" (Figure 17). The form should include pictures or sketches of the items to be purchased. Amounts may be penciled in next to each article (e.g., 1 dozen, 5 pounds). Encourage students to check off each article as it is purchased.
2. Once the student has developed his own individualized meal chart, take him on a trip to a supermarket or grocery store. Walk him around the store and match each of the foods on his chart with its actual counterpart.
3. Begin making purchases by concentrating first on buying the foods needed for breakfast. As you place each item in the shopping basket, comment on the fact that it is a good breakfast food. Show the student the quantity to buy. Make a chart for breakfast shopping; for example, a dozen eggs, a container of milk, a loaf of bread, bacon, cereal, and juice. Indicate on the chart the next shopping day and the quantity needed to take the student to that date. Put the exact number or amount of each article by showing pictures that indicate the exact quantity. For example, a picture of two cans of orange juice could be used to indicate the exact purchase needed.

4. Repeat Activity 3 for lunch foods and then for dinner foods.
5. Gradually reduce the amount of assistance given to the student until he has reached the point when he can "solo" in the supermarket or grocery. Reward him for his independent performance. (*Note:* Whenever the student purchases an item that can be used for several meals, this should be indicated.)

Functional Emphases   In designing your own instructional activities and plans, emphasize the following elements:

1. Location of stores that sell nutritious foods.
2. Calculation of the cost of different foods.
3. Awareness of the different food groups.
4. Identification of directories within a store.

Figure 17. Shopping list form.

5. Knowledge of information found on meal charts and shopping lists.
6. Calculation of the amount of money available for food purchases.
7. Estimation of the cost of purchases.
8. Selection of appropriate currency and coins.
9. Verification of change.
10. Verification of store receipts for accuracy.

Specific Objective C

The student, after shopping, stores food in appropriate places before eating or cooking.

Functional Settings and Suggested Instructional Activities

School

1. In the case of fresh fruits and vegetables, indicate that they go in the refrigerator so they will last longer. Conduct a demonstration by refrigerating part of a purchase of fruit or vegetables while not refrigerating the other part of the same purchase. Show the student the spoilage that occurs, including the discoloration, shriveling, and odor of the unrefrigerated fruits and vegetables. Praise the student for putting fresh fruits and vegetables in the refrigerator. (*Note:* Teach handling of bananas separately.)
2. Indicate that jars or bottles that have been opened should be refrigerated. (*Note:* Although there are some items in opened jars and bottles that do not need to be refrigerated, it is best to teach the general practice because it might be unhealthy not to refrigerate some open jars, such as mayonnaise, whereas it is not unhealthy to refrigerate open jars that do not need refrigeration.)

Home

1. Ask the parents to demonstrate to their child how to unpack the groceries after grocery shopping. Tell them to assist him in unpacking the bags and in separating the food items into three groups: those to be refrigerated, those to be put in the freezer, and those to be stored in cabinets. Use a "Food Storage Chart" (Figure 18) to which he may refer when necessary. The parents should establish a routine to assist him (for example, canned goods are always put in the same closet), and encourage him to unpack and store food as soon as he returns from shopping. Tell the parents to label the cabinets, refrigerator, and freezer, if necessary, by attaching small pictures of the appropriate items to them. Actual labels from products purchased may also be used.
2. Ask the parents to relate for their child the storing of the items at home to the way they are arranged in the store. When removing an item from a store shelf, they should say to him, "This can go on a shelf at home." They should remind him to notice that the item is not cold and say, "It isn't kept

cold at the store, so we don't have to keep it cold at home before using it."
(*Note:* This is true in most cases except for fresh fruits and vegetables,
which must be taught as an exception.) Similarly, when a refrigerated item
is purchased, they should indicate to him that it is cold because it is being
kept in the store's refrigerator, so he must put it in his refrigerator when he
gets it home. They should also point out the difference in the frozen food
storage bins and display cases and the hardness of the frozen items, and
indicate that items kept in the store's freezer are to be put in the home
freezer.

Figure 18. Food storage chart.

Functional Emphases In designing your own instructional activities and plans, emphasize the following elements:

1. Knowledge of where to find specific foods within a store (e.g., in the freezer department).
2. Knowledge of where to store food within the home.
3. Selection of the right temperature to store food needing refrigerating or freezing.
4. Awareness of when foods have spoiled or have been contaminated.

Specific Objective D

The student opens and closes food packages without the use of tools.

Functional Settings and Suggested Instructional Activities

School The activities listed below can also be done at home. The parents should be encouraged to teach the opening of a variety of types of packages that are normally found in the child's home and immediate environment.

1. For each of the food items included in the student's food charts, demonstrate to the student how to open the package before using it. Begin by opening packages that require only the use of the hands.
2. Demonstrate opening and closing boxes that simply require lifting the top flap out. Assist the student in indentifying the top of the package. Point out pictures on the package as a guide to the top and bottom of each box. If a package has no pictures, try showing the student the difference between upside down and right side up letters. If this is not possible, furnish the student with a reference chart of familiar packages (Figure 19) to which he can match his package. Pictures may be drawn to size, or actual box fronts may be pasted on to aid in recognition. Remind him to close the box and put it away.
3. Demonstrate opening and closing boxes that require the pulling of tear strips on cellophane wrappers, such as a box of tea bags. Assist the student. Practice opening the top of the box. Give the student a taste of the food or beverage if possible. Remind him to close the box and put it away. Assist him.
4. Demonstrate opening and closing boxes that require the pulling of cardboard tear strips, such as a package of Jello. Point out the pull tab and assist him in opening the package and removing the contents. Prepare the food and give the student his share. If there is unused material, remind the student to close the box and put it away.
5. Demonstrate opening and closing boxes that require removing a cellophane strip placed over a pour spout, such as a box of salt. Point out the cellophane or adhesive strip and assist the student in removing it and

opening the pour spout. Assist him in closing the pour spout. Remind him to put the box back where he found it.

6. Demonstrate opening and closing boxes with attached cap tops or snap tops, such as spice containers and bread crumbs. Assist the student in opening the container and in shaking out or removing the contents. Remind him to close the container and put it away.

7. Demonstrate opening and closing containers with a pull-up cylindrical spout such as a mustard container. Assist the student in squeezing out just enough of the food and moving the spout back into its closed position.

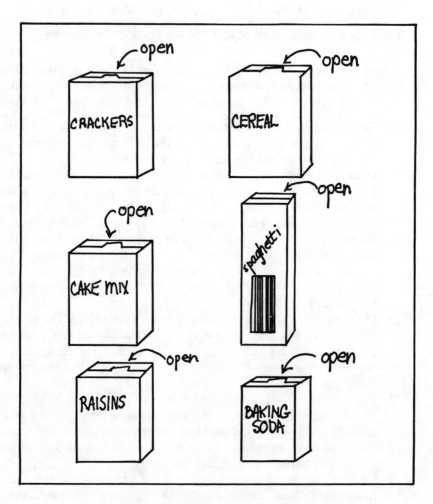

Figure 19. Familiar packages chart.

Remind him to wipe the spout and to clean and return the jar to its storage place.

8. Demonstrate opening and closing containers with a tab zip-top such as a can of soda. Assist the student in doing so. Point out the danger of cuts. (*Note:* Some students may cut their tongues because they like to stick their tongues into the opening.) Remind him to throw away the empty can or place the unused portion in the refrigerator. Caution the student to dispose of the tab top before drinking the beverage.

9. Demonstrate opening and closing boxes that require pressing in a tab and pulling a strip or section of the box open. Assist the student in removing the contents and closing the package. Remind him to return the package to its storage place.

10. Demonstrate opening and closing a container of milk, juice, or lemonade. Assist the student in doing so. Remind him to return the container to its storage place. Use different-size containers of milk.

11. Demonstrate opening and closing a carton of eggs. Assist the student in doing so. Remind him to return the container to its storage place.

12. Demonstrate opening and closing a wrapped loaf of bread. Demonstrate the use of a twist tie in closing the package. Assist the student in doing so. Remind him to return the container to its storage place.

13. Demonstrate opening and closing packages (often contained in boxes) that require tearing off the top, such as dry soup mixes. Assist the student in locating the top strip and tearing it open. Remind him to close the package and store it.

14. Demonstrate opening and closing containers with wheel tops, such as spice containers. Assist the student in opening the container, shaking out the contents, closing the container, and putting it back.

15. Demonstrate opening and closing tops of bottles and jars that require no tools. Assist the student in opening and closing jars or bottles. Reward him with a taste of the food or beverage. Remind him to store the remainder in the refrigerator.

16. Demonstrate opening and closing a lidded can, such as powdered flavor (Quick or cocoa) or baking powder. Assist the student in using the handle of a spoon to do so. Observe safety precautions. Assist him in closing the container and remind him to return it to its storage place.

Functional Emphases   In designing your own instructional activities and plans, emphasize the following elements:

1. Development of motor skills necessary to open and close packages.
2. Knowledge of safety procedures to use in opening food packages.
3. Awareness of "opening and closing" directions found on food packages.
4. Avoidance of purchasing food packages that are difficult to close.
5. Awareness of health considerations when closing food packages (i.e., wiping lids, cleaning ingredients off of bottles or packages, and tightening lids to prevent moisture).

Specific Objective E

The student opens food packages using various can and bottle openers.

Functional Settings and Suggested Instructional Activities

School   The activities listed below can also be done at home. Exposure to opening as many types of food packages as possible is recommended.)

1. Demonstrate opening a can with ridged edges on the top and the bottom using a manually operated can opener. Help the student to identify cans with ridged edges. Assist him in opening the can. Follow safety precautions. If available, use an electric can opener. Do not rely solely on the electric can opener, however, because the student must not be so reliant on an electric can opener that he would not be able to open a can if the electric opener breaks or the electricity goes off.
2. Demonstrate opening a can without ridges by using a "church key" or a juice opener. Assist the student in opening a juice can and pouring himself and others glasses of juice. Help the student open a can of evaporated milk. Use the evaporated milk in a cooking activity.
3. Demonstrate opening a bottle without a twist top by using a bottle opener. Assist the student in opening a bottle of carbonated beverage and pouring drinks for himself and a friend.
4. Demonstrate opening a can with a key that is attached to the top or bottom of the can (e.g., a can of sardines). Help the student remove the key. Assist him in finding the metal starting strip, turning the key, and wrapping the metal on the key. Observe safety precautions.

Functional Emphases   In designing your own instructional activities and plans, emphasize the following elements:

1. Knowledge of how to use various can and bottle openers.
2. Use of safety procedures when operating can or bottle openers or related equipment.
3. Awareness of health factors created when openers are not clean or are not cleaned after use.
4. Avoidance of openers that are poorly made or that appear unsafe.
5. Modification of openers when appropriate (e.g., wrapping tape around handle of opener, elevating or lowering electric can opener to appropriate level).

Specific Objective F

The student throws out food that is spoiled or contaminated.

Functional Settings and Suggested Instructional Activities

School

1. Indicate to the student that if something he normally eats tastes bitter or smells unpleasant, he should not eat it. Encourage him to use taste and smell as monitoring devices for rejecting food that might be spoiled.
2. Demonstrate how to check a can for swelling. Show the student samples of swollen cans. Assist him in throwing these cans out. When discarding these cans, indicate verbally and/or through gestures that the contents are not good to eat. Also use this checking activity in purchasing foods. Encourage the student not to purchase dented cans.

Home

1. Ask the parents to point out food that is decayed. Tell them to show their child "before" and "after" samples and point out the visual signs of decay, including molds, wilting, and curdling. Tell them to indicate unpleasant odors as a sign of decay. (It is the contrast in appearance and smell between the good and bad samples that is the key.) Tell them to join him in eating the good sample and in rejecting the spoiled sample. Tell them to smile with satisfaction when eating the good sample, and to look upon the spoiled sample with disgust and push it aside, perhaps with an "Ugh!" or gesture of disgust.
2. Ask the parents to encourage their child to check food that he has stored for visual or odor signs of spoilage. Tell them to reward him for checking foods before cooking and/or eating.
3. Ask the parents to help their child to check uncooked eggs for cracked shells. Tell them to encourage him to throw out cracked eggs or to return them to the store.

Functional Emphases   In designing your own instructional activities and plans, emphasize the following elements:

1. Awareness of when food is spoiled.
2. Knowledge of how to dispose of spoiled food.
3. Awareness of purchasing canned goods and dated food packages before their expiration period.
4. Identification of signs that point to spoiled foods found in stores.

Specific Objective G

The student effectively and safely uses kitchen utensils.

Functional Settings and Suggested Instructional Activities

School   The activities listed below can also be done at home. Using kitchen utensils appropriately is an especially critical area in terms of eating, cooking, and socialization skills and should be taught carefully and practiced often.

1. Use a chart to identify different kinds of knives (Figure 20). Pictures may be sketched or cut from magazines, or real tableware may be attached to heavy cardboard for identification purposes. Show the student pictures of various knives, including butter knives, potato peelers, paring knives, steak knives, and electric knives.
2. Demonstrate how to use various knives in preparing, cutting, and eating foods. Explain the safety rules to follow and demonstrate the precautions.
3. Use a chart (see Figure 20) and/or pictures to help the student identify different kinds of forks (regular, salad or cake, and long fork).
4. Demonstrate how to use various forks. Assist the student in using each of these forks in preparing and eating foods.
5. Demonstrate how to use a knife and fork together in cutting meat. Assist the student in doing so, and cut and eat some slices of meat.
6. Use a chart (see Figure 20) and/or pictures to identify different types of spoons, such as a wooden spoon for mixing, a basting spoon, a tablespoon for soup, and a teaspoon.
7. Demonstrate the use of various spoons. Assist the student in actually using spoons in preparing and eating foods.
8. Use a chart and/or pictures to identify various measuring spoons and cups (Figure 21).
9. Demonstrate how to use measuring spoons and cups for measuring. Assist the student in using them to prepare simple snacks or parts of a meal.

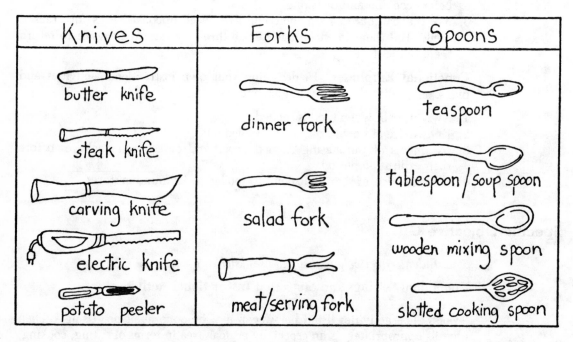

Figure 20. Knives, forks, and spoons chart.

10. Use a chart and/or pictures to identify various pots and pans used for boiling, frying, broiling, roasting, and baking (Figure 22). Color code pots and pans according to their use (e.g., red = oven, blue = top of stove). For more advanced use, color code for boiling, baking, and frying.
11. Demonstrate how to use various pots and pans for cooking. Assist the student in using each of them in preparing a snack or part of a meal.

Functional Emphases In designing your own instructional activities and plans, emphasize the following elements:

1. Awareness of safety procedures when using kitchen utensils.
2. Selection of utensils that are clean and appropriate.

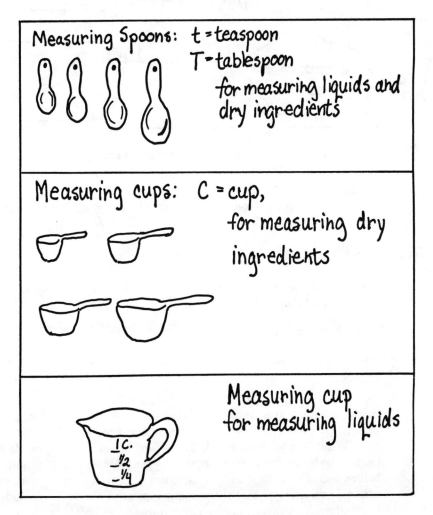

Figure 21. Measuring spoons and cups chart.

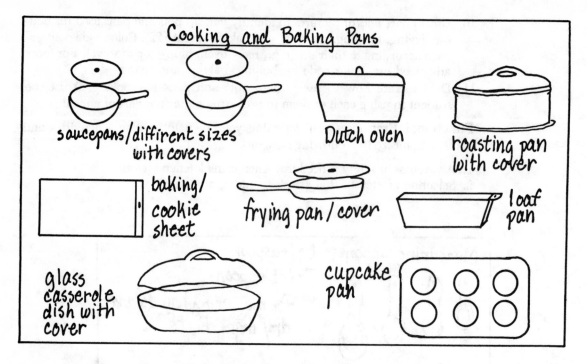

Figure 22. Cooking and baking pans chart.

3. Modification of utensils when necessary.
4. Use of utensils made from different materials and in different sizes.

Specific Objective H

The student prepares simple, nutritious snacks or parts of meals that require no heating or cooking.

Functional Settings and Suggested Instructional Activities

School   The activities listed below can also be done at home. Use of nutritious snacks instead of "junk food" needs to be stressed to both parents and child.

1. Demonstrate to the student how to prepare foods that require peeling before eating (e.g., tangerines, bananas, and hard-boiled eggs). Help the student peel each of these foods. Praise and encourage him throughout the task. When the food is peeled, allow him to eat it at appropriate times.
2. Demonstrate to the student how to prepare foods that require washing before eating (e.g., apples, peaches, pears, plums, grapes, leafy vegetables, carrots, and celery). Tell the student to wash each of these foods, indicating that each of them may be eaten immediately after being washed clean with no further preparation needed.

3. Demonstrate to the student how to prepare foods that merely require pouring from a container (fruit juices and milk). Assist the student in opening and pouring these liquids and enjoy the snack at an appropriate time.

4. Demonstrate to the student how to prepare foods that can be eaten directly from the container: finger foods such as peanuts, raisins, dry cereals, dried fruits, and pickles; and foods that require utensils, such as cottage cheese, yogurt, applesauce, canned fruits, pickled beets, sauerkraut, three-bean salad, pig's feet, gefilte fish, and sardines. Assist the student in preparing these foods and eating them. (*Note:* Pay attention to the student's individual tastes, special dietary needs, and cultural and religious backgrounds.)

5. Demonstrate how to prepare foods that require cutting (tomatoes, cucumbers, peppers, celery, carrots, grapefruit, and oranges) and trimming (lettuce, celery, and carrots) before eating. Assist the student in preparing each of these foods and follow through by eating them at appropriate times.

6. Demonstrate the preparation of foods that require spreading, such as mayonnaise, butter, margarine, mustard, ketchup, jellies, jams, spreadable cheese, and peanut butter. Assist the student in spreading each of these on bread, crackers, or celery. Eat the prepared snacks at appropriate times.

7. Demonstrate how to make sandwiches. Identify foods that can be used as sandwich filler (e.g., meats, cheese, spreadables, and salads). Assist the student in preparing sandwiches with the above foods either singly or in combination (peanut butter and jelly or ham and cheese). Assist the student in adding condiments such as mustard or mayonnaise.

8. Demonstrate how to prepare foods that may be mixed, such as vegetable, tuna, chicken, ham, cottage cheese, and fruit salads, fruit, cereal, milk (also instant powders such as skim milk), frozen concentrates, peanuts, and raisins. Assist the student in preparing each of these snacks. Eat the prepared meals at appropriate times.

Functional Emphases In designing your own instructional activities and plans, emphasize the following elements:

1. Selection of foods that have nutritional value.
2. Preparation of nutritional foods.
3. Awareness of special dietary needs.
4. Knowledge of recipes that use nutritional foods.
5. Awareness of cultural and religious patterns in types of foods and in special recipes.

Specific Objective I

The student effectively and safely operates major appliances, including a stove, microwave oven, and dishwasher.

Functional Settings and Suggested Instructional Activities

School   Find a stove in school that can be used for cooking activities and practice the following activities.

1. Demonstrate regulating flames underneath pots and pans. Encourage the use of a low flame (flames should never extend out beyond the sides of the pan). Assist the student and praise him for effectively and safely carrying out the cooking task.
2. Demonstrate the checking of water levels, cooking status of the food, and boiling levels to prevent boiling over or burning of foods. Demonstrate turning the burner off.
3. Demonstrate the use of a pot holder to remove lids and to remove pots and pans from the stove. Warn the student that he should be careful of escaping steam. Assist the student in these processes and reward him for effectively and safely doing them. Hang up or put away the pot holder after using it.
4. Demonstrate turning an oven first on and then off. Indicate that an oven is helpful for heating foods, for baking cakes, bread, and cookies, and for broiling and roasting foods. Warn that an oven can be dangerous.
5. Demonstrate turning the oven dial to various levels. Use an enlarged teacher-made dial or gauge for practice purposes. Assist the student in doing so safely and effectively.
6. Help the student to identify temperatures on packages to be heated in an oven. Tell him to match the numbers to corresponding ones on an oven dial.
7. Prepare foods that require the use of an oven. Encourage the student to become familiar with his oven, especially with how long it takes for the oven to go on (automatic pilot).
8. Assist the student in removing foods from the oven safely, including sliding of trays, use of pot holders, and waiting for some cooling to occur.
9. Practice the above activities for a variety of social occasions.

Home

1. Ask the parents to take their child into the kitchen and point out the stove. Tell them to indicate to the child in some way that the stove is needed to help cook food. Tell them to stress that a stove can be dangerous if it is not used correctly and point out hazards such as gas escaping because the burner has failed to light, has gone out, or is partially turned on. Tell them to warn the child of the heat of the flames or coils (electric), the heat occurring during cooking, and the heat remaining in pots, pot lids, and pot handles just used for cooking. The child should be reminded never to leave metal cooking utensils in pots because they retain heat and could burn his hand if he grasps them.
2. Ask the parents to demonstrate turning each burner on and off. Tell them to make continuous reference to safety hazards and safety checks through-

out. Remind them to indicate that, if the burner fails to light, it should be turned back off immediately.

3. Ask the parents to demonstrate putting pots and pans on the stove. Tell them to indicate that the child should make sure handles are on tight and that, when the pot or pan is placed on the stove, the handle should not be over another burner or hanging over the front of the stove. Tell them to help the child to do this and praise him for doing it effectively and safely.

Functional Emphases   In designing your own instructional activities and plans, emphasize the following elements:

1. Development of motor skills necessary to operate major appliances.
2. Knowledge of operating directions for stoves, ovens, dishwashers, and other major appliances.
3. Awareness of safety procedures to be observed when operating major appliances.
4. Avoidance of appliances that appear unsafe or are not working properly.
5. Awareness of aids used in cooking and washing dishes (e.g., pot holders and dishwasher detergent).
6. Knowledge and use of numbers found on oven dials and switches.
7. Awareness of procedures to follow in case of a fire.

Specific Objective J

The student effectively and safely operates simple appliances used in cooking.

Functional Settings and Suggested Instructional Activities

School   Activities 2 and 3 can also be done at home using the same or similar appliances.

1. Plan a party that requires the students to open cans (e.g., making lemonade or orange juice). Observe whether the student uses the can opener appropriately and safely. Praise him if he does it correctly.
2. Demonstrate the use of a toaster. Show the student how to plug the toaster in and show him that the dial is color or number coded. Warn the student of the following points: (1) always keep the dial or arrow in the middle, (2) never butter bread before you toast it, and (3) never insert anything but food in the toaster or in any electrical appliance. Tell the student that, if toast does not pop up in time or if it starts burning or smoking, he can push the button up to make it pop up. Demonstrate how to push the button up and remove the toast from the toaster. Show the student how to unplug the toaster. Urge him never to wrap cords around appliances or cover appliances while they are still warm and never to immerse electrical appliances or cords in water.
3. Demonstrate the use of a can opener to the student by following these steps. First, put the plug in the outlet. Second, demonstrate how to lift the

lever, and explain to him that the blade and magnet are on the lever. Holding the can by the bottom, put the can directly against the can opener and push the lever down using force. The blade should cut the can on the edge and the can will begin to rotate. After the can is completely opened, hold the can by the bottom and lift or release the lever. Remove the can and empty the contents from it. Using your index finger and thumb, carefully remove the lid from the magnet. Then place the lid in the empty can and dispose of it and unplug the appliance. (*Note:* Never plug in or unplug an appliance with wet hands.)

Functional Emphases In designing your own instructional activities and plans, emphasize the following elements:

1. Development of motor skills necessary to operate simple appliances.
2. Knowledge of operating directions for simple appliances.
3. Awareness of safety procedures to be observed in operating simple appliances.

Specific Objective K

The student prepares simple, nutritious snacks or part of meals requiring heating or minimal cooking.

Functional Settings and Suggested Instructional Activities

School

1. Demonstrate the use of a toaster for waffles, Pop Tarts, bread, English muffins, and bagels. Assist the student in doing so safely and effectively. Eat the prepared food as part of a regular meal.
2. Demonstrate the use of frying for cooking eggs, bacon, sausage, meats, and fish. Show the student how to put oil in the pan first. Practice. Assist the student in safely and effectively preparing these fried foods. Eat the prepared foods as part of a regular meal.

Home

1. Ask the parents to demonstrate to their child the use of boiling water for cooking vegetables, rice, macaroni, noodles, potatoes, prepared packages, soups, eggs, frankfurters, bouillon, tea, and hot chocolate. Tell them to assist him in doing so safely and effectively. The prepared food should be served as part of a regular meal.
2. Ask the parents to demonstrate to their child the use of the oven for heating frozen dinners, frozen pies, cakes, cookies, and bread, and for baking, roasting, and broiling. Tell them to assist him in doing so safely and effectively. The prepared food should be served as part of a regular meal.

Functional Emphases In designing your own instructional activities and plans, emphasize the following elements:

1. Awareness of nutritional foods.
2. Awareness of safety procedures used in using cooking utensils and appliances.
3. Knowledge of recipes.
4. Identification of cooking directions found on food and food products.

Specific Objective L

The student prepares simple, nutritious meals using cooking utensils and appliances.

Functional Settings and Suggested Instructional Activities

School

1. Visit the school cafeteria and observe the utensils that are used for cooking. Return to the class and discuss what was observed, and ask the student to explain why certain utensils are used for certain foods.
2. Repeat the activities discussed in the Home activities using classmates or guests from the school.

Home

1. Ask the parents to assist their child in preparing breakfast or one of the other daily meals. Tell them to provide an opportunity for him to use appliances and cooking utensils. The prepared meal should be served.
2. Ask the parents to plan a party with their child. Tell them to suggest that he invite a few friends or family members. Tell them to assist him in preparing for the party by planning a menu and cooking food (e.g., spaghetti, fruit drink, and pudding).

Functional Emphases In designing your own instructional activities and plans, emphasize the following elements:

1. Awareness of nutritional foods and food groups.
2. Awareness of safety procedures used in working wtih cooking utensils and appliances.
3. Knowledge of recipes.
4. Identification of cooking directions found on food and food products.

Specific Objective M

The student sets the table for serving informal meals.

Functional Settings and Suggested Instructional Activities

School

1. Assist the student in setting the table.
2. Demonstrate and then assist the student in folding a napkin. Guide him in placing it on the place setting or table.

Home   Ask the parents to practice the Class activities at home with their child.

Functional Emphases   In designing your own instructional activities and plans, emphasize the following elements:

1. Development of motor skills necessary to set a table (e.g., folding a napkin and serving a meal).
2. Identification of the different types of tableware and serving utensils.

Specific Objective N

The student washes, dries, and stores kitchen equipment, dishes, glasses, and silverware.

Functional Settings and Suggested Instructional Activities

School

1. After a party or eating, ask the student to help you in washing and drying the dishes. Praise him for doing a good job.
2. Bring the student to the school cafeteria and point out the various equipment, dishes, and silverware. Point out how the dishes are washed (both by hand and by machine).

Home

1. Ask the parents to identify the dish washing detergent to be used and distinguish it from other cleaning agents. Tell them to demonstrate the cleaning of dishes to their child.
2. Tell the parents to demonstrate different water temperatures to their child. Tell them to first help him fill three dishpans with water, and then ask him to feel the water in each pan (be sure none is too hot). They should select the water temperature that is most suitable for dishwashing and tell him why they selected it (e.g., hot water cuts grease, kills germs).
3. Ask the parents to display a dishcloth, dish towel, dishpan, scouring pad, dish rack, and draining board for their child to identify.
4. Ask the parents to stack the dishes on the counter in preparation for washing. Tell them to place the glasses in soapy water before storing table leftovers, and to use a wet dishcloth or sponge to wash off the table.
5. Ask the parents to demonstrate to their child washing first the glasses, then the china, then the silverware, and then the pots and pans. Remind them

to show the proper use of scouring pads and the placement of dishes on the drain board. Tell them to encourage the child to imitate their actions and practice washing the dishes.

Functional Emphases In designing your own instructional activities and plans, emphasize the following elements:

1. Development of motor skills necessary to wash and dry hands.
2. Knowledge of how to measure appropriate amounts of detergents and cleaners.
3. Awareness of how and where to store kitchen equipment and materials.
4. Use of cleaning and washing aids (e.g., drain boards, silverware racks, and scouring pads).
5. Awareness of water temperatures and how to regulate them.

Specific Objective O

The student stores unused and/or leftover food in appropriate wrappings, containers, and places.

Functional Settings and Suggested Instructional Activities

School Repeat the Home activities when appropriate (i.e., after covered dish dinners or parties).

Home

1. Ask the parents to demonstrate to their child wrapping an unused portion of meat or meat leftovers in aluminum foil or clear plastic wrap. The child is to imitate their actions and to wrap leftovers. Remind them to indicate that all leftover meats or unused portions of meat are to be put in the refrigerator. Tell them to assist him in refrigerating the meat and to warn him in some way that defrosted meats and other things go into the refrigerator and never back into the freezer.
2. Ask the parents to demonstrate to their child placing non-meat leftovers and unused portions of food into covered bowls, Pyrex containers, Tupperware, and cleaned used jars. Tell them to assist their child in doing so. They should indicate that all leftovers and all unused portions of foods that were not originally in paper or cardboard packages are to be stored in the refrigerator. Tell them to assist the child in doing this and reward him.

Functional Emphases In designing your own instructional activities and plans, emphasize the following elements:

1. Development of motor skills necessary to wrap food.
2. Knowledge of types of containers used to store food.
3. Knowledge of health hazards that can be created by not refrigerating food properly.

4. Awareness of how to use temperature dials in refrigerators and freezers.
5. Avoidance of saving small amounts of food that will not be used and may get lost in the refrigerator.

General Objective II

The student will be functionally independent in purchasing and maintaining his clothes in a manner that allows him to perform optimally.

Specific Objectives

The student:

A. purchases needed clothes.
B. cleans his clothes, linens, and towels.
C. sews and mends his clothes.
D. sends his clothes to an appropriate person or place for cleaning, major repairs, and/or alterations.
E. stores clothes after purchasing or cleaning.
F. packs clothes for trips and outings.

Specific Objective A

The student purchases needed clothes.

Functional Settings and Suggested Instructional Activities

School

1. Make a list of clothes the student should have on hand, including shoes, socks or stockings, undergarments, and outer garments. The list should include the quantity of each article required to meet his individual needs. Help the student determine the colors, fabrics, and style that best suit his needs, age, body type, and coloring.
2. Make a "Clothing Chart" (Figure 23) to which the student may refer for the purpose of determining whether his clothing stock is complete. This chart should include his size for each article of clothing and the quantity needed. Also indicate the price range for each item appropriate to his economic status. Update the chart periodically as his economic situation changes and as his sizes change. For nonreaders, use pictures of clothing rather than the written word.

Student's Name			
Article	Number Needed	Size	Approximate Price
Shorts	10	34	3/8.00
T-Shirts	10	34	3/8.00
Socks	10	9½	1.19 each
Work Shirts	5	Medium	12.00 each
Work Pants	3	34 Regular	18.00 each
Pajamas	2	Medium	12.00 each
School Shirts	5	Medium	14.00 each
School Pants	3	34 Regular	18.00 each
Sport Jacket	1	34	55.00 each
Winter Coat	1	34	85.00 each
Misc.			

Figure 23. Clothing chart: sizes, numbers, and prices.

Home and Community

1. Ask the parents to demonstrate checking their child's articles of clothing for excessive wear and tear. Tell them to show him samples of clothing that are no longer serviceable and contrast these with samples of clothing of varying condition and age that are still wearable. Tell them to assist him in making comparisons and in separating the wearable from the unwearable.
2. Assist the student in making a wallet-size card on which has been written or typed his sizes for various items of apparel (update when necessary). Indicate that he should use the card for reference and/or for communicating information to a salesperson. On this card, also include the price range for each article of clothing. Go on a shopping trip and first check his purchases each time, then spot-check after he shows some success.

Functional Emphases In designing your own instructional activities and plans, emphasize the following elements:

1. Selection of clothes that are well made, nonflammable, and not overly expensive.
2. Awareness of material that might cause an allergic reaction.
3. Location of stores and places that sell clothes in the sizes and price range needed.
4. Awareness of how clothes should fit (i.e., not too tight or too loose).

Specific Objective B

The student cleans his clothes, linens, and towels.

Functional Settings and Suggested Instructional Activities

School

1. Demonstrate the use of an automatic washing machine, including the use of coins, detergents, and powdered bleaches. Separate clothing to be machine washed into two categories: colored fabrics and white fabrics. Assist the student in using the washing machine.
2. Demonstrate the use of the automatic dryer. Assist the student in using the dryer.

Home and Community

1. Ask the parents to assist their child in separating his clothes that are dirty and need washing from clothes that are still clean enough to wear. Tell them to show him how to examine clothes for dirt marks, grease, and other stains.
2. Ask the parents to establish a routine schedule for washing their child's clothes—for example, undershorts and undershirts are to be washed after one day's wear, bed linens and towels after one week's use. Tell them to make a clothing wear and washing chart indicating the day of the week for washing clothes, and the number of days each article of clothing is to be worn.
3. Ask the parents to assist their child in separating dirty clothes, linens, and towels into cleaning categories. Suggest that they use rebus labels sewn into garments to indicate how each article is to be cleaned, (i.e., a sketch of a washing machine for washable clothes, a sink for hand washing, and a store front for dry cleaning). Tell them that color labels may be substituted for rebuses when appropriate.
4. Ask the parents to demonstrate to their child how to hand wash items in the sink. Tell them to assist him in washing and help him in hanging up

clothes for drying in a suitable place. Suggest that they use Woolite or a similar product to protect garments from shrinking and fading.

5. Take the student to a laundromat and assist him in using the washing and drying machines. Point out any special washing instructions and supervise him as he does his laundry.
6. Assist the student in preparing clothes to be dry cleaned for the dry cleaner. Take a trip to the dry cleaner or arrange for a laundry pick-up service.

Functional Emphases In designing your own instructional activities and plans, emphasize the following elements:

1. Use of automatic washing machines and dryers.
2. Knowledge of how to measure exact amounts of detergent, bleach, or fabric softeners when doing a wash.
3. Location of community laundromats and/or cleaners.
4. Recognition of information on labels that designate poison (e.g., on bleach bottles).
5. Awareness of the appropriate times when clothes need to be cleaned.

Specific Objective C

The student sews and mends his clothes.

Functional Settings and Suggested Instructional Activities

School

1. Demonstrate how to replace a missing button. Assist the student in selecting a suitable button.
2. Plan a project that requires sewing using appropriate needles and materials. Ask the student to bring in a garment of his that needs mending and use this for his sewing project.

Home

1. Ask the parents to demonstrate to their child how to sew a seam that has come apart. Tell them to assist him in threading a needle, knotting one end of the thread, and closing the seam. Tell them to practice with the child and reward him for accomplishing the task.
2. Tell the parents to demonstrate to their child how to sew a patch on jeans, pants, and shirts when appropriate. Tell them to review threading a needle and knotting the thread. Tell them to assist him in placing the patch over a hole. Suggest that they help him to pin the patch in place and to stitch around the inner edge of the patch, and remind him to remove and replace pins.

Functional Emphases In designing your own instructional activities and plans, emphasize the following elements:

1. Development of motor skills necessary for sewing and mending.
2. Knowledge of when clothes may need some simple mending or when they should be taken to a tailor.
3. Knowledge of safety skills needed when using needles, pins, and scissors.
4. Awareness of different types of threads, mending, and patching materials.

Specific Objective D

The student sends his clothes to an appropriate person or place for cleaning, major repairs, and/or alterations.

Functional Settings and Suggested Instructional Activities

School

1. Explain to the student that we sometimes need help from other people in sewing. Indicate in some way that there are people called tailors who perform special sewing tasks for money.
2. Show the student the kinds of repairs and alterations that require the service of a tailor (these should be determined by the individual skills of the student). Such services might include shortening sleeves, taking in or letting out of seams, or putting cuffs on.

Home and Community

1. Ask the parents to gather their child's clothes that need cleaning. Tell them to point out where the clothing is soiled or dirty. Tell them to take him to a dry cleaner and indicate that this is where his clothes can be professionally cleaned.
2. Tell the parents to take a trip through the community with their child. Tell them to point out businesses that do cleaning, tailoring, and/or alterations.
3. When the student has the need for tailoring services, take him to a tailor for this purpose. When the garment is ready, praise his appearance in the altered garment.

Functional Emphases In designing your own instructional activities and plans, emphasize the following elements:

1. Awareness of when clothes need to be cleaned, repaired, or altered.
2. Knowledge of places in the community that do dry cleaning and tailoring.
3. Awareness of the cost for tailoring and alterations (this information should be continuously updated because these costs change rapidly).

Specific Objective E

The student stores clothes after purchasing or cleaning.

Functional Settings and Suggested Instructional Activities

School and Community

1. Take the student on a trip to a department store. Once there, visit the area of the store that sells garment bags. Point out how garment bags are used and which ones are appropriate for certain clothes.
2. At the end of a season visit a dry cleaning store that provides for clothes storage. Bring in some clothes (e.g., winter coats and work clothing) that you would like to have professionally stored. Explain to the student that, although this is an excellent way of protecting clothes, it can be expensive.

Home

1. Tell the parents to bring their child with them when they have to pick up dry cleaning. Tell them to show the child where they put the clean clothes (e.g., in a closet, garment bag, or chest) when they arrive home.
2. Tell the parents to point out to their child where certain clothes are stored, (e.g., coats, rainwear, and seasonal outfits). Tell them to check at certain times to see if he is putting his clothes away appropriately.

Functional Emphases In designing your own instructional activities and plans, emphasize the following elements:

1. Awareness of the chemicals used in the storing of clothes (i.e., moth balls and flakes).
2. Selection of an appropriate place within the house to store clothes.
3. Knowledge of special directions on labels of clothing that pertain to their storage.

Specific Objective F

The student packs clothes for trips and outings.

Functional Settings and Suggested Instructional Activities

Home and Community

1. Tell the parents to show their child how to pack his clothes in a suitcase and, when appropriate, a garment bag when planning a trip. Tell them to start the packing and then urge him to finish.
2. Tell the parents to plan an outing with their child as part of a leisure experience. Tell them to prepare for the outing by having the child pack

sports clothes in a duffel bag or knapsack. Tell them to monitor how well the child packs his clothes and provide praise when appropriate.

3. Plan to have the student visit a relative. Have him pack for the trip, taking into consideration the type and amount of clothes needed and the projected weather conditions.

4. Plan to have the student stay overnight with a friend. Once these arrangements have been made, tell him to pack the right amount of clothes for the trip. Emphasize the need for toiletries, sleepware, and any special medications.

Functional Emphases   In designing your own instructional activities and plans, emphasize the following elements:

1. Awareness of how to pack clothes in a suitcase, garment bag, or duffel bag/knapsack.
2. Awareness of what to pack according to projected weather conditions.
3. Identification of bags and suitcases according to size, strength, and weight.

General Objective III

The student will be functionally independent in caring for his living quarters, appliances, and furnishings in a manner that allows him to perform optimally.

Special Objectives

The student:

A. purchases appropriate equipment and materials necessary for the maintenance of his living quarters.
B. appropriately uses the appliances needed to keep his living quarters clean.
C. uses cleaning materials appropriately.
D. stores small appliances and cleaning materials in appropriate places.
E. follows a schedule for general house cleaning.
F. appropriately uses furniture and household accessories.
G. makes his own bed.
H. makes minor household repairs.
I. seeks appropriate help for repairs to household appliances and accessories when necessary.

Specific Objective A

The student purchases appropriate equipment and materials necessary for the maintenance of his living quarters.

Functional Settings and Suggested Instructional Activities

School

1. Look through Sears, Wards, hardware, or discount store catalogs, newspaper ads, and circulars with the student. Find the equipment needed for the maintenance of his living quarters. Put markers in the catalogs to note where the materials are. Cut out ads from newspapers and circulars for needed cleaning equipment such as mops, brooms, vacuum cleaners, or electric brooms.
2. Point out the prices for a variety of cleaning equipment. Make a language experience chart, and list the equipment needed and the prices for each catalog or circular.

Home and Community

1. Ask the parents to show their child different cleaning equipment and materials. Tell them to explain and demonstrate the use of mops, brooms, dustpans, a vacuum cleaner, dust cloths, sponges, furniture polish, cleanser, and window cleaner when they are cleaning the house.
2. Take the student on a shopping trip to different stores to buy cleaning equipment and materials. Make the student responsible for buying the particular items needed for his living quarters from his own pay, social security, allotments, allowance, or school funds.

Functional Emphases   In designing your own instructional activities and plans, emphasize the following elements:

1. Identification of well made and safe cleaning equipment.
2. Adaptation of equipment to make it easier to use (e.g., wrapping tape or padding around the handles on brooms and/or mops).
3. Awareness of stores that sell cleaning equipment.
4. Knowledge of information on warning and instructional labels.
5. Awareness of safety rules when using electrical appliances.
6. Selection of cleaners and chemicals that are nontoxic and safe.

Specific Objective B

The student appropriately uses the appliances needed to keep his living quarters clean.

Functional Settings and Suggested Instructional Activities

School

1. Invite the custodian to come to the classroom as a guest lecturer to discuss the importance of a clean building, stressing health, safety, and appearance factors.
2. If the student lives in a residential setting, make him responsible for cleaning his own living area. Perhaps take mini–field trips to each student's room to see how well he maintains it. This should encourage the student to keep his quarters neat.

Home

1. Ask the parents to demonstrate equipment they use during house cleaning (i.e., broom, mop, dustpan, vacuum cleaner, and electric broom).
2. Ask the parents to make a housekeeping chart. As their child completes his work for the week with a particular piece of equipment, the parents should evaluate his work. If he has mastered the use of the equipment, they should place a small picture of that piece of equipment beside his name on the chart and assign him another job. If he has not mastered the use of the equipment, they should praise him for trying hard and assign him the same job for the next week. Tell them to explain to him why he did not get a picture on his chart.

Functional Emphases   In designing your own instructional activities and plans, emphasize the following elements:

1. Selection of safe and well-made appliances.
2. Recognition of information found on warning labels and in appliance direction booklets.
3. Maintenance of equipment after it is used.
4. Selection of the right or most appropriate piece of equipment for the job.

Specific Objective C

The student uses cleaning materials appropriately.

Functional Settings and Suggested Instructional Activities

Home

1. Ask the parents to demonstrate the use of window cleaners, cleansers, sponges, dustcloths, household cleaners, and furniture polish. (*Note:* Because of its poisonous contents, it is best if furniture polish is used in a spray can or squeeze bottle rather than in a bottle that requires pouring). Tell them to remind him of safety precautions and review with him the things that are for eating and drinking and the things that are not.
2. Ask the parents to present various cleaning situations to their child and ask what materials would be needed for each. Encourage them to ask him to

point to the objects and carry out the operation: for example, sink stains—cleanser and sponge; dusty furniture—furniture polish and dust cloth; fingerprints on doors or woodwork—household cleanser and sponge.

Functional Emphases In designing your own instructional activities and plans, emphasize the following elements:

1. Selection of safe cleaning materials (i.e., nontoxic fumes).
2. Recognition of stores that sell cleaning materials.
3. Selection of appropriate-size containers.
4. Measurement of wet and dry chemicals for mixing.
5. Identification of "key" warning words on labels.
6. Knowledge of directions found on container labels or in brochures supplied with the cleaning product.

Specific Objective D

The student stores small appliances and cleaning materials in appropriate places.

Functional Settings and Suggested Instructional Activities

School

1. Take the student to the custodian and ask the custodian to show the student the storage places for cleaning materials. Stress the necessity for storing cleaning materials in appropriate places and that it is safer for children and pets if materials are stored in high or locked places.
2. Upon returning to the classroom, instruct the student to assemble the cleaning equipment and materials. Help him to choose an appropriate storage place for them—perhaps a part of the clothing closet that is not in use or that has separate shelves. Put the name or a picture of the item in or on the storage area.

Home

1. Ask the parents to take their child around the home and point out all the small appliances. Tell them to point out places where these appliances are kept when not in use. Also tell them to show the child where appliances used daily (e.g., toaster or electric can opener) are kept. Ask them to emphasize that, when stored, all the appliances should always be clean so they will not attract insects or create an unsanitary condition.
2. Tell the parents to discuss the storage of cleaning materials and appliances with their child. Tell them to explain that appliances need care and should be stored carefully in a closet or kitchen. They should stress that cleaning materials contain dangerous chemicals and are flammable, and should never be stored with food or in hot places; a separate box, bag, or bucket is the safest place for the storage of cleaning materials.

Functional Emphases In designing your own instructional activities and plans, emphasize the following elements:

1. Selection of appropriate places for storing.
2. Knowledge of how to store specific cleaning materials and small appliances, i.e., in a well-vented area, away from heat or excessive cold.
3. Avoidance of storing volatile cleaning materials in the home.

Specific Objective E

The student follows a schedule for general house cleaning.

Functional Settings and Suggested Instructional Activities

School

1. During the class day, encourage the student to do specific cleaning jobs at specific times of the day. For example, the student can wash off the tables after eating, empty wastebaskets at the end of the school day, and wipe the sink after grooming time.
2. Make a schedule chart (Figure 24) for the student's classroom duties. Instruct the student to check daily to find his job assignment and the time to do it.

For older or reading students

Duty Schedule

Students' Names	Date											
John	Sink	Waste basket	Table	Floors								
Mary	Table	Sink	Doors									

For younger or non-reading students

Job Chart

Name	Waste Basket	Windows	
Mike	✓		
Peter		✓	
Stephen			
Madelyn			
Billie			

Figure 24. Class duty schedule and job chart.

Home

1. Ask the parents to discuss schedules with their child. Ask them to talk about doing certain things at the same time each day (e.g., getting up, eating, and going to bed). Tell them to help the child make up a daily schedule.
2. Tell the parents to provide their child a place to hang his schedule. Tell them to talk about the daily cleaning jobs he does and when he can do them: for example, make the bed after I get up; wash up after I make my bed; get dressed after I wash up.

Functional Emphases In designing your own instructional activities and plans, emphasize the following elements:

1. Knowledge of how to read a schedule.
2. Knowledge of how to tell time or decode time symbols.
3. Calculation of the time needed to perform a job.

Specific Objective F

The student appropriately uses furniture and household accessories.

Functional Settings and Suggested Instructional Activities

School

1. Use scale model furniture or pictures of furniture, and ask the student to name each piece of furniture and its use.
2. Help the student to make posters or pictures illustrating the do's and don'ts for using household things, and add them to a safety bulletin board.

Home

1. Ask the parents to discuss household accidents with their child, making the key point that accidents are often the result of careless and inappropriate use of household furniture.
2. Ask the parents to tell their child to choose a household article or piece of furniture (chair, table, lamp, toaster) in the home. Tell them to ask him to name its proper use and discuss the danger of misuse. Tell them to do this with each piece of furniture and appliance he can think of or those he comes in contact with.

Functional Emphases In designing your own instructional activities and plans, emphasize the following elements:

1. Knowledge of the safety rules involved in using household accessories.
2. Selection of furniture and accessories that are well made, cost effective, and warranted.
3. Calculation of the money needed to purchase furniture and household accessories.

Specific Objective G

The student makes his own bed.

Functional Settings and Suggested Instructional Activities

School

1. Show the student the linen needed to make a bed. For making the bed, the student will need two sheets, a pillow case, one or two blankets, and a bed-spread. (Flat sheets are recommended as top and bottom sheeets; although fitted sheets are a better fit, they are difficult to get on.) Ask the student to name or identify each item and to demonstrate its use.
2. On a "Housekeeping Chart," place a picture or sketch of a bed next to the student's name once he independently makes his bed.

Home

1. Ask the parents to demonstrate making a bed to their child.
2. Ask the parents to engage their child in making a bed after he has had the opportunity to observe the activity several times. Tell the parents to make the bed themselves until the last step (i.e., tucking the spread under the pillow), and then have the child do the last step. Once he has mastered this last step, the parents should make the bed for him until the next to the last step and have him then do the last two steps. They should proceed in this way until he can make a bed independently.

Functional Emphases In designing your own instructional activities and plans, emphasize the following elements:

1. Knowledge of how to make a bed.
2. Selection of appropriate-size (full, king, queen, or twin) bed materials.
3. Avoidance of purchasing poorly made bed materials or those that are not permanent press.

Specific Objective H

The student makes minor household repairs.

Functional Settings and Suggested Instructional Activities

School

1. Discuss with the student those occasions when screws and a screwdriver would be needed for home repairs (i.e., to tighten handles of cooking pots and to tighten screws on doorknobs or switch plates).
2. Allow one or two of the students to bring in a small object that requires a minor repair, e.g., a plug on a lamp (be sure to get the parents' permission). Demonstrate how to repair the object.

Home

1. Ask the parents to show their child a lamp with a burned-out light bulb. Tell them to explain that the lamp will not work until the light bulb has been changed. Tell them to demonstrate changing a light bulb.
2. Ask the parents to discuss with their child those occasions when hammering would be used in the home: hanging pictures, fastening down loose floor molding when nails are protruding, and securing parts of objects.

Functional Emphases   In designing your own instructional activities and plans, emphasize the following elements:

1. Knowledge of when a simple repair can be made or when the object should be sent to a repair shop.
2. Safety factors involved in making simple repairs (e.g., carefully handling light bulbs, unplugging lamps or appliances before working on them, and carefully and appropriately using aids such as stepladders).
3. Knowledge of tools and materials needed for simple repairs.
4. Use of instruction/repair manuals or booklets when appropriate.

Specific Objective I

The student seeks appropriate help for repairs to household appliances and accessories when necessary.

Functional Settings and Suggested Instructional Activities

School   Many of the activities listed below can also be done at home. (*Note:* It is best to teach these types of activities only after consultation with the parent for appropriateness.)

1. With the less able student, it is best to tell him to go to an adult for assistance (e.g., to a resident manager, a familiar neighbor, ward personnel, or parents). Show him how to explain the problem or take the adult to the problem.
2. Make a pictorial list (pictures from catalogs) of household appliances and accessories. Discuss with the student the possibility that they may break. Ask the student what he would do if his toaster, TV, toilet, or sink broke. During the discussion, mention that there are people called repair persons who can help. Stress that these people are specially trained to fix things.
3. Play a question-and-answer game while referring to the list made in Activity 2. Ask the student, "If your _____ broke, who would repair it?" _____. For example, ask about a broken television (TV repair person), toaster (small appliance repair shop), or iron (small appliance repair shop), or a clogged sink or toilet drains that overrun (plumber or apartment maintenance person/landlord).
4. If the student is able to use the phone, and has permission, teach him the

information number and how to use information to find numbers for various types of repair shops.

Functional Emphases   In designing your own instructional activities and plans, emphasize the following elements:

1. Knowledge of when repairs to household appliances and accessories require professional help.
2. Knowledge of where to seek help for repairs.
3. Use of the yellow pages to look up repair services.
4. Calculation of how much it will cost to repair an appliance versus purchasing a new one.

General Objective IV

The student will operate simple appliances, objects, conveniences, and home accessories.

Specific Objectives

The student:

A. plugs in and unplugs appliances.
B. uses light switches and switches that turn appliances and conveniences on and off.
C. locks and unlocks catches, locks, and chains on doors.
D. picks up and dials a regular and a pushbutton phone and engages in a telephone conversation.
E. raises, lowers, and adjusts venetian blinds and window shades.
F. opens and closes cabinets, cupboards, drawers, and doors.
G. uses cooking utensils, including pots, pans, and kettles.
H. operates small and large electrical appliances.
I. uses bathroom facilities and accessories.
J. uses grooming accessories and appliances.
K. winds and sets clocks.
L. operates recreational appliances for entertainment and information, including video games, televisions, radios, stereos, and videotape recorders and disks.
M. adjusts thermostats.
N. operates cleaning equipment and appliances.
O. uses coin-operated machines and equipment.
P. operates ticket machines found in bakeries, supermarkets, and stores.
Q. uses self-service elevators.

R. uses personal aids.

S. puts on and adjusts jewelry.

Specific Objective A

The student plugs in and unplugs appliances.

Functional Settings and Suggested Instructional Activities

School

1. Assign jobs to the student within the learning area. As one of his jobs, make the student responsible for unplugging the record player and taperecorder each afternoon just before dismissal. Expect the student to plug in the equipment the next morning so that it is ready for the day's use. Rotate jobs so that each student has a turn at each job.
2. Show the student an electric percolator. Point out the various parts: the pot itself, the detachable cord, the receptacle for the plug, and the plug that goes into the electrical outlet. Be certain to stress the difference between the plug that goes into the pot and the one that goes into the electrical unit.

Home

1. Ask the parents to show their child the plugs on various household appliances and equipment. Tell them to point out two- and three-pronged plugs. (A three-pronged plug may be found on grounding plugs on heavy equipment such as dishwashers, clothes washers, clothes dryers, and air conditioners.)
2. Ask the parents to show their child electrical wall outlets that are found throughout the home and point out the two or three slots in the outlet. Tell them to hold the appliance plug near the outlet and show the child that the prongs on the plug fit into the slots or openings in the electrical outlet. Tell them to warn him that appliances must be turned off before inserting the plug into the outlet.

Functional Emphases In designing your own instructional activities and plans, emphasize the following elements:

1. Awareness of safety procedures when using plugs.
2. Selection of appliances that are well made and bear the Underwriters' Laboratories (UL) seal.
3. Awareness of when cords or plugs should not be used because of damage, wear, or inappropriate size.
4. Avoidance of overloading appliances or using them to do work they are not designed to do.

Specific Objective B

The student uses light switches and switches that turn appliances and conveniences on and off.

Functional Settings and Suggested Instructional Activities

School

1. Show the student a variety of lamps with various types of on-off switches. Include a regular turning type of switch, one that is shaped like a key, a push-button such as that on most fluorescent lamps, and a switch that is pushed in one direction to turn the light on and in the opposite direction to turn the light off. Demonstrate using each type of switch. Tell the student to imitate your actions and practice using the various types of switches.
2. Take the student to the homemaking unit or any place in the building with carpeting. Tell the student to turn the vacuum cleaner on, vacuum the carpet, and turn the vacuum cleaner off.
3. Bring a few flashlights into the classroom or learning area. Show them to the student and point out the various parts of the flashlight: the body, the switch, and the lens. (Plastic flashlights are best because they are light-weight, easy to handle, and unbreakable.) Demonstrate turning a flashlight on and off. Do this a number of times, telling the student what you are doing as you do it. Tell the student to imitate your actions and to practice turning the flashlight on and off.

Home

1. Tell the parents to show their child a vacuum cleaner. Tell them to point out the on-off switch and demonstrate its use. The child should vacuum a carpet when appropriate.
2. Tell the parents to demonstrate to their child turning an air conditioner or fan on and off. Tell them to allow the child to turn the air conditioner or fan on and off at appropriate times.

Functional Emphases In designing your own instructional activities and plans, emphasize the following elements:

1. Awareness of safety procedures to follow when using switches (e.g., not using a switch with wet hands).
2. Knowledge of when a switch needs replacing.
3. Avoidance of switches that appear unsafe or are poorly made.
4. Experience in using a variety of switches.

Specific Objective C

The student locks and unlocks catches, locks, and chains on doors.

Functional Settings and Suggested Instructional Activities

School

1. Construct a locking board. Secure a variety of locks, chains, and catches on a heavy piece of wood. Tell the student to practice locking and unlocking the various locks, chains, and catches on the board. After this activity find the same type of locks on doors and point them out.
2. Take the student to a door with a lock that locks and unlocks with a skeleton key. Show the student the skeleton key. Point out the section of the key that is inserted into the keyhole. Insert the key into the keyhole and turn it until the door locks. Encourage the student to imitate your actions and to practice locking and unlocking the door.

Home

1. Ask the parents to take their child to a window with a lock on it. Tell them to close the window tightly, and lock and unlock the window. The child should imitate their actions and practice locking and unlocking the window.
2. Ask the parents to take their child to a door with a safety chain. Tell them to point out the chain and the slot into which the chain slides, and to grasp the end of the chain with a thumb and forefinger. Next they should place the end of the chain into the wide end of the slot and slide the chain down or across to secure it. The child should imitate their actions and practice securing the safety chain.
3. Ask the parents to take their child to an aluminum storm door or screen door. Tell them to point out the small button or catch that locks and unlocks the storm door (this is usually located directly below the doorknob or handle). Tell them to lock and unlock the door and to ask the child to imitate their actions and lock and unlock the screen door.

Functional Emphases In designing your own instructional activities and plans, emphasize the following elements:

1. Development of motor skills necessary to use a variety of locks, catches, and chains on doors.
2. Use of a variety of locks in a variety of areas.
3. Awareness of safety hazards when using locks, catches, and chains on doors.
4. Use of locks that are well made.

Specific Objective D

The student picks up and dials a regular and a pushbutton phone and engages in a telephone conversation.

Functional Settings and Suggested Instructional Activities

School

1. Demonstrate dialing both dial and pushbutton telephones. Tell the student to imitate your actions and to practice using these telephones.
2. Role play phone conversations. Divide students into twos and assign each duo a topic of conversation (e.g., reporting an emergency or making arrangements to meet someone). Be sure the student picks up the receiver and talks into the phone.
3. Print phone numbers on flash cards (e.g., the weather and time). Tell the student to practice dialing the printed phone numbers on both types of telephones.

Home

1. Ask the parents to show their child the telephone (both dial and pushbutton styles). (*Note:* they may borrow practice phones and teletrainers from the phone company.) Tell them to point out the similarities and differences between them. The child should use the phones.
2. Ask the parents to give their child a personal list of important phone numbers. Tell them to assist him in making calls to his family and friends.

Functional Emphases In designing your own instructional activities and plans, emphasize the following elements:

1. Development of motor skills necessary to dial a phone.
2. Use of a variety of phones made by a variety of companies.
3. Use of appropriate manners when engaging in phone conversations.
4. Awareness of when a phone is not working properly and of steps to follow to correct the situation.

Specific Objective E

The student raises, lowers, and adjusts venetian blinds and window shades.

Functional Settings and Suggested Instructional Activities

School

1. Point out window shades in the classroom or take the student to the cafeteria, homemaking room, or a part of the school building where there are window shades. Point out the window shades, and demonstrate how to

raise and adjust each. Tell the student to imitate your actions and to practice raising and lowering the window shades. Tell the student to adjust the shades all the way down, all the way up, and halfway open. When showing filmstrips, assign different students the job of raising, lowering, and adjusting the window shades.

2. Tell the student to imitate your actions and to raise and adjust venetian blinds.

Home

1. Ask the parents to demonstrate raising and lowering a window shade to their child. Tell them to describe what they are doing as they do it.
2. Ask the parents to demonstrate raising, lowering, and adjusting venetian blinds to their child. Tell them to describe what they are doing as they do it.

Functional Emphases In designing your own instructional activities and plans, emphasize the following elements:

1. Development of motor skills necessary to raise, lower, and adjust shades and blinds.
2. Use of a variety of sizes and shapes of blinds and shades.
3. Avoidance of purchasing shades and blinds that are poorly made.

Specific Objective F

The student opens and closes cabinets, cupboards, drawers, and doors.

Functional Settings and Suggested Instructional Activities

School

1. Assign the student jobs involving opening cabinets and cupboards (art cupboards, kitchen cabinets, and storage cabinets). Tell the student to place art supplies in cupboards, pots, pans, and canned goods in kitchen cabinets, and mops, brooms, and buckets in storage cabinets at appropriate times.
2. Send the student on errands outside the classroom. Require him to close the classroom door.
3. Demonstrate closing a drawer that is crooked to the students. First center the drawer in the middle of its opening, allowing an equal amount of space on each side of the drawer (for example, if it is too far to the left, push the drawer to the right to even it out). Then close the drawer from the middle.

Home

1. Ask the parents to remind their child to close the door when he uses the bathroom. Tell them to stress privacy and to remind him to close the door each time he uses the bathroom.
2. Tell the parents to demonstrate opening and closing the refrigerator and freezer compartment drawers. Tell them to do this a number of times and to tell their child to imitate their actions and to practice opening and closing the refrigerator.
3. Tell the parents to demonstrate opening and closing a cabinet or cupboard door with a knob. Ask them to tell their child what they are doing as they do it.

Functional Emphases   In designing your own instructional activities and plans, emphasize the following elements:

1. Development of motor skills necessary for opening and closing doors, drawers, cupboards, and cabinets.
2. Awareness of safety factors to follow when closing drawers and doors (e.g., avoiding catching fingers).
3. Modification of drawers, cupboards, and cabinets when appropriate (e.g., using large knobs).
4. Appropriate ways of opening and closing doors, drawers, cabinets, and cupboards.

Specific Objective G

The student uses cooking utensils, including pots, pans, and kettles.

Functional Settings and Suggested Instructional Activities

School

1. Bring a selection of pots and pans with lids into the classroom. Show the student the various sizes of pots and pans and their corresponding lids. Practice matching them.
2. Do simple cooking activities that require placing lids on pots, pans, and casserole dishes and removing the lids.

Home

1. Ask the parents to demonstrate placing a lid on a pan and removing it and then have their child imitate these actions.
2. Tell the parents to demonstrate placing a lid on a casserole dish and removing it. Tell them to remind their child that casserole dishes are more fragile than pots and pans, so he should be gentle when placing the lids on casseroles and removing them.

3. Ask the parents to show their child a capped-spout tea kettle. Tell them to explain that the spout must be opened and closed to pour water in and out of the kettle. Tell them to show the two most common types of spout control: the kettle with a button on the handle that opens and closes the spout and the kettle with a curved hook under the handle that opens and closes the spout.

Functional Emphases In designing your own instructional activities and plans, emphasize the following elements:

1. Development of motor skills necessary to use cooking utensils, pots, and pans.
2. Use of a variety of cooking utensils, pots, and pans.
3. Awareness of safety procedures when using cooking utensils, pots, and pans.
4. Avoidance of utensils or pots and pans that are worn or are in poor shape.

Specific Objective H

The student operates small and large electrical appliances.

Functional Settings and Suggested Instructional Activities

School

1. Bring an electric can opener into the classroom or learning area. Demonstrate its use. Tell the student to imitate your actions and to practice lifting and lowering the lever of the can opener. Give the student clean empty cans and let him practice opening the unopened end.
2. Following physical education or cooking activities, take the student to a laundry room or area where there is an automatic clothes washer. Tell the student to lift the lid of the washing machine and to put gym suits or soiled dish towels into the washing machine. Demonstrate how to use the washing machine.

Home

1. Ask the parents to demonstrate to their child the small appliances found in the kitchen. Tell them to allow him to first observe and then practice using the appliances.
2. Ask the parents to prepare a simple breakfast of juice and toast, frozen French toast, or waffles that are cooked in the toaster. Tell them to make their child responsible for putting the bread into the toaster, pushing the lever down, or removing the bread from the toaster.
3. Ask the parents to prepare a simple lunch (canned soup or canned spaghetti, canned vegetables, and canned fruit). Tell them to have their child open the cans.

Functional Emphases In designing your own instructional activities and plans, emphasize the following elements:

1. Use of a variety of small and large electrical appliances.
2. Awareness of safety factors involved when using appliances.
3. Avoidance of purchasing appliances that do not have the Underwriters' Laboratories (UL) seal.
4. Avoidance of purchasing appliances that appear to be poorly made or that contain no warranty.

Specific Objective I

The student uses bathroom facilities and accessories. For instructional activities and functional emphases, refer to Chapter 2, General Objective I.

Specific Objective J

The student uses grooming accessories and appliances.

Functional Settings and Suggested Instructional Activities

School

1. Tell the student to wash his hair as part of classroom grooming activities. Once his hair has been washed, tell the student to use the hair blower or hair dryer to dry his hair.
2. As part of grooming, assign the student a partner. Ask the partners to take turns washing and drying each other's hair, using the hair dryer and blower.

Home

1. When appropriate ask the same-sex parent to show his or her child how to use an electric shaver, and to tell the child that one should shave regularly in order to maintain a neat appearance. Suggest that the parent allow the child to try a variety of electric shavers until one is found that is best suited for him or her.
2. Ask the female parent to show her child how to set her hair. Tell her to practice using a variety of curlers, hot rollers, or curling irons.

Functional Emphases In designing your own instructional activities and plans, emphasize the following elements:

1. Use of a variety of grooming accessories and appliances, as appropriate.
2. Selection of grooming accessories and appliances that are safe and warranted.

3. Awareness of safety procedures and rules to follow when using grooming accessories and appliances.

Specific Objective K

The student winds and sets clocks.

Functional Settings and Suggested Instructional Activities

School

1. Bring a number of alarm clocks that require manual winding into the classroom or learning area. Show the student the winding key and demonstrate winding the clocks.
2. Set the alarm clocks for different times: lunch, physical education, bus, bathroom, and recess. Tell the student to wind the clocks so that they will go off at the appropriate times, and remind the student to proceed to the next class or activity.

Home

1. Ask the parents to show their child a variety of clocks found within the home. Tell them to point out which ones need to be wound (nonelectrical) and which ones run by electricity or battery.
2. Ask the parents to encourage their child to use an alarm clock to wake himself up in the morning. Someone else may be responsible for setting the clock while he may be responsible for winding it.

Functional Emphases In designing your own instructional activities and plans, emphasize the following elements:

1. Development of motor skills necessary to wind and set a clock.
2. Use of a variety of clocks including electric, winding models, and battery operated.
3. Recognition of numbers 1 to 12 and other ways of indicating position on the clock.
4. Knowledge of how to tell time or estimate time to the quarter hour, half hour, or hour.

Specific Objective L

The student operates recreational appliances for entertainment and information, including video games, televisions, radios, stereos, and videotape recorders and disks.

Functional Settings and Suggested Instructional Activities

School

1. Bring a cassette tape recorder into the classroom. Demonstrate the use of the cassette recorder, and tell the student what you are doing as you do it. Point out the various parts of the recorder: cassette ejection button, record button, stop button, play button, etc. You may want to color code the buttons for the student's convenience (e.g., red on the stop button, green on the play button, yellow on the record button, blue on the cassette ejection button, black on the rewind button, and orange on the volume button).
2. Make a chart using the color codings of the tape recorder buttons, showing the students the order to follow in using the cassette tape recorder (Figure 25).
3. Use tape cassettes with coordinated storybooks.

Home and Community

1. Ask the parents to demonstrate using a television set or stereo with a knob that turns for on and off.
2. Tell the parents to repeat the above activity using a television or stereo with a push-pull on-off switch or a rocker-type on-off switch.
3. Tell the parents to demonstrate to their child how to adjust the volume control on the entertainment appliances within the home. Tell them to

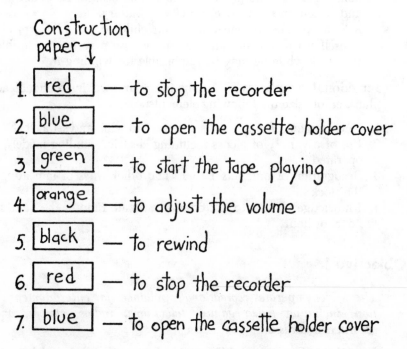

Figure 25. Color coding chart for sequence of steps in playing a cassette tape recorder.

encourage the child to imitate their actions and, at appropriate times during the day or evening, to put him in charge of raising and lowering the volume.
4. At the beach, place the student in charge of the radio. Warn him not to play it too loud because it will disturb others.

Functional Emphases   In designing your own instructional activities and plans, emphasize the following elements:

1. Use of a variety of recreational appliances.
2. Knowledge of directions and/or operating instructions.
3. Awareness of safety procedures to follow when using recreational appliances.
4. Avoidance of recreational appliances that are poorly made or that appear unsafe.

Specific Objective M

The student adjusts thermostats.

Functional Settings and Suggested Instructional Activities   This activity is best done at home because adjusting thermostats in school may pose problems with the school's Heating and Cooling Plant.

Home

1. Ask the parents to show their child a thermostat that is located in the home or living quarters. Tell them to point out the movable dial, the indicator, the arrow, and the numbers that represent the degrees of temperature.
2. Ask the parents to place a red dot above the number on the thermostat that indicates the desired temperature for the room in which the thermostat is located (e.g., 68° in a bedroom). Tell them to show him how to line up the arrow on the movable dial with the dot above the number. The child should imitate their actions and practice adjusting the thermostat by matching the arrow and the dot. (For the child's living quarters, they may want two different-color dots: one for daytime temperature and one for evening or sleeping temperature. This would, of course, depend upon the individual child.)

Functional Emphases   In designing your own instructional activities and plans, emphasize the following elements:

1. Comprehension of numbers and words found on a thermostat.
2. Awareness of when a thermostat needs to be adjusted.
3. Knowledge of whom to contact when a thermostat is not functioning properly.

Specific Objective N

The student operates cleaning equipment and appliances.

Functional Settings and Suggested Instructional Activities

School

1. If a washing machine is available, ask the student to wash his dirty gym clothes in the school's washer. Point out the settings and the amount of detergent needed for the wash.
2. Develop classroom jobs that include using an electric broom or vacuum cleaner. Assign a cleaning job to the student that requires him to use the cleaning appliances.

Home and Community

1. Tell the parents to provide opportunities for their child to help in cleaning the house or his room. Tell them to demonstrate the use of the vacuum cleaner or electric broom, including how to empty its bag or cup when it is full. Tell them to monitor how appropriately he uses the appliances.
2. Tell the student to offer to clean the room where he is staying when he is a guest in a home for a period of time. Tell the student to vacuum the rug or floor as part of his cleaning.

Functional Emphases   In designing your own instructional activities and plans, emphasize the following elements:

1. Use of a variety of cleaning equipment and appliances.
2. Knowledge of how to follow directions found on cleaning equipment and appliances or in their instruction booklets.
3. Awareness of safety rules required when using cleaning equipment and appliances.
4. Knowledge of where to find community laundromats.

Specific Objective O

The student uses coin-operated machines and equipment.

Functional Settings and Suggested Instructional Activities

School

1. Take the student to an automat or lunch room with vending machines. Demonstrate operating the various types of vending machines, including those with push buttons and pull out-type knobs. Insert the appropriate coin(s) into the coin slot. Make your selection and operate the machine.

Tell the student to watch what you are doing and to imitate your actions, and have him practice operating vending machines.

2. Take the female student to a bathroom with a sanitary napkin vending machine. Insert the appropriate coin into the coin slot. Grasp the handle, and turn it until the sanitary napkin is released. Tell the student to watch what you are doing, and tell her what you are doing as you do it. Tell the student to imitate your actions and to practice operating the sanitary napkin vending machine.

Community

1. Take the student to a subway or other place having a turnstile that is operated by inserting a token. Buy a token and encourage the student to insert the token into the turnstile.
2. Buy bus tokens and take the student on a public transportation bus. Tell the student to insert a token into the token box as he steps onto the bus.
3. Take the student to a laundromat or laundry room with coin-operated machines. Tell the student to identify which coin(s) the machines require and choose the appropriate coin(s). Tell the student to grasp the coin between his thumb and forefinger and to insert the coin into the slot.

Functional Emphases In designing your own instructional activities and plans, emphasize the following elements:

1. Use of a variety of coin-operated machines.
2. Knowledge of how to obtain change and verification of change received.
3. Development of motor skills necessary to effectively use coin-operated machines.
4. Awareness of when coin-operated machines are out of order, broken, or will accept only specific coins.
5. Identification of words that illustrate operating instructions.

Specific Objective P

The student operates ticket machines found in bakeries, supermarkets, and stores.

Functional Settings and Suggested Instructional Activities

Community

1. Take the student to a bakery or supermarket that has a ticket machine. Demonstrate operating the ticket machine. Tell the student what you are doing as you do it. Tell the student to imitate your actions and to operate the numbered ticket machine.
2. Schedule a small luncheon for your class. Take the student to the supermarket to buy luncheon food. (There often is a ticket machine at delicates-

sen and bakery counters.) The student must take a ticket at the delicatessen, wait his turn, and order his portion of cold cuts. The student must then go to the bakery, take a ticket, wait his turn, and order rolls, bread, or pastries for the luncheon.

Functional Emphases In designing your own instructional activities and plans, emphasize the following elements:

1. Location of ticket dispensing machines.
2. Use of a variety of ticket machines found in stores.
3. Development of motor skills necessary to operate ticket machines.
4. Awareness of numbers found on tickets and what they represent (i.e., waiting until one's number is called).

Specific Objective Q

The student uses self-service elevators.

Functional Settings and Suggested Instructional Activities

School

1. Show the student flashcards of numbers and "B" and "L" for basement and lobby. Drill the student until he recognizes the numbers and letters.
2. Construct an elevator push-button panel out of corrugated cardboard. Paste or draw on buttons. Tell the student to find buttons with specific numbers and/or letters.

Community

1. Visit apartment buildings with self-service elevators (if possible) when the student wishes to visit friends. Observe to see how the student uses the elevator.
2. Take the student to a store or office building with a self-service elevator. Practice pushing the buttons of the self-service elevator. (You may want to check with the building superintendent to find out the times when the elevators are least busy.)

Functional Emphases In designing your own instructional activities and plans, emphasize the following elements:

1. Knowledge of how to use self-service elevators.
2. Comprehension of numbers and letters found on self-service elevator switch panels.
3. Avoidance of using self-service elevators that appear broken, dirty, or dimly lit or are in unsafe areas.
4. Awareness of how to enter and exit self-service elevators.
5. Awareness of what to do in case self-service elevators break down while in the process of being used.

Specific Objective R

The student uses personal aids.

Functional Settings and Suggested Instructional Activities

School

1. Bring sunglasses into the classroom (the student who wears glasses may use his own glasses). Point out the various parts of the glasses: the lenses, the frame, the bridge, and the earpiece.
2. Demonstrate the use of a hearing aid to the student. Check the hearing aid to be sure it is off (hearing aids should always be off before the earpiece is inserted into the ear). Read the directions on how to use the hearing aid and allow the student to demonstrate its use. Tell him to watch what you are doing and explain what you are doing as you do it. Tell the student to imitate your actions and to practice operating the hearing aid.

Home

1. Tell the parents to demonstrate putting glasses on and removing them. Tell them to have their child watch what they are doing and to explain each action as they do it. Tell the parents to remind their child not to put his fingers on the lenses and to handle glasses with care.
2. Tell the parents to encourage their child who uses a hearing aid to wear it whenever appropriate. If the child does not wear a hearing aid, they should tell him to be understanding and supportive of a person who does.

Functional Emphases   In designing your own instructional activities and plans, emphasize the following elements:

1. Awareness of professionals who can help in selecting and/or evaluating the need for personal aids.
2. Awareness of personal aids that may prove helpful.
3. Knowledge of how to use personal aids.
4. Knowledge of simple maintenance techniques for personal aids.
5. Awareness of where to purchase personal aids.

Specific Objective S

The student puts on and adjusts jewelry.

Functional Settings and Suggested Instructional Activities

School

1. Bring watches with buckle-type watchbands into the classroom or learning area. Demonstrate opening and closing the buckle on the watchband. Tell

the student to watch what you are doing and explain what you are doing as you do it. Tell the student to imitate your actions and to practice opening and closing the buckle on the watchband.

2. Bring a variety of necklaces and neck chains into the classroom or learning area. Demonstrate opening and closing the clasp of the necklace or chain. Tell the student what you are doing as you do it. Tell the student to imitate your actions and to practice opening and closing the clasps of necklaces and chains.

Home and Community

1. Tell the parents to assist their child in selecting and putting on jewelry. Tell them to point out that there are times when a lot of jewelry is not appropriate (funerals) and when it may be dangerous (when working with machines in which jewelry may get caught).
2. Take the student to plays, movies, or the theater. Have the student dress for the occasion by wearing jewelry as accessories.

Functional Emphases In designing your own instructional activities and plans, emphasize the following elements:

1. Selection of jewelry that is well made.
2. Selection of jewelry that will not cause an allergic reaction when it comes in contact with the skin.
3. Avoidance of jewelry that has clasps that appear flimsy or will be easily broken.
4. Awareness of the relative cost of jewelry.
5. Knowledge of when the use of jewelry is inappropriate.

Special Materials List

Books/Pamphlets

Sharing an Apartment by Durlynn Anema, and Getting Around Cities and Towns by Winifred Ho Roderman. Janus Book Publishers, 2501 Industrial Parkway West, Department E246, Hayward, CA 94545.

Kits

Planning Your Apartment. Chaselle, Inc., 9645 Gerwig Lane, Columbia, MD 21046.
Social Perceptual Training Kit for Community Living by B. Edmonson, E. Leach, and H. Leland, Educational Activities, Inc., P. O. Box 392, Freeport, NY 11520.
Independent Living Evaluation—Training Program. Stout Vocational Rehabilitation Institute, University of Wisconsin–Stout, Menomonie, WI 54751.

Community Signs—Reading. Exceptional Education, P. O. Box 15308, Seattle, WA 98115.

Independent Living Skills Curriculum. Research and Training Center, University of Oregon, Eugene, OR 97403.

Photo Sequence Cards Set 3: Daily Living Activities. Modern Education Corp., P. O. Box 721, Tulsa, OK 74101.

Suggested Readings/References

Amary, I. B. (1979). *Effective meal planning and food preparation for the mentally retarded and developmentally disabled: Comprehensive and innovative teaching methods.* Springfield, IL: Charles C Thomas.

Arithmetic skill text for daily living. (1977). Huntington, NY: Special Service Supply.

Barnard, J. D., Christophersen, E. R., & Wolf, M. M. (1977). Teaching children appropriate shopping behavior through parent training in the supermarket setting. *Journal of Applied Behavior Analysis, 10,* 49–59.

Bastian, H. (1972). Teaching trainable level retarded students to prepare hot cereal. In L. Brown & E. Sontag (Eds.), *Toward the development and implementation of an empirically based public school program for trainable mentally retarded and severely emotionally disturbed. Part II.* Madison, WI: Madison Public Schools.

Bastian, H., Johnson, P., & Sontag, E. (1972). Teaching educable level retarded students to use a cooking oven. In L. Brown & E. Sontag (Eds.), *Toward the development and implementation of an empirically based public school program for trainable mentally retarded and severely emotionally disturbed. Part II.* Madison, WI: Madison Public Schools.

Bastian, H., Milbauer, L., Brown, L., & Sontag, E. (1972). Teaching trainable level students to use a clothing iron. In L. Brown & E. Sontag (Eds.), *Toward the development and implementation of an empirically based public school program for trainable mentally retarded and severely emotionally disturbed. Part II.* Madison, WI: Madison Public Schools.

Bastian, H., Milbauer, L., Hammerman, J., Brown, L., & Sontag, E. (1972). Teaching trainable level retarded students to use a kitchen stove. In L. Brown & E. Sontag (Eds.), *Toward the development and implementation of an empirically based public school program for trainable mentally retarded and severely emotionally disturbed. Part II.* Madison, WI: Madison Public Schools.

Bastian, H., & Ruff, S. (1972). Teaching trainable level retarded students to prepare toast. In L. Brown & E. Sontag (Eds.), *Toward the development and implementation of an empirically based public school program for trainable mentally retarded and severely emotionally disturbed. Part II.* Madison, WI: Madison Public Schools.

Bauman, K. E., & Iwata, B. A. (1977). Maintenance of independent housekeeping skills using scheduling plus self-recording procedures. *Behavior Therapy, 8,* 554–560.

Belina, V. S. (1975). *Planning your own apartment: Text-Workbook and Teacher's Guide; Reading Level, 3.0; Interest Level, Grades 7-12/ABE.* Belmont, CA: Fearon-Pitman Publishers.

Bellamy, T., & Buttars, K. (1975). Teaching trainable level retarded students to count money: Toward personal independence through academic instruction. *Education and Training of the Mentally Retarded, 10,* 18–26.

Bender, M., & Valletutti, P. J. (1982). *Teaching functional academics: A curriculum guide for adolescents and adults with learning problems.* Austin: PRO-ED.

Bender, M., Valletutti, P. J., & Bender, R. (1976). *Teaching the moderately and severely handicapped (Vols. I, II, & III).* Austin: PRO-ED.

Brown, V. (1976). On reviewing cookbooks: From kitchen to classroom. *Journal of Learning Disabilities, 9,* 63–68.

Certo, N., Schwartz, R., & Brown, L. (1975). Community transportation: Teaching severely handicapped students to ride a public bus system. In L. Brown, T. Crowner, W. Williams, & R. York (Eds.), *Madison's alternative to zero exclusion: A book of readings (Vol. 5).* Madison, WI: Madison Public Schools.

Certo, N., & Swetlik, B. (1976). Making purchases: A functional money use program for severely handicapped students. In L. Brown et al. (Eds.), *Madison's alternative to zero exclusion: Papers and programs related to public school services for secondary age severely handicapped students.* Madison, WI: Madison Public Schools.

Coon, M. E., Vogelsberg, R. T., & Williams, W. (1981). Effects of classroom public transportation instruction on generalization to the natural environment. *The Journal of the Association for the Severely Handicapped, 6,* 46–53.

Crnic, K. A., & Pym, H. A. (1979). Training mentally retarded adults in independent living skills. *Mental Retardation, 17,* 13–16.

Cronin, K. A., & Cuvo, A. (1979). Teaching mending skills to mentally retarded adolescents. *Journal of Applied Behavior Analysis, 12,* 401–406.

Cuvo, A. J., Jacobi, L., & Sipko, R. (1981). Teaching laundry skills to mentally retarded students. *Education and Training of the Mentally Retarded, 16,* 54–64.

Doyle, E. (1980). *Skills for daily living series.* Baltimore: Media Materials.

Floor polish and floor care. (1972). Consumer Information Series No. 9. Washington, DC: General Services Administration.

George, R. (1978). *The new consumer survival kit:* Adapted from the series produced by the Maryland Center for Public Broadcasting. Boston: Little, Brown.

Johnson, B., & Cuvo, A. J. (1981). Teaching cooking skills to mentally retarded adults. *Behavior Modification, 5,* 187–202.

Knox, C. (1980). *Using the telephone directory.* Baltimore: Media Materials.

Laus, M. D. (1977). *Travel instruction for the handicapped.* Springfield, IL: Charles C Thomas.

Leff, R. B. (1975). *How to use the telephone: The dial-a-phone kit.* Peoli, PA: Instructor/McGraw-Hill.

Levy, L., Feldman, R., & Simpson, S. (1976). *The consumer in the marketplace; Interest Level, Grades 7–12.* Belmont, CA: Fearon-Pitman Publishers.

MacWilliam, L. J. (1977). You can get there from here. Travel and community experience for multiply handicapped students. *Teaching Exceptional Children, 9,* 49–51.

Matson, J. L. (1979). A field tested system of training meal preparation skills to the retarded. *British Journal of Mental Subnormality, 25,* 14–18.

Matson, J. L. (1980). A controlled group study of pedestrian skill training for the mentally retarded. *Behavior Research and Therapy, 18,* 99–106.

Matson, J. L. (1981). Use of independence training to teach shopping skills to mildly mentally retarded adults. *American Journal of Mental Deficiency, 86,* 178–183.

Neef, N., Iwata, B., & Page, T. J. (1978). Public transportation training: In vivo versus classroom instruction. *Journal of Applied Behavior Analysis, 11,* 331–344.

Nettlebeck, T., & Kirby, N. H. (1976). Training the mentally handicapped to sew. *Education and Training of the Mentally Retarded, 11,* 31–36.

Nietupski, J., & Williams, W. (1976). Teaching selected telephone related social skills to severely handicapped students. *Child Study Journal, 6,* 139–153.

Page, T. J., Iwata, B. A., & Neft, W. A. (1976). Teaching pedestrian skills to retarded persons: Generalization from the classroom to the natural environment. *Journal of Applied Behavior Analysis, 9,* 433-444.

Robinson-Wilson, M. (1977). Picture recipe cards as an approach to teaching severely and profoundly retarded adults to cook. *Education and Training of the Mentally Retarded, 12,* 69–73.

Roderman, W. H. (1979). *Getting around cities and towns: A Janus Survival Guide.* Hayward, CA: Janus Book Publishers.

Sarber, R. E., Halasz, M. M., Messmer, M. C., Bickett, A. D., & Lutzker, J. R. (1983). Teaching menu planning and grocery shopping skills to a mentally retarded mother. *Mental Retardation, 21,* 101–106.

Schutz, R. P., Vogelsberg, R. T., & Rusch, F. R. (1980). A behavioral approach to integrating individuals into the community. In L. Heal and A. Novak (Eds.), *Integration of the developmentally disabled into the community.* Baltimore: Paul H. Brookes.

Shultheis, P., Paine, R., Morgan-Brown, A., Smith, S., & Hanson, R. (1980). *Household mathematics.* Baltimore: Media Materials.

Shultheis, P., Paine, R., Morgan-Brown, A., Smith, S., & Hanson, R. (1980). *Shopping mathematics.* Baltimore: Media Materials.

Shultheis, P., Paine, R., Morgan-Brown, A., Smith, S., & Hanson, R. (1980). *Traveler's mathematics.* Baltimore: Media Materials.

Sowers, J. A., Rusch, F. R., & Hudson, C. (1979). Training a severely retarded young adult to ride the city bus to and from work. *AAESPH Review, 3,* 15–24.

Smith, M., & Meyers, A. (1979). Telephone-skills training for retarded adults: Group and individual demonstrations with and without verbal instruction. *American Journal of Mental Deficiency, 83,* 581–587.

Stacy-Sherrer, C. J. (1981). *Skills necessary for contributive family and home living: Applicable to the moderately to severely retarded child & adult: A task analysis manual for teachers, parents and houseparents.* Springfield, IL: Charles C Thomas.

Thompson, T. J., Braam, S. J., & Fuqua, R. W. (1982). Training & generalization of laundry skills: A multiple problem evaluation with handicapped persons. *Journal of Applied Behavior Analysis, 15,* 177–182.

Tiller, C., & Wyllie, C. (1978). *An activities of daily living curriculum for handicapped adults.* Twin Falls, ID: Magic Valley Rehabilitation Services, Inc.

Triebel, J., & Manning, M. (1976). *I think I can learn to cook or I can cook to think and learn.* San Rafael, CA: Academic Therapy Publications.

VanDenPol, R. A., Iwata, B. A., Ivancic, M. T., Page, T. J., Neef, N. A., & Whitley, F. P. (1981). Teaching the handicapped to act in public places: Acquisition, generalization & maintenance of restaurant skills. *Journal of Applied Behavior Analysis, 14,* 61–69.

Vogelsberg, R. T. (1980). Access to the natural environment: The first step to community independence. In R. DuBose and K. Stonecipher (Eds.), *Illinois' best practices for teaching severely handicapped students.* Springfield, IL: Illinois

State Board of Education.

Vogelsburg, R. T., & Rusch, F. R. (1979). Training severely handicapped students to cross partially controlled intersections. *AAESPH Review, 4*, 264–273.

Walls, R. T., Crist, K., Sienicki, D. A., & Grant, L. (1981). Prompting sequences in teaching independent living skills. *Mental Retardation, 19*, 243–246.

Wheeler, J., Ford, A., Nietupski, J., & Brown, L. (1979). Teaching adolescent moderately/severely handicapped students to use food classification skills and calculator-related subtraction skills to shop in supermarkets. In L. Brown, M. Falvey, D. Baumgart, I. Pumpian, J. Schroeder, & L. Gruenewald (Eds.), *Madison's alternative to zero exclusion: Strategies for teaching chronological age appropriate skills to adolescent and young adult severely handicapped students (Vol. 9)*. Madison, WI: Madison Public Schools.

Wheeler, J., Ford, A., Nietupski, J., Loomis, R., & Brown, L. (1980). Teaching moderately and severely handicapped adolescents to shop in supermarkets using pocket calculators. *Education and Training of the Mentally Retarded, 15*, 105–112.

Williams, R. D., & Ewing, S. (1979). Consumer roulette: The shopping patterns of mentally retarded persons. *Mental Retardation, 19*, 145–149.